What Your Colleagues Are Saying . . .

"If you are looking for the magic that successful teachers use—you have found it in this book! Whether you are a beginning teacher looking for ways to engage your students or an experienced teacher seeking inspiration, this book is for you. *Real Talk About Classroom Management* shares the behind-the-scenes secrets that teachers use to maintain their balance, stay inspired, and keep the joy in teaching. Thank you, Serena, for sharing your wisdom."

Carol Pelletier Radford
Author, *"When I Started Teaching I Wish I Had Known . . .":
Weekly Wisdom for Beginning Teachers;
The First Years Matter; and Mentoring in Action*

"*Real Talk About Classroom Management* offers a fresh, much-needed perspective on student-centered practices that should be on every educator's shelf, no matter their experience level! The focus of every practice rests squarely on ensuring that students feel seen, valued, and heard. Serena Pariser's strategies are highly practical, universally relevant, and easy to apply, making the text a perennial resource for all grades and subject levels taught."

Lindsay Prendergast
Region 3 Support Lead, Clark County School District

"*Real Talk About Classroom Management* provides a true, intimate look at many layers of what goes on behind the scenes in a classroom. The book is filled with real-life examples, scenarios, and quotes from teachers and students; readers at all experience levels will easily connect with this content. Serena Pariser knows that true classroom management relies on a balance of mind, body, and soul—but most importantly, it's centered in the heart."

Darius Phelps
Associate Professor and PhD Candidate in English Education,
Teachers College, Columbia University

"I appreciate Serena Pariser's obvious skill, experience, and creativity in working with students. Her insights and strategies are grounded in mutual respect between students and adults and provide an authentic roadmap to strengthening classroom management."

Natalie Bernasconi
Educator, Santa Cruz, California

Real Talk About Classroom Management

Second Edition

This book is dedicated to the person who encouraged me to submit my very first book to publishers. You've transformed my life, just as you have done for many others. Thank you, Edward Deroche.

Real Talk About Classroom Management

57 Best Practices That Work and Show You Believe in Your Students

Second Edition

Serena Pariser

FOR INFORMATION:

Corwin

A SAGE Company

2455 Teller Road

Thousand Oaks, California 91320

(800) 233-9936

www.corwin.com

SAGE Publications Ltd.

1 Oliver's Yard

55 City Road

London EC1Y 1SP

United Kingdom

SAGE Publications India Pvt. Ltd.

Unit No 323-333, Third Floor, F-Block

International Trade Tower Nehru Place

New Delhi 110 019

India

SAGE Publications Asia-Pacific Pte. Ltd.

18 Cross Street #10-10/11/12

China Square Central

Singapore 048423

Vice President and
   Editorial Director: Monica Eckman

Executive Editor: Tori Mello Bachman

Associate Content
   Development Editor: Sarah Ross

Content Development Editor: Sharon Wu

Product Associate: Zachary Vann

Production Editor: Tori Mirsadjadi

Copy Editor: Shannon Kelly

Typesetter: C&M Digitals (P) Ltd.

Cover Designer: Scott Van Atta

Marketing Manager: Margaret O'Connor

Copyright © 2024 by Corwin Press, Inc.

All rights reserved. Except as permitted by U.S. copyright law, no part of this work may be reproduced or distributed in any form or by any means, or stored in a database or retrieval system, without permission in writing from the publisher.

When forms and sample documents appearing in this work are intended for reproduction, they will be marked as such. Reproduction of their use is authorized for educational use by educators, local school sites, and/or noncommercial or nonprofit entities that have purchased the book.

All third-party trademarks referenced or depicted herein are included solely for the purpose of illustration and are the property of their respective owners. Reference to these trademarks in no way indicates any relationship with, or endorsement by, the trademark owner.

Printed in the United States of America

Library of Congress Cataloging-in-Publication Data

Names: Pariser, Serena, author.

Title: Real talk about classroom management : 57 best practices that work and show you believe in your students / Serena Pariser.

Description: Second edition. | Thousand Oaks, California : Corwin, 2024. |

Series: Corwin teaching essentials |
Includes bibliographical references and index.

Identifiers: LCCN 2023039206 | ISBN 9781071922552 (paperback) | ISBN 9781071932353 (epub) | ISBN 9781071932360 (epub) | ISBN 9781071932377 (pdf)

Subjects: LCSH: Classroom management. | Effective teaching.

Classification: LCC LB3013 .P28 2024 | DDC 371.102/4—dc23/eng/20230928
LC record available at https://lccn.loc.gov/2023039206

This book is printed on acid-free paper.

24 25 26 27 28 10 9 8 7 6 5 4 3 2 1

DISCLAIMER: This book may direct you to access third-party content via web links, QR codes, or other scannable technologies, which are provided for your reference by the author(s). Corwin makes no guarantee that such third-party content will be available for your use and encourages you to review the terms and conditions of such third-party content. Corwin takes no responsibility and assumes no liability for your use of any third-party content, nor does Corwin approve, sponsor, endorse, verify, or certify such third-party content.

Contents

List of Videos — xi

Acknowledgments — xiii

About the Author — xv

Introduction — 1

Part 1. First Weeks of School — 8

Best Practice #1: Build Mutually Respectful Relationships With Students From Day 1 — 10

Best Practice #2: Nurture a Belonging Classroom — 15

Best Practice #3: Make It About the Students and the Importance of Student Collaboration on Day 1 — 19

Best Practice #4: Set Your Routine and Structures Early . . . and Keep Them! — 23

Best Practice #5: Use Empowering Language Instead of Controlling Language — 27

Best Practice #6: Create Purposeful Seating Charts — 32

Best Practice #7: Create Room Environments That Foster Student Belonging — 42

Part 2. Forming Positive Relationships With Your Students — 46

Best Practice #8: Recognize Your Power and Use It Positively — 49

Best Practice #9: Celebrate Mistakes as Learning Opportunities — 55

Best Practice #10: Strengthen Inclusion and Belonging for All Students — 58

Best Practice #11: Stick With the Students Who Challenge Us the Most — 62

Best Practice #12: Become a Teacher Detective to Discover Why Students Aren't Performing Well Academically — 67

Best Practice #13: Focus on the Positive and Create Positive Students — 74

Best Practice #14: Dig Deeper With Connection Kids — 78

Best Practice #15: Reward Students — 84

Best Practice #16: Motivating Students in Elementary, Middle, and High School and How That Might Look Different — 87

Best Practice #17: Consider Behavior Contracts — 90

Part 3. Engagement and Instruction — 102

Best Practice #18: Make Learning Powerfully Authentic and Make It Transferable — 105

Best Practice #19: Learn and Grow Using Trusted Sources — 109

Best Practice #20: Pick up the Pace — 113

Best Practice #21: Use Arm's Length Voice — 116

Best Practice #22: Use Technology in Lessons to Enhance, Not Replace — 118

Best Practice #23: Be One or Two Steps Ahead of the Class — 122

Best Practice #24: Keep Everything Contextualized (Including SEL Lessons) and Do Projects! — 126

Best Practice #25: Tap Into Students' Curiosity With Problem-Based Learning — 131

Best Practice #26: Rely on Formative Assessment to Drive Instruction — 136

Best Practice #27: Be a Warm Demander to Challenge and Support Students — 139

Best Practice #28: Lean Into Learning Activities That Are More Engaging, Fun, and Collaborative Rather Than Relying on Direct Instruction — 143

Best Practice #29: Take Risks in Your Lessons — 148

Best Practice #30: Prepare Ahead for When You Just Can't Be There — 151

Best Practice #31: Implement Creative Discipline	155
Best Practice #32: Vary Levels of Noise in the Classroom	160
Best Practice #33: Make Groupwork Work	164
Best Practice #34: Let Their Creative Juices Flow	169
Best Practice #35: Teach Every Different Type of Learner	172
Best Practice #36: Have *No* Doubts . . . but Be Prepared to Have (Just a Few) Lessons Flop	180

Part 4. Partnering and Cultivating Relationships With Stakeholders — 184

Best Practice #37: Work With Parents and Caregivers as Partners	192
Best Practice #38: Make Coteaching Work	197
Best Practice #39: Lean on Social Workers and School Counselors	204
Best Practice #40: Find a Mentor	208
Best Practice #41: Watch and Learn	211
Best Practice #42: Listen With Your Mind	213
Best Practice #43: Earn the Respect of Administrators	215

Part 5. Spins That Will Wow Your Students — 222

Best Practice #44: Host Guest Speakers	226
Best Practice #45: Know That Students Are Ready to Have Power and Voice	231
Best Practice #46: Show Your Students You Care	235
Best Practice #47: Laugh Together, Learn Together	240
Best Practice #48: Give Gifts Without Strings Attached	244
Best Practice #49: Empower Students With Student-Led Conferences	247
Best Practice #50: Use Peer Mediation to Teach Conflict Resolution Skills, Foster More Positive Classrooms, and Make Your Life Easier	251

Best Practice #51: Get Students to Behave When You're Covering a Colleague's Class — 256

Best Practice #52: Surprise! — 260

Part 6. Staying Afloat — 266

Best Practice #53: Balance Your Life — 270

Best Practice #54: How to Turn Around a Potentially Difficult Parent or Caregiver Meeting — 275

Best Practice #55: Be Aware of Secondary Trauma and Compassion Fatigue — 280

Best Practice #56: Cultivate Healthy Relationships With Colleagues — 286

Best Practice #57: How to Navigate Colleague Conflict — 289

Handy To-Go List of Fifty-Seven Teaching Dos and Don'ts — 294

The End . . . of the Beginning — 298

Real Advice: Teacher to Teacher — 300

References — 305

Index — 307

List of Videos

Note from the Publisher: The author has provided video and web content throughout the book that is available to you through QR (quick response) codes. To read a QR code, you must have a smartphone or tablet with a camera. We recommend that you download a QR code reader app that is made specifically for your phone or tablet brand.

Videos may also be accessed at **resources.corwin.com/realtalk2e**.

Part 1. First Weeks of School

6.1 Purposeful Seating Charts

Part 2. Forming Positive Relationships With Your Students

9.1 Creating an Environment Where It's Safe to Make Mistakes

12.1 Teacher Detective

Part 3. Engagement and Instruction

Opener: Jeff Kirschbaum Explains How Instruction Directly Affects Classroom Management

25.1 Solving Global Issues

26.1 Ways to Do Formative Assessments

27.1 What Is a Warm Demander?

28.1 Strategies That Engage Learners

32.1 Incorporating Music Into a Classroom

35.1 Add Variety to Your Instruction

Part 4. Partnering and Cultivating Relationships With Stakeholders

38.1 What Coteaching Can Look Like

38.2 Utilizing Your Coteacher's Strengths

Part 5. Spins That Will Wow Your Students

45.1 Give Students Power and Voice

47.1 Show Students Your Sense of Humor

50.1 Peer Mediation in Elementary School

50.2 Peer Mediation in Middle or High School

52.1 How Surprises Can Increase Student Engagement

Part 6. Staying Afloat

Opener: Tips on Staying Afloat from Rebekah Madren

53.1 Work-Life Balance

53.2 Teacher Self-Care

54.1 Positively Engaging Parents

57.1 Positively Engaging Colleagues

Acknowledgments

A teacher's journey relies on many people and lessons along the way. I'd like to acknowledge those who have helped my journey and sincerely express my gratitude to those listed below.

To my first sixth-grade math class in West Philadelphia, who taught me that you must connect with students before and during teaching content. And thank you for also showing me what happens when you do not!

To all of my students who sat in desks in front of me day after day, you truly were my teachers through the years. Thank you.

Thank you to Gompers Preparatory Academy and Vincent Riveroll for showing me what it truly means to connect with a child.

Thank you Mel, Dad, Ellen, Carla, Ron, Joe, Rob, Pam, and Mom.

Thanks to my nieces, Sydney, Aria, Sam, Sloane, and Skylar, for unknowingly giving me inspiration to write this book in the hopes you'll have progressive classrooms that challenge, engage, and support you academically, emotionally, and socially all through your schooling.

Zippy and Carl, thank you for your support and kindness.

Corwin has been supportive, always, in my book writing journey. Thank you for taking a chance on me in the very beginning.

And finally, I'd like to express endless gratitude to Tori Mello Bachman, executive editor at Corwin, for going above and beyond and bringing this book to life.

Publisher's Acknowledgments

Corwin gratefully acknowledges the contributions of the following reviewers:

Darius Phelps
Associate Professor, Teachers College, Columbia University
New York NY

Natalie Bernasconi
Educator, UC Santa Cruz
Spreckels, CA

About the Author

Serena Pariser is the best-selling author of several professional books for educators, including *Real Talk About Classroom Management: 50 Best Practices That Work and Show You Believe in Your Students* (Corwin, 2018) and *Real Talk About Time Management: 35 Best Practices for Educators* (Corwin, 2020). She is a coauthor of *Five to Thrive: Answers to Your Biggest Questions About Creating a Dynamic Classroom* (Corwin, 2022) and *It Starts in the Classroom: Character Education for a Better Tomorrow* (Rowman & Littlefield, 2022).

Serena taught English language arts for many years, primarily in San Diego, California, and in Philadelphia, Pennsylvania. She has experience working with most grades in a variety of school settings across the spectrum, from underresourced urban public schools to affluent private schools. Serena was honored as Teacher of the Year at Gompers Preparatory Academy, located in San Diego.

She served as assistant director of field experience at the University of San Diego, where she taught graduate and undergraduate classes for teachers in training. In addition, Serena was selected to be a national evaluator for Schools of Character.

A Fulbright scholar, Serena coaches educators across the United States and around the globe, from California to Kathmandu. Her passions include progressive classroom management best practices, bringing curriculum to life, time management for teachers, and weaving character education into the curriculum.

In her spare time, Serena travels and loves to experience the world for weeks at a time with just a backpack strapped to her back and a smile on her face.

Serena's website can be found at www.serenapariser.com, where she writes educational articles that are enjoyed by a large audience of teachers. She is most active on social media on X @SerenaPariser and maintains a blog at www.serenapariser.com, where she writes articles for educators. She can also be directly contacted at serena.pariser@gmail.com.

Introduction

The only constant is change. As teachers, how do we adjust to these ever-changing times while keeping our confidence and cool?

The reality is that we are preparing the students in our classrooms for jobs that might not even exist yet. Let that sink in for a second.

In 2021 Education Week surveyed executives at some of the nation's leading companies, including companies that specialized in everything from consulting to hospitality to automotive, with the prompt, "Tell us what you'll want and expect from today's K–12 students when you're eventually hiring them, and make suggestions for how schools can provide students with those skills" (Education Week, 2021). The responses included these skills:

- **Agility and flexibility.** Ability to sense unpredictability and act quickly in response; ability to identify new ideas and approaches. Demonstrate curiosity—ask questions and have the courage to move quickly.

- **Growth mindset and resilience.** Desire to continuously learn. Ability to recover and bounce back from adversity and hardships. Take ownership and accountability; develop strategies for reflection and learning.

- **Teamwork and collaboration.** Desire to work with others different from yourself—different backgrounds, genders, functions, geographies, cultures—to create better, more durable results. Ability to work as a member of a team to achieve an agreed set of goals.

- **Learning to learn.** The world is changing fast, and successful companies are evolving even faster to serve their customers and remain competitive. Associates with the ability to identify and anticipate changes in the environment and who can acquire new knowledge and skills will be needed and effective in this environment.

- **Conflict resolution.** Workers in all fields will need to be able to independently resolve conflict.

Read the full Education Week article here.

To read a QR code, you must have a smartphone or tablet with a camera. We recommend that you download a QR code reader app that is made specifically for your phone or tablet brand.

These skills are specifically taught and practiced in classrooms where students become a community of learners, where students are encouraged to ask questions and challenge each other, where critical thinking is more valued than rote memorization, and where every student is seen and heard. This is where I want to offer a helping hand, because it's not always easy to create that type of classroom.

In this book I'll tell it like it is to you, teacher to teacher. I'll share real best practices that have worked time after time, real anecdotes to illustrate those best practices, real conversations I've had with my students, and real classroom management scenarios I've experienced in my classroom. (The only aspect of the book that isn't real is the student names.) I would like to share what I have learned with those who are in need or perhaps just curious to build on what they already know.

The beautiful thing about our profession is that you will always be needed. And you will most likely always laugh with your class every day because Camille said something outrageous, or Javier glued his hands together by accident, and yes, students still pass gas in class at every grade level. That's never going to change. Here's more good news: Your students are more aware today than ever, they are more curious about our changing world more than ever, and they are more empathetic than ever. Let's take advantage of that in our classrooms and help them keep up with today's world.

It's important to hold on to why we first went into this profession and cherish that feeling we get when a lesson goes really well. Teaching K–12 students is one of the most rewarding professions when we lead with love, follow our gut instincts, and know we are shaping the adults of tomorrow. To give students the opportunity to thrive we need to create and nurture classrooms where positive energy flows, students are collaborating, academic rigor is high and engaging, and strong student-to-student as well as student-to-teacher relationships exist. I'm here to help you get there because I've messed up, but then I figured it out and thrived. I want the same for you and your students because we are in one of the most noble professions in the world. This book will get vulnerable at some parts and I'm okay with that. So, here's a bit of my story.

Who Am I? And Why Am I Writing This Book?

The first classroom management strategy I tried in my first year was good old-fashioned yelling. I figured if I could get my voice louder and stronger than the students', I could startle them into listening. It's really all I could think to do with a rowdy class of twenty-nine sixth graders. I eventually realized yelling is only a short-term—*very* short-term—and detrimental solution.

The first time I realized yelling can be detrimental not only to a classroom but also to your health was around the middle of my very first year in the classroom. I noticed my ears ached after class. The pain became so unbearable that I eventually went to an ear doctor. The doctor told me both of my eardrums were very swollen, which was causing the pain. He asked what I did for a living, and I told him I was a sixth-grade teacher. He chuckled and replied, "That's why your eardrums are swollen." My ears did return to normal, but it was literally a painful wake-up call as to how much I was raising my voice in the classroom. Something had to change. If *my* ears were in pain, I couldn't even imagine how my students felt. Something was off, and I was determined to find a better way to teach. This is where my quest to find the best practices in teaching began.

I've always considered myself fearless. I've bungee jumped and skydived in New Zealand on the same day, rafted through class-four rapids, free-fall jumped from casinos in Las Vegas, snorkeled with sharks, backpacked solo through Australia and Costa Rica, canoed down deadly hippopotamus-infested waters in Zimbabwe, and jumped in frozen lakes for fun—twice. None of these adventures comes close to the accomplishment I felt when I finally figured out what makes classrooms work. Most of us, including myself, make mistakes trying to figure out what works. Most new teachers have little help, a few teaching books, and maybe a classroom management course or two to guide us. I'd like to give back to the profession and tell you everything I know and direct you to practices that most teachers say work. I'm here to make it easier for you.

I am not claiming to know the only right way to teach. What makes teaching so difficult, so complex, and so beautiful is that there are many right ways and more are being discovered every day. However, many best practices form a common thread among good teachers. I am sharing my knowledge and insights about what has worked for me and my peers. What is revealed in this book is just the tip of the iceberg, and it took me years to figure it out through trial and error, through tears and triumph. I hope to save you from some of the mistakes I made and share with you the many joys I had in the classroom and how I got there.

I wrote this for you, so you can spend less time on the errors and more time on discovering what works for you and your students. Many of my chapters are inspired by *real questions* teachers have asked me as we were walking down the hallway, during lunch, during my prep period, after school, or through e-mail. Every time a teacher asked me a question, I immediately started developing a new chapter for this book, because if one person is asking, there's every chance that other people have the same question.

Achieving these insights took me years of practice, trying any and every teaching method, reading the research, working closely with a mentor, and working in challenging school settings. Through my growing determination, curiosity about what works in teaching, passion to always be better, and my love of the students, I earned Teacher of the Year in my school and was awarded a Fulbright Distinguished Teacher grant to coach educators in Botswana, Africa, on student engagement, technology, and student-centered lessons. I've coached teachers in Kathmandu, Nepal, on student-centered lessons and empowering students. I've worked with students from Eastern Europe and Russia, taught K–12 classes in Turkey, and taught graduate-level classes at the University of San Diego to teacher candidates entering our beautiful profession. I've been invited to keynote education conferences and have consulted with districts around the country. What I'm saying is these strategies work.

What I found from coaching teachers and working with students around the world is that even despite language barriers, there are universal best practices that consistently bring success to teachers and students. I knew I had to share what I learned and accomplished with others. These positive and powerful moments are what got me up way too early in the morning and what kept me working countless hours after school. I hope you can use this book to build on my experiences for even greater successes in your own classrooms and homes.

And before we move any further, understand that in these pages I'm by no means saying do more; I'm suggesting that you think differently. When we think of classroom management, we traditionally think of ways to keep students quiet, well behaved, and on task. However, in order to prepare students for today's world, we should think of classroom management as guiding students to work collaboratively, communicate with each other, and listen to their classmates' thoughts and opinions. We now know classroom management practices that are better for students than what has been done in the past. Older classroom management practices traditionally focus on compliance, while more modern, progressive practices focus on student well-being, social-emotional learning, belonging, equity, and engagement. Classroom management is about building students up, not breaking them down. This means we are starting to shift our own perspective.

> We should think of classroom management as guiding students to work collaboratively, communicate with each other, and listen to their classmates' thoughts and opinions.

Times are changing. According to a study conducted by Child Trends, Inc. (2015), there are five critical skills most likely to increase the odds of success across all outcomes and which employers expect employees to have. The first three are social skills, communication, and higher-order thinking skills (including problem-solving, critical thinking, and decision-making). These three are supported by the intrapersonal skills of self-control and positive self-concept.

Here's a real-world statistic to support this: It has been reported that 85 percent of those who are terminated from jobs are let go because of inadequate social skills. According to a *Forbes* article discussing what skills employers look for, "Employers also want new hires to have technical knowledge related to the job, but that's not nearly as important as good teamwork, decision-making and communication skills, and the ability to plan and prioritize work" (Adams, 2014). Today, companies are hiring people who can work independently just as well as they can with others. Obedience is not valued as much as other 21st century skills, which has teachers rethinking how this translates to classroom management for us. How do we prepare our students for the real world?

Perhaps you've already heard of a few of these best practices. Or perhaps you have your own twists on the practices, which are perfect to share with your colleagues in the discussion questions at the end of each chapter. The point is that each of these practices warrants discussion because they are all critical parts of what makes learners engaged, confident, empowered, and independent.

Why Teach?

They say the person you fall in love with should bring out the best in you, making your light shine. The same goes for the job you fall in love with. Teaching is one of the most vulnerable professions out there, yet it should make your best qualities shine, lighting you up from the inside out. Teaching did this for me. It brought out characteristics in me that I did not know existed. It also exposed my raw weaknesses. However, those moments when my weaknesses were most glaring motivated me to work toward becoming a better teacher.

The kids out there need you. There might be times you mess up a lesson or a conversation with a student. That's more than okay, it's expected—you're human. It's all part of the process. As educators, we get to be exactly what they need, imperfections and all. How lucky are we?

There is something special about teaching. We all have our own reasons that drew us to this profession, and they are all unique from one another. I'm not sure if any of my teachers from middle or high school know I became a teacher. I'm pretty sure if you told them that I was a teacher, it would surprise them. Until college, I was never particularly motivated as a student. I flew under the radar and did just enough not to draw attention to myself. I wonder what was going on all of those years in the classroom when I was passing notes to my friends. (I filled an entire box of notes. My friends and I earned an *A* in note-writing, not note-taking.) My junior year of college is when my light switch went on and I actually started feeling smart. I became a different student.

My academically apathetic history is probably the single most important factor in why I have succeeded as a teacher. I understand why students get bored, feel unengaged, fall asleep, get rowdy, etc. I get it. But I also know how to convert that energy into engagement and excitement in the classroom.

I bet you can't find one teacher who hasn't shed a tear of joy the first time they found success in a student. If you look around any teacher's desk, you'll probably see a thank-you card hanging up from a student. These cards bring us so much joy. That's why I've included actual quotes from real students at the beginning of each chapter. Students remember the way we make them feel. You'll see the light switch turn on in a child's eyes when you explain a concept well and they get it. When you ask a teacher what they do, they'll usually smile as they explain what grade and subject they teach. You can't say that about many other professions. This book will show you ways to make your students feel good while learning. The emotional element is a significant part of the process for teacher and student alike.

A time will come in your teaching career when you feel lucky just to be a person in your students' lives every day, because they are phenomenal. And there's a point where your students, even when they are difficult, will feel lucky just to be in your class. With love, patience, skill, and creativity you will actually be working and changing a person's life in your classroom every day.

There's going to be a point where you are working way too hard, and that's where I'd like to come in and help take some of the load off of you. Whatever classroom management frustration you've had in your classroom, I've most likely been there (times two). I'm listening, I understand, and I can help. To all the teachers reading this book: Thank you for joining our beautiful profession. We need people like you.

—Serena

PART 1
FIRST WEEKS OF SCHOOL

A Memorable Day 1 . . .

On Day 1 of ninth-grade history, another teacher walked into the classroom and asked to borrow some paper and our teacher completely flipped out and made a scene. We all watched in disbelief. Then, after it was over, she asked us to write down what we saw, including every detail from the color of the shirt the other teacher was wearing, the length of time the confrontation went on, and exact quotes said in the interaction. She/we read all of them afterwards and there were so many variations of what everyone witnessed. Then she went on to say that much of history is like that as well. I'll never forget it.

—Amy, Age 38

What do the first weeks of school have to do with classroom management?

Everything. First of all, we want to be prepared and not only on time but early, so the above doesn't happen. The first weeks of school will establish routines in your classroom, set your expectations for behavior and participation, and teach healthy student collaboration skills. This will be the time your students form good habits in your classroom. This is also the time you will start to build a relationship based on mutual respect with students and set boundaries and structures. A strong first few weeks of the year almost always predicts a strong school year. Make these few weeks count.

Build Mutually Respectful Relationships With Students From Day 1

....

> All of my years as a student I went through a countless number of teachers. I have had cool teachers, strict teachers, laid-back teachers. I have always thought, *I wish I could have a teacher that knows how to be all of those, when they need to.*
>
> —Sammy, Grade 9

I chose to complete my four-month student teaching assignment at a boarding school in rural Pierre, South Dakota, with a student population that was 100 percent Natives from the surrounding reservations. We were told these students were mandated to be at this boarding school because they were unable to live in their homes for one reason or another. Needless to say, although it was a powerful student teaching experience, often classroom management was an issue because of my limited expertise. I remember the first time the classroom teacher allowed me to administer my own quiz. Finally I had my own class, if only for a few minutes. I handed out the papers and started walking around the room as I gave directions. One eighth-grade girl yelled in a snarky tone, "Hey, what's your first name anyway?" I replied, trying to sound as authoritative as possible, "Serena, but *you* have to call me Ms. Pariser!" I shot her a look that I thought screamed, "Don't mess with me." She must have interpreted it as, "I'm going to demand your respect and you're going to give it to me." That rarely works, I quickly learned, unless you're looking for respect through intimidation. As a student teacher, I was anything but intimidating.

She thought for a second and then yelled, "Hey, Serena!" I fell into her trap and replied, "Ms. Pariser!" She laughed and yelled even louder, "Serena, Serena, Serena!" This went back and forth for a little while. My face was boiling red. I let loose with my final I'm-going-to-teach-you comeback: *"Ms. Pariser! You are a student!"*

BAM.

A spiral-bound 100-sheet notebook hit the side of my face. She had thrown it at me, with perfect aim, in a successful attempt to shut me up. My eyes started to water in fright. Had a student really just thrown a notebook at my face? Was I bleeding? What was the rest of the class thinking? I said in my calmest voice, "Call security," but I was shaking. This is how I learned that you have to build mutually respectful relationships with students in order to be truly respected by them. The students don't owe you anything.

Does Amazon sell respect? It seems like some teachers have it from their students and some do not. How do those successful teachers do it? Let me start by saying if the students respect and like you as a person, your job will be a lot easier. Unlike a boss who doesn't like an employee, you can't fire a student. You can spend your entire year trying to fix a fractured relationship that is broken due to lack of respect. Here are some guidelines to help earn the respect of your students (not an easy task):

First: You are part of the class. It's not you versus the class.

Is your goal to get the kids to listen to you or to help each of them succeed? Think hard about this. Do you have the same goals in mind? Now, you may be thinking, *Yes, but how do I help them succeed if they don't even listen when I am talking?* You're not the only one who's been on the verge of tears. I soon learned that when there is a battle in the classroom (you versus them), they can and will overpower you. They outnumber you. Scary thought, right? The secret is that you can't let them know that. That's the difference between an unsuccessful teacher and a successful one. Successful teachers know this and work with their students. Unsuccessful teachers seem to fall into the trap of testing their power, using a loud voice to try to overpower. Power struggles rarely work in the long run. It leads to intimidation, which isn't an ideal learning environment. Yes, I've been overpowered. I've had students walk out of my classroom, curse in my face, and laugh when I discipline them. It's not a pleasant situation when a student or whole class shows disrespect. It's also hard to earn respect back once it's lost. However, once the students trust—yes, trust—that you have their interests in mind, they will let their guard down and get ready for the educational journey. They will *want* you to lead them. They will *ask* you what they are going to learn today.

> If you want them to take seriously their job as a student, do your job by being prepared to teach.

They will *give up* the fight because they realize you are both on the same side. How do you do this? You don't tell them, you show them that you have their interests in mind by using the following tips.

Tips for Building Mutually Respectful Relationships With Your Students

- **Focus on your goal.** Know that whatever you focus on is what will thrive in the classroom. If you focus on negative behaviors, that is what will thrive. If you focus on classroom rules, students will learn those rules, but when will they learn content? My advice is to always have your lesson prepared. Focus on the learning. Show students that learning is always the first priority. That is your job. If you want them to take seriously their job as a student, do your job by being prepared to teach. If you focus on your lesson plan, you will feel confident and the rest will follow suit.

- **Let students know you believe in their success.** Tell your students that you believe in their success. Do you think they will rise to the occasion if you challenge them? Here's a secret: If you believe in them and tell them so, they will believe in themselves. If you don't believe that your students will succeed, they won't believe either. For example, say

    "Nathan, I really want you to do well today. How can I help you with that?" instead of, "Nathan, you have an *F* in my class, don't you *want* to get a good grade? Why can't you behave?"

    Both statements show Nathan that he is accountable for his behavior. The first statement, however, shows him you believe in his success and it is his choice how he behaves. You are rooting for him, yet he has agency. The second statement puts a student on the defensive, which rarely works. Be smart with your words and work on the relationship. The way you communicate makes a big difference in how your words are received by the students.

- **Be the teacher you are.** This seems like a simple statement, but I have always found it profound. Be your best self inside your classroom. What excites you that you can use in the classroom to accelerate learning? Use your personality strengths in your teaching. Do you love acting? Then use it in your teaching. Are you a great artist but feel insecure teaching math? Draw out some math problems! Do you love playing the piano? Why don't you play to the students as they are working? Your strengths are one of the biggest assets to your classroom. I love being silly and playful in life, but for many years I tried to run a very serious classroom because I was afraid of doing anything different as a new teacher. Once I brought my silly side to the learning, my students' test scores jumped, the students were happier, and I was a happier teacher. We know there are still serious times in the classroom, but we also know when we can laugh together. Weave your personality into the lesson. If you are a golf-loving science teacher, why not bring in your nine irons on the day you teach force? If you do this, you are much more likely to be a better and "real"—as the students like to say—teacher.

- **Work on your weaknesses.** In addition to using your strengths to become a "real" person in the students' eyes, you have to be willing to work on your weaknesses if that is what the students need. Let them know you learned how to do this specifically for them. You are a student as well. Think of yourself as a caretaker. This is the work you have to do outside of school hours (or during your prep if you're super efficient). This is what your students need. Say two inexperienced teachers are discussing groupwork. One teacher says, "Groupwork is just not my thing. It's easier to just have them work independently." The second teacher says, "I know groupwork is better for the students but I also know this is my weak spot. I'm going to learn how to do it." Which teacher do you think the students will respect more and will have more prepared, engaging lessons?

- **Use discipline sparingly.** If you discipline, do so for a specific purpose and tell students why. They will respect your authority and admire that you rarely have to use your power. Anger or disappointment can be effective only if used very rarely. Anger used often is completely ineffective. Discipline once, within the first two months of school, and only after you have taught the structures of your classroom. This establishes boundaries. Students need you to be stern when they cross your boundaries. For example, you could address your class with, "Do you remember the classroom agreements we discussed? Do we need something added to address side conversations? I want to make sure we're on the same page. If there's a misunderstanding, I can certainly address that. I know you're not trying to be malicious, but you are in fact breaking an agreement." Learn to pick and choose your battles. I always asked myself, *Is this affecting the learning of the whole class?* If the answer is yes, it is your job to correct the behavior. If the answer is no, do not stop the classroom for just one student. It's not fair to the other students, unless you are using it as a teachable moment.

- According to one metastudy (Marzano et al., 2003), teachers who have strong relationships with their students have 31 percent fewer behavioral issues in their classrooms. This statistic has a huge impact on the amount of learning that goes on the classroom and the amount of quality teaching that happens, as well as on your general well-being. Building a mutually respectful relationship with a student starts the minute they know you know their name and you use it often when speaking with them. Strong relationships with students don't happen by chance. They happen through the way we decide, consciously or unconsciously, to interact with students from Day 1.

Your Turn

1. What are your teaching strengths? Are they the same or different from what other teachers have recognized as your strengths? How do you use this information to maximize student learning?

   _____
   _____
   _____
   _____
   _____
   _____

2. When was the last time you disciplined a full classroom? Can you remember a teacher who did this? Do you think it worked or not? If not, how could you or that teacher do it differently next time?

   _____
   _____
   _____
   _____
   _____
   _____

3. How can you show your students that you respect them, care for them as human beings, and believe in their success from Day 1?

   _____
   _____
   _____
   _____
   _____
   _____

Nurture a Belonging Classroom

> You rescued me from a lonely life.
>
> —9th Grade Student

There's a phrase that has grown quite popular in the educational field the past few years: Maslow's before Bloom's. Basically, it's saying that we have to tend to Maslow's hierarchy of needs before students can get very far up on Bloom's taxonomy. So, if a student doesn't feel like they completely belong or doesn't have a sense of connection with the other students in the classroom, any sort of deeper learning may not happen throughout the school year as they will continue to struggle with Maslow's hierarchy and most likely eventually check out or shut down. (If you're not familiar with the concepts of Maslow and Bloom, look to Figure 2.1.)

As teachers it's our job to make Maslow's hierarchy happen very early in the school year, starting even on Day 1. You see, on Day 1 we are already working to create bonds between students. We want students to feel a sense of connection to each other, to feel accepted, and to start creating friendships with their classmates.

How can we create belonging classrooms from Day 1? Here are a few strategies that work.

- **Teach students not to shame, laugh, or ridicule each other for giving incorrect answers.** I used to do table points in a class-wide token reward system. When a student would accidentally laugh at another student for giving a way-off-track answer, I would reward the student who was ridiculed with table

Figure 2.1 Maslow's Before Bloom's

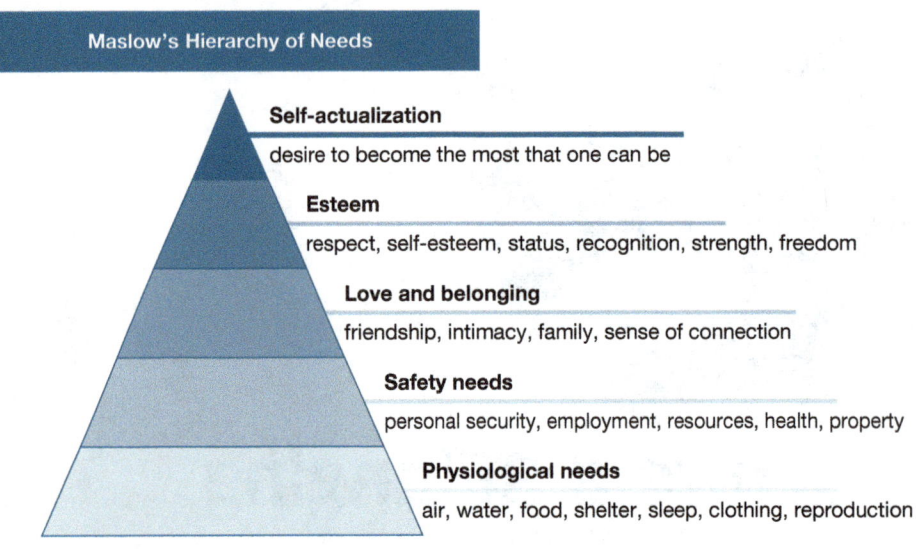

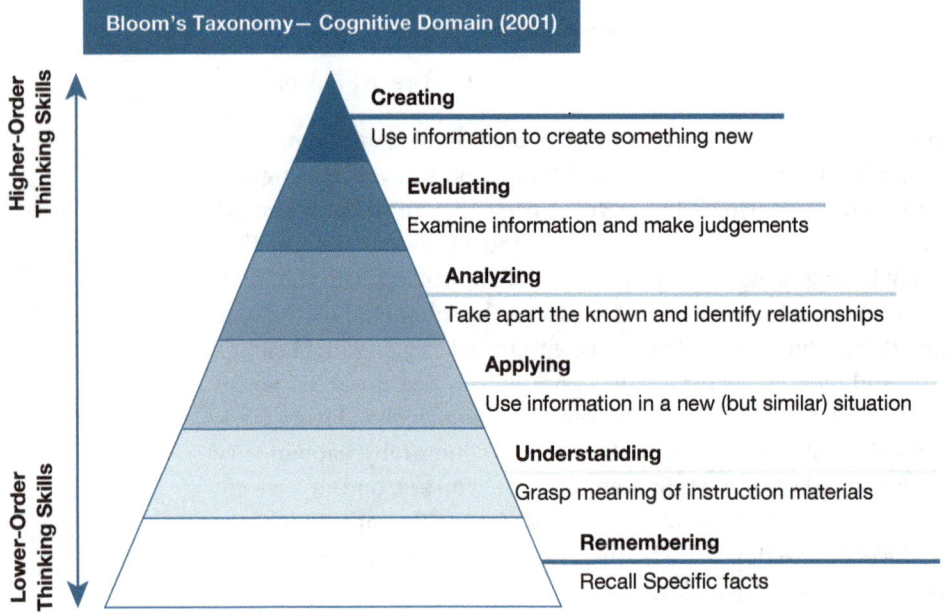

Source: Adapted from Maslow's Heirarchy of Needs and Bloom's Taxonomy.

points. If the perpetrator apologized, I would give a few points to him or her, but not as many as the ridiculed student. This gave the power back to the student who was ridiculed. Pretty soon the laughter stopped because students knew that inside our classroom this was not okay.

- Create a "family board" or area of the classroom dedicated to student pictures so students can feel seen in the classroom. It's okay if not every student is up there right away (especially if you are a middle or high school teacher and have multiple classes) because they will be at some point. Students who might not feel initially connected to the class, their peers, or the teacher might need to be on the family board in the first round to gain a sense of belonging in the class early on. Another benefit of family boards is that if you post group photos or photos with more than one student in it, many students feel seen in the classroom at once, which builds a sense of belonging. For an example of a family board, see Figure 2.2.

Figure 2.2 Family Board

Source: Pariser and DeRoche, (2020).

- **Hold morning meetings daily (with the same format to provide structure and comfort to students) or weekly.** Morning meetings are a powerful way for students to come together on a regular basis and "gather around the dinner table," as you would with any functional family.

Your Turn

1. Did you ever have a class in K–12 or even university or graduate school where you really felt like you belonged? What contributed to that?

   _____
   _____
   _____
   _____
   _____
   _____

2. On the other hand, think of a time when you felt like you didn't belong to a class or a group somewhere. What contributed to that?

   _____
   _____
   _____
   _____
   _____
   _____

3. How does creating a belonging classroom help increase learning in the classroom and lead to fewer behavioral issues and higher engagement?

   _____
   _____
   _____
   _____
   _____
   _____

Make It About the Students and the Importance of Student Collaboration on Day 1

The first day of school should be all about the students. We need to learn their names as fast as possible. The faster we know their names, the more we care about them. At least that's what they're thinking, I promise. Referring to your seating chart will help you learn the names the quickest. My seating chart is virtually attached to my hands the first few weeks of school until I learn all of the students' names. Make sure the seating chart is always on a clipboard that you walk around the classroom with. The students don't know what is on your clipboard, so the fact that you are addressing them by name will be impressive to them. Every other adult in your room should have a copy of the seating chart so they know names as well.

In the first couple of days, you may not have a seating chart yet and students may still be enrolling in the school or your class. However, you can still start learning student names in a few creative ways.

Tips for Learning Students' Names

- **Learning students' names Method #1 (basic).** If you're a little hesitant and would rather take a conservative approach to learning names, that's fine. My mentor taught me an effortless trick. Have the students take an index card and write their first name on it, preferably with marker and as large as possible so you can see it easily. They then fold the cards in half and place them on their desks with the names facing you. This will work for the first few days. Then make a seating chart as soon as possible to get a handle on the names fast. You could also use name tags, but index cards are reusable and easier on your wallet. Most schools provide index cards to teachers at the beginning of the school year.

- **Learning students' names Method #2.** Use student pictures. Most attendance programs now can make seating charts with student pictures on them. If you don't want to take the time to construct one, you can either cut and paste the student pictures onto your seating chart or keep a reference of student pictures on your clipboard behind your seating chart.

- **Learning students' names Method #3 (advanced).** I read this strategy in Kelley's (2003) *Rookie Teaching for Dummies* and still use it every year. The students get a kick out of it, and it's really effective for learning names. It also shows the students that you are creative and they may never know what to expect.

    1. Start at one edge of your classroom and ask the student her or his first name.
    2. Move on to the student behind her or him.
    3. Go back and forth a few times between the two of them, repeating their names as you look into their faces.
    4. Move on to student number three, repeat the name, and review all the names you've learned so far.
    5. Repeat this process until you learn the entire class, and then spend some time picking out students at random and trying to remember their names.
    6. When you feel comfortable with the names, turn your back and ask the students to change desks.

My goal was always to find out about my students on the first day (make it about them). Show them you care who they are as learners. I like to do an activity to get them talking to each other, problem-solving, or working as a team to try to create something. Remember, they are as nervous as you are. They want to know about you, but they also want to know each other. You will need your students to be friendly with each other to have a productive year, so it pays off if they can learn to communicate with a bit of structure and enjoy speaking with and learning from each other. This is why structured team-building or icebreaker activities are priceless on this day.

On the first day you want your students to smile, be able to communicate with each other, start raising hands, and start learning each others' names. Save the rest for later. The introductory activities I enjoyed the most required students to be up and out of their seats, moving around the room, and trying to solve a puzzle in a group or team. Tons of these activities can be found online, in books, or in the minds of your colleagues. A book I recommend for icebreakers and team-building activities that can carry you throughout the year is Thiagarajan's *100 Favorite Games* (2006). This book is filled with activities for grade school up to adult learners to help build a community of leaders and critical thinkers in your classroom. My copy lives on the bookshelf beside my desk.

Table 3.1 shows the traditional way of conducting Day 1 contrasted with a more effective way that will engage your students.

In Best Practice #6, you'll see why having students speak to one another on Day 1 will help you build a seating chart the first week. You have to get a glimpse of their personalities. Day 2 is when students can begin to take notes, learn the classroom rules, understand your expectations and consequences, and get ready to learn. Day 1 shows them you are curious about *them*, hear *their* voices, and and learning *their* names.

Table 3.1 Engaging Your Students on Day 1

OLD WAY OF DAY 1	FRESH AND ENGAGING IDEAS FOR DAY 1
Teacher goes over class rules and expectations.	Students do a collaborative icebreaker or structured collaborative activity. Teacher saves rules and expectations for Day 2.
Students leave with an idea of the teacher's personality.	Teacher is more interested in seeing the personalities of the students.
Students do not know their classmates and may be resistant to collaborating the next day.	Students start to know their classmates and collaboration is easier the next day.
Student voice is not heard.	Student voice is heard.
Students leave the room understanding rules and expectations.	Students leave the room smiling and excited for the next day of class. Teacher goes over rules and expectations to class on Day 2.
Students do not talk to each other on Day 1. The teacher talks to them most of the time.	Most of the period is a collaborative team-building activity where teacher can start to see the personalities of the students to help build a seating chart.

Your Turn

1. What is one of your favorite Day 1 activities? Why do you like it so much?

   _____
   _____
   _____
   _____

2. What message does doing a fun and collaborative activity on Day 1 relay to your students?

   _____
   _____
   _____
   _____

3. Why is it important to have students talking to each other on Day 1 in a structured activity? How will this facilitate student collaboration in your classroom?

   _____
   _____
   _____
   _____

4. Think about a successful Day 1 you've had in the past. What were some of the long-term positive results that came out of what you did?

   _____
   _____
   _____
   _____

Set Your Routine and Structures Early . . . and Keep Them!

If you've ever substitute taught or covered a colleague's classroom, you know that you can tell a good teacher the moment you walk into their class. Even when their usual teacher isn't there, the students know what do to. They enter a certain way, they go to their seats, they do a specific procedure first, they ask to do certain things and know not to ask to do others. This classroom routine shows the teacher set structures early. These types of classrooms run like a well-oiled machine, especially in the first five to ten minutes of class. Routines should be taught in the beginning of the school year, just as content is taught.

Setting structures early almost guarantees a successful year. Let students own the routine. Humans tend to keep habits. Without habit, classroom and life may be exciting, but we start to feel out of place. Give students a habitual way to start and end your class.

Tips for Establishing Classroom Structures

- **Make it easy.** Make sure your structures are not too tedious. If a student needs to get a pencil, do they have to sign ten release forms? Or is there a basket always in the same place that holds

(Continued)

(Continued)

pencils? If the structures make sense and show you value the students, then they will work.

- **Consistency is key.** Don't change your structures too often. I'm not saying don't *ever* change structures, but having an established routine makes students feel comfortable. Students learn to remember and do daily things automatically. If you keep changing things—even if the new structures are better—they'll forget what the newest structure is and just follow none. Decide on structures that work early on.

- **Structure the beginning of class.** Give structure to the beginning of your class period by asking the students to do the same type of thing at the beginning of class every day. Think about how your own personal morning routine before you get to school sets you up for the rest of the day. This way, if kids come in groggy they will know what to do automatically. An example of a great daily structure is outlined in the following steps:

    1. Go directly to your seat and sit.
    2. Place your backpack on the back of your chair or on the floor.
    3. Take out your homework log and record your homework.
    4. Start the warm-up exercise on the board.

Once you do the same routine for about seven days, the students will get in the habit of doing it, and the routine will become comforting to them. They will feel successful since they are following the rules. Remember to praise students each and every time they follow your routine, no matter how easy. Post the opening routine somewhere in the room for your visual learners or any students who need a gentle reminder. It will save you a lot of frustration if you can just say the student's name and point to the routine instead of repeating yourself. I have found a PowerPoint slide helps with this. Split your computer screen and project that slide (so you can take attendance as students do the morning routine). Pro tip: Place a smiley face on the slide somewhere and "Good morning/afternoon Period _____." All you have to do is change the period number or class name, project the slide, and boom—you're free for the first several minutes of class to take attendance and get ready for the lesson. Posting the routine on a screen also creates student agency, builds confidence, and projects positive vibes from the start of your class.

> Remember to praise students each and every time they follow your routine, no matter how easy.

Routines that need to be set as early as possible in Week 1:

- Technology sign-out
- Tardy student policy
- Students assigned technology numbers; this is most effective if technology numbers are on student names on seating chart
- Classroom books sign-out
- Bathroom pass/log (if necessary)
- Where are assignments turned in?
- Where can missing work be found for absent students?
- Where is homework written on the board for students to record?
- Cell phone/electronic device policy for your classroom

Your Turn

1. Look at the above list of routines. What is a structure or routine that you've seen work well in a classroom for one of the items?

   _____
   _____
   _____
   _____
   _____
   _____

2. In your opinion, are there any of the above items that do not need a structure and/or routine? Why?

   _____
   _____
   _____
   _____
   _____
   _____

3. Do you think it's more important to have a routine to begin the class, a routine to end the class, or both? Why?

   _____
   _____
   _____
   _____
   _____
   _____

Use Empowering Language Instead of Controlling Language

....

> Your class is a place I look forward to coming to every day.
>
> —Carmen, Grade 9

Even though students are mandated to attend school daily, don't take advantage of that. Strive to make your classroom a place they look forward to being in. Strive to make it a place where they feel good and comfortable. After my third year teaching, a close teacher friend gave me one of the most meaningful presents I have ever received. She handed me *Positive Words, Powerful Results* (2004), a book by Hal Urban.

Inside the front cover was a handwritten note regarding how teaching is all about what we say and how we say it. This message stayed with me. It took me a few months before I started reading the book. I mean, who had time to read books for fun with all those papers to grade, right? Urban's book was the beginning of my journey of realizing that teaching is all about making the students feel empowered, challenged, successful, and supported. There's a quote by an unknown author I stumbled upon recently that sums it up perfectly: "If speaking kindly to plants helps them grow, imagine what speaking kindly to humans can do." Our job as teachers is to help our students grow academically, socially, and emotionally. That's a big responsibility. The climate in the classroom begins with your words: what you say, *how* you say it, and the tone you use while saying it. It is an art and a science. Some of us are born with the ability to *give* not *take* from others with our subconscious choice of words. This wasn't the case for me; I had to learn. The book was one of the most meaningful presents to me because it cracked the door to show me that our words and tone can be either our biggest ally or our biggest hurdle in becoming a great teacher.

I can use my words and tone more effectively now, but I remember a time during my third year of teaching where I failed. I was walking my ninth graders down the hallway and they were supposed to be silent. One notoriously defiant student—I'll call him Adam—continued to talk. I first threatened to make the whole class turn around (secretly hoping I didn't need to go there because I wasn't even sure if they would listen to me enough to turn around). Adam continued to talk away, however, unafraid of my threats. I stopped the class, stuck out my first finger—otherwise known as the teacher finger of shame—and waved it with every word I said.

"*Stop talking!*"

Adam laughed.

"*I. Said. Stop. Talking!*" I spoke a bit louder this time and with a face more red, my head leaned downwards and eyes of fire (or so I thought) staring at Adam.

He turned around to not only laugh but also show his classmates he didn't care with a snarky glance. This was probably not the first time a teacher had tried to overpower him and was probably not the first time it hadn't worked. Adam had zero fear of me, and fear was the emotion I was trying to trigger in him to get obedience. Needless to say, the story ended with my head almost flying off because of all of the blood that had rushed to it. Adam eventually stopped talking but just to get out of the school gates. I lost. He left laughing and I took an aspirin. This story is just one of many where I was not using empowering language but instead using controlling language.

> We have to be careful not to beat ourselves up for the times we mess up. These are the times when we are learning, and these times will be your biggest teachers.

Just writing about this story today triggers a painful feeling. As teachers, we have to be careful not to beat ourselves up for the times we mess up and resort to controlling language because we're at our wit's end. These are the times when we are learning, and these times will be your biggest teachers.

Tips for Improving How We Can Use Empowering Language

- **Use "I" statements.** If you want a student to do something, especially when correcting behavior, never say, "*You* need to . . ." Always start with, "*I* need you to . . ." Students can't really argue

#5. Use Empowering Language Instead of Controlling Language

with an "I" statement. It's very easy for a student to argue with a "you" statement.

- When speaking to a seated student one-on-one, try to kneel down to their level or below them. This is less intimidating for students and they will be more likely to open up to you.

- **Say the student's name when speaking to them, but not in a threatening way.** People love hearing their own name. In fact, according to Carnegie's (1981) *How to Win Friends and Influence People*, "A person's name is to that person the sweetest and most important sound in any language" (p. 83). Dale Carnegie knew how to win people over. This is why this tactic will work for your class. Saying a student's name in a respectful and even loving way will connect them with you as you are talking to them or asking them to do something.

- **Put yourself in your students' shoes.** Think of the last time you spoke to your class. Would you appreciate being spoken to like that? If the answer is yes, well done! Great job! You are ahead of where most are, including myself, in the first year or two of teaching. I equate the first years of teaching as fighting with a significant other in an unhealthy relationship. You say things you don't mean; you apologize; you lose control at times; you wonder why they don't care about all the preparation or work you are putting in. However, the great news is that as you become more experienced, you realize that you are on the same team as the students and not fighting against them. You will have more control and stronger connections with your students this way. Yes, you will still lose your cool, but it will happen rarely and for a specific reason. Yes, you will disagree, but you will keep your composure as you see the issue for what it is. How can you start growing? Speak with respect to the students with the goal to empower them. They will do what you want them to do more often and because they want to, not because they are afraid of you or sick of hearing you nag.

The student sees the first comment as him doing the teacher a favor, but he sees the second comment as a threat or challenge, and he thinks you are using your power to hold it over his head that you can give him detention. Ironically, you could give detention in both cases; you are just making Jorge feel like he is doing you a favor with the first comment.

> Empowering comment: "Jorge, I need you to sit down, please. Thank you."
>
> Instead of a controlling comment (in the mind of a student): "Sit down or you will have detention."

(Continued)

(Continued)

EMPOWERING LANGUAGE	CONTROLLING LANGUAGE
"I need you to . . ."	"You need to . . ."
"Do me a favor and sit down."	"Sit down *now*!"
"Can you do me a favor and listen up please."	"Why aren't you listening?"
"Could you please stop talking to your neighbor and listen a bit more closely?"	"Why can't you stop talking?"
"I" statements	"You" statements

I will admit that sometimes you can get faster results with controlling language, but when we do that we are breaking the students down and they may resent you in the long run. Empowering language helps build students up.

Your Turn

1. Can you remember a teacher who made you feel not good because of their words? What did they say and how did they say it?

   _____
   _____
   _____
   _____
   _____
   _____

2. Now think of an instructor who made you feel great every time you heard them speak to the class or to you. Do you remember specific words they said or just the way the words made you feel?

   _____
   _____
   _____
   _____
   _____
   _____

3. Practice using "I" statements and statements using a student's name in a respectful and loving way aloud. The more you hear yourself say it, the more likely you are to do this naturally.

   _____
   _____
   _____
   _____
   _____
   _____

Best Practice #6

Create Purposeful Seating Charts

Watch for more about creating purposeful seating charts.

A big part of classroom management is giving every student opportunities to succeed. Have you ever seen a class that is doing a word search? Do you ever wonder why it drops down to almost silent immediately? *It's because they all can do the task.* The problem is that the task is too easy. Often misbehaviors occur because students are underchallenged and become bored, or they are overchallenged without academic support. This is where the tool of a purposeful seating chart can and will help both your classroom management and the academic abilities of the class. With a purposeful seating chart, even with a challenging curriculum students will always be in close proximity to those that can help them. A purposeful seating chart will foster a community of learners.

My mentor taught me a strategy for making seating charts that changed my teaching career. Before this strategy, I used to break up students who "shouldn't sit together" and then sprinkled the rest around and hoped for the best. This isn't the way to go. Making a purposeful seating chart means you look at students' academic abilities, learning disabilities, and language barriers and then make a chart from there. *I suggest having a seating chart done by Day 3 of the first week of school.* The earlier the better or students will start finding who they want to sit next to and then you'll have an extra battle on your hands. On the first day, if you do a student-centered activity where students are given ample opportunity to talk and work with each other, you'll have the opportunity to observe how the students interact with each other and what personalities stand out (and some will). Take notes as you observe student interactions on Day 1. You'll need these observations to make a purposeful seating chart.

Tips for Preparing a Purposeful Seating Chart

Step #1: Acquire a list of students with individualized education programs (IEPs) in your class. You can usually find this on your attendance roster. It's helpful to have a description of the disability if available. Sometimes IEPs trickle in later in the school year, but work with what you have at the beginning of the school year.

Step #2: Find the list with the students who are multilingual. Usually you can acquire this list from the speech pathologist at your school or from the school counselor. It's easiest to get this information on your attendance roster, so check there first.

Step #3: Acquire a list of students identified as GATE (gifted and talented). This information is often found on your attendance roster.

The rest of your students should be general education students.

Draw how you want to arrange the desks in your room. I recommend groups of four to six, which research also suggests is best for larger projects (Teaching & Learning Transformation Center, n.d.) and will leave more space in your classroom for movement. Situate the groups so students' backs are not toward the front of the room. You will be talking to the whole class many times and do not want students to constantly have to flip their chairs around.

Step #4: Place your students with IEPs first. *Spread them out from each other*. Some students may have preferential seating in their IEP, meaning they are legally mandated to sit in the front, back, or side of the room depending on their needs and what is most beneficial to their learning.

Step #5: Also *spread your multilingual students out from each other*. I usually put these students next to vocal general education students who speak often in class. If the general education student speaks the multilingual student's native language, even better. Vocal students will usually be eager to help a struggling multilingual student when needed. This makes a difference. Spread out the advancement via individual determination (AVID) students you may have from each other, if you have that data.

Step #6: *Spread out* your students identified as GATE and AVID from each other.

You may be thinking, *Why would I spread out all of my students with IEPs, multilingual students, or students who need extra support when I work with them all together?* The answer is that you spread them out to create the most heterogeneous seating chart possible so that instead of students forming cliques with like students that sit near them, the class as a whole has a strong chance of becoming a community that

(Continued)

> (Continued)
>
> collaborates and learns from each other as well as from you. Also, every student has somebody near them who can help them access the content and build on social-emotional skills. Let's face it, in tomorrow's world students will need to be able to empathetically work with people different than they are and still reach a common goal.

You don't want to have a seating chart with *IEP* and other indicators written all over it, but you want to be able to identify these students when you are teaching. Perhaps use a different color highlighter to color their names or put a dot next to them. This way you can remember what types of learners you have in the class as you are teaching.

A carefully planned seating chart in a class might look something like that in Figure 6.1.

Figure 6.1 A Seating Chart

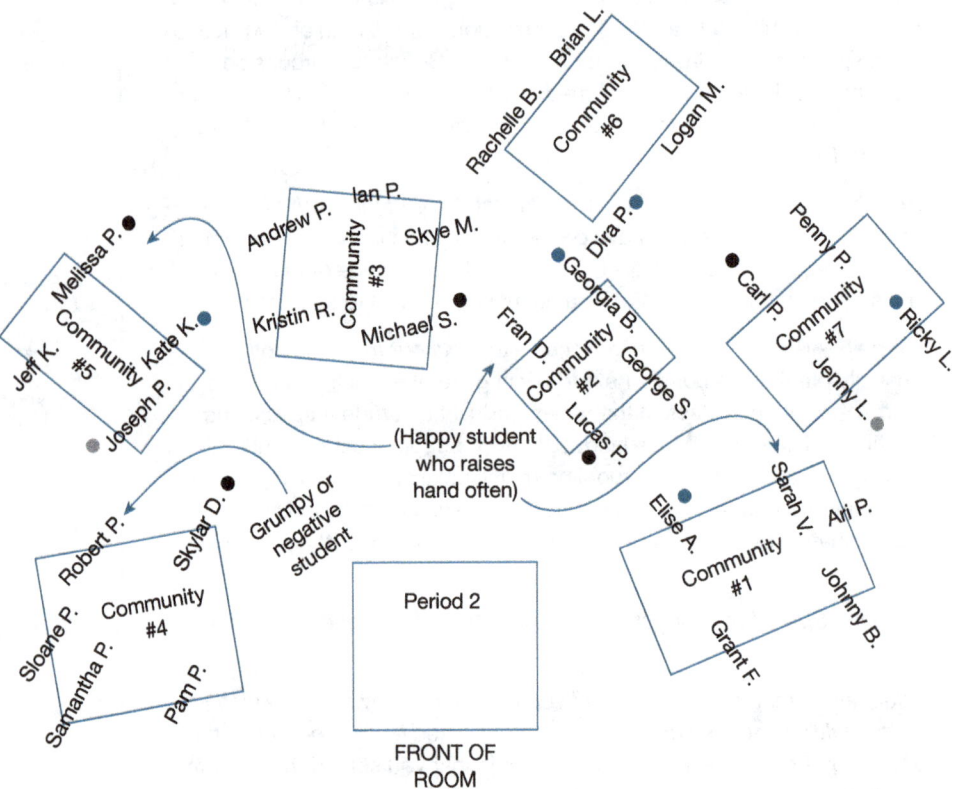

- student with IEP
- student identified as ELL (Keep in mind that advanced or early advanced ELLs may function quite similarly to general education students.)
- GATE student

A coded seating chart is most effective if it is always visible to the teacher. Dedicate a special place on your desk or on your clipboard where it is always in plain sight as you are teaching. You might want to put the code somewhere near your desk, but be careful about labeling student abilities right on the seating chart as students will figure out who is who and feelings could be hurt. Also, of course, that information is legally confidential.

As you create your seating chart, you may also want to keep in mind these possible participants in your classroom:

- **One-on-one adults in your room.** if you have an adult who is a one-on-one with a child, great! This student will be put in a group and the adult will be in the group as another member. It can be beneficial to put a "negative" student in this group because the constant attention and proximity of another adult could turn a negative personality around because they won't have to fight for attention. It's worth a shot; I've seen it work. Just make sure the one-on-one adult and negative student aren't a personal clash and that the negative student isn't an explosive student. This isn't fair to anyone. It's a good idea to have a talk first with the adult to let them know about the other students in the group so they feel empowered to work with all of them.

- **Happy students.** I usually wait two days before making the seating chart so I can pick out the happy students who raise their hands often in the classroom. Happy and consistently engaged students will reveal themselves fast, so usually I can spot them by Day 2. I try not to change seats after I make the seating chart on Day 3. I'll stick one happy student dead center in the front and one dead center in the back. This keeps the class joyful and gives every table in the room a change to have engagement. Have you ever noticed a table of four students with all of their heads down sleeping? Humans tend to mimic behaviors near them that they see. If they see the person next to them raising their hand, they will be more likely to follow suit. (See Best Practice #8 for more details on how spreading positivity in the classroom can help maximize learning for students.)

- **Chronically grumpy or angry students.** As much as I'd like to wave a magic wand and have a smile appear on all students' faces, it's just not always possible. The fact is, the learning must go on. And we know that a grumpy or angry student doesn't learn as much as a happy student. Chronically grumpy and angry students may need the most help, but their negative attitude shouldn't get most of your attention. If placed incorrectly, they may try to bring the entire class down with their negativity. Once you make sure the learning of the class isn't being hindered by a chronically grumpy or negative student, then you can go deeper into looking at the root causes of these emotions and help the student one-on-one.

I'll usually seat them on the side of the room in front so they don't get lost in the back of the room or create a peanut gallery, and so their negative energy doesn't bleed into the class. We want happy and engaged students to become role models for these students, not the other way around. When identifying these students you are looking for one trait: negativity. Most of the time these students can be identified as quickly as the happy students.

▶ **Vocal students.** Make sure there's one vocal student at each community table. *Vocal* means a student who loves to share out or even perhaps just talk to others around them. Using vocally gifted students as an asset can greatly increase engagement and increase participation for shy students. *I mark these students on my class roster Days 1 and 2 so I know to spread them out.* These are usually also the students who like to talk to their friends, too, and that's okay. Sometimes the vocal students are the lowest-level multilingual students, and I love when this happens. You want the student to be vocal (regardless of language or academic ability) because you want a focus of your class to be on raising hands to answer and having a voice. It's fascinating how these students can encourage others to raise their hands as well. Use vocal students as resources to get strong participation from your classes. If each community group has someone raising their hand in the beginning, that will lead to others in the group following suit.

If you need to do a few seat swaps later, you can (the sooner the better), but make sure you still have the IEP, multilingual, GATE, and gen ed ratios evenly spread out. Most years I do one or two seat swaps in the first week and then leave the seating as is. The bottom line is that as teachers we have to figure out a way to ensure that the whole class learns together.

With all these things considered, I then check the seating chart to make sure of the following:

▶ Every low-level multilingual student is placed next to a gen ed student for academic support. It's even better if that gen ed student can speak the local language of the multilingual student.

▶ Two students with IEPs are not seated in the same group if possible.

I also ask myself the following:

▶ Do I have any students who might need a bit of extra room for body size or wheelchairs? Are they going to be comfortable where they are seated? You'll be able to see this on Day 1 and make sure to jot it down discreetly.

▶ Do I have space for other adults in the room to sit so they feel part of your classroom?

This will give you a happy, mixed-ability class that has the most potential for success. Each student has a fighting chance to succeed. And if you make a seating chart in the first week of class, you will learn student names much faster. It's a win-win.

In Figure 6.1, you'll notice I placed the two hand-raising, happiest students in the center front and toward the center back because *I want their energy to spread out to the class.* I then placed grumpy and/or angry students in Community #4. I now have a classroom where all students are given a chance to academically succeed. It's useful to keep your seating chart with you when you are teaching to check in on these students. If one table isn't grasping a concept, look at what learners you have at each table. Were three lower-level multilingual students accidentally placed together?

There's a small chance that if you explain to someone how you decided on the seating for your class, they may be offended because you're looking at cognitive abilities rather than other factors. But what you are actually doing is making the focus of your class academic success, collaboration, and engagement, and you're giving each student a chance to succeed based on the skills and knowledge they have. If you want to teach challenging curriculum and help students be able to perform academically, this way works.

Tips for Making a Seating Chart

1. Print out a class roster before Day 1 of the school year.
2. During class, mark:
    a. happy, engaged students
    b. grumpy, angry students
    c. vocal students (please use just one letter or codes so students can't interpret)
3. Keep an eye on the same students for Day 2. Are they marked accurately?
4. Before the suggested day to have a seating chart ready (Day 3), print out your list of IEP, multilingual, GATE, and AVID students (this information usually can be found on your attendance roster if you look closely).
5. Arrange the desks the way you'd like first, before Day 3.
6. Draw a seating chart for each class. First, place your IEP and multilingual students based on where they will learn best. Next, place GATE and AVID students. Then, place your happy students definitely first toward the center and then spread out evenly. Finally,

(Continued)

> (Continued)
>
> place your negative students on the side where they have room and aren't physically bumped often by accident. These students usually like space.
>
> 7. Spread out the gen ed students in the remaining seats.
>
> 8. Color code your chart based on type of student so you have a reference during class to check for understanding. Be as discreet as possible when making the color code legend on the seating chart. Assume a student will see it at some point during the year so be sure they aren't able to understand the legend.
>
> Step #8 is especially important if you have to switch somebody's seat (this usually happens). You can make sure the switch still supports the class as a whole being balanced out academically.

Changing It Up in Middle and High School

In middle or upper grade levels, the students are able to move their desks into different formations depending on the learning plan that class period. Doing this once a week is usually enough to make this type of arrangement "special" and can really spice up a lesson. High school students can move desks around fast for you, so you can have a bit more flexibility with desk arrangement to best fit the discussion needs of the lesson without having to do all of the work yourself. The seating chart you created using the tips above can be your "home base" arrangement.

In middle or upper grade levels, depending on your subject, you may want to rearrange seats in a way that fosters the *type of conversations* you have in the classroom. For example:

- In an ELA classroom, if the space allows, a circle or horseshoe makes sense for having discussions about text in a seminar-type lesson.

- In a history class, a class divided down the center makes sense to debate two different sides of a story or historical event.

- In a math class, groups make sense to foster working collaboratively in teams to solve math problems.

- In a science class, groups make the most sense to complete labs.

In each of these seating arrangements, the students' cognitive levels should be spread out.

You could also use this type of dynamic seating style the second half of the year in an upper grade middle school classroom. They may just need more help arranging the desks (maybe project a visual of what each shape should look like when you ask them to move the desks), and you might leave a few more minutes to get the desks back in their original spots.

I'd change seating arrangements sparingly in the middle school grades—maybe once per unit during a debate, Socratic Seminar, or other special activity.

Flexible Seating

Flexible seating means that students choose their own seats based on where they feel most comfortable and/or learn best. In flexible seating students often have unique seating options, such as bean bags, the carpeted floor, or swivel stools. Although flex seating has certain benefits and is often preferred by students, it can take strong classroom management for students to be able to sit where they want one day then go back to their home base seats the next. You might consider using it very sparingly in your first few years of teaching. Here are a few reasons why:

- Something to keep in mind with this is that students are unaware of others' data, meaning students do not know each other's English language (EL) levels, who has an IEP, or which of their classmates are GATE, so they're not likely to keep the mix that you'd be able to create with a seating chart. Flexible seating should still provide students with opportunities for collaboration.

- If your class is on a full-class behavior modification program based on groups or communities, flexible seating can disrupt this because students may be constantly changing their seats. Also, with flexible seating, self-chosen student groups will likely be academically uneven in skill level. In my experience with flexible seating, usually the students with low EL levels are grouped together, the students with high academic ability are grouped together, and so on. Human beings tend to naturally gravitate to people like them.

- Students may be so excited to be able to have flexible seating that they agree to be more focused. However, we know that a quiet classroom does not always mean that students are learning the most or grappling with the material. Remember the word search example from the beginning of this section? It's a fine balance.

Tips for Flexible Seating

If you are curious about trying flexible seating, I suggest you do the following:

- Use the seating arrangement proposed in the tips for creating a seating chart as the students' home base or normal seating. The home base seats usually work best for instruction time and should be where the students are the most often. It's amazing how fast students can forget where they sit.

- Try flexible seating out in small ways first. For example, if students are working in table groups, you could let the groups choose where they want to sit in the room during work time. The groups should stay together. In another example, during groupwork time, one group may go to the carpet together and sit in a circle if that works for them and they are more comfortable.

- Use flexible seating at first with classes that need less academic or language scaffolding, such as a class with mostly gen ed students. The seating arrangement created from the tips above provides solid academic support. So, students who need less academic support might do better with flexible seating.

- Have a mini-lesson teaching students how to pick the seat best for them.

- Try flexible seating out with just one class first.

Teachers often ask me how often to change a seating chart. The answer is that it really depends on you, the teacher. I personally like to keep the same home base seats all year or at least half the year. Why?

- Building a community of learners means they have to trust each other academically, socially, and emotionally, and that takes time. Keeping the same seats builds deeper relationships between students.

- Because the seating chart is done so thoughtfully, all student needs should be met. For example, students who need preferential seating or students who need to be closer to the board to see should be taken care of.

It's important to point out that if students are grouped together with people not at their table for a group project, they would sit with the project groups while working. The seating chart is always their home base seating.

Your Turn

1. What are your thoughts on the heterogeneous seating chart and spreading out students with IEPs, general education students, multilingual students, etc.?

   _____
   _____
   _____
   _____

2. How would you do small group instruction in your room? Would you have a designated area?

   _____
   _____
   _____
   _____

3. What are your thoughts on spreading out happy, engaged students and negative students? Do you think this has benefit to a classroom?

   _____
   _____
   _____
   _____

4. Do you have another way you would like to do a seating chart? Talk to your coteacher or another colleague about this and gather some ideas. (Remember, if you want the focus of the class to be on academics and engagement, then you have to look at this criterion—i.e. the data—first when arranging students.)

   _____
   _____
   _____
   _____

Best Practice #7

Create Room Environments That Foster Student Belonging

....

> We treat this classroom as if we were home.
>
> —Michelle, Grade 8

We want our classrooms to feel like a second home to our students. Heck, sometimes our classrooms are the most consistent environment for students who are highly mobile or live in overpopulated or disorganized households. Some of our students might have even experienced living with different relatives at different times. Students should feel comfortable, calm, and at peace in our classrooms. This is when true learning can begin. Here are some tips for creating this environment.

Ways to Create Room Environments Where Students Feel Comfortable, Calm, and at Peace

- Have a few plants around the room. Give students leadership in taking care of them.
- Add some lamps, string lights, or some sort of dimmer lighting around the room.

- Have students wipe down their own desks at the end of class so they take responsibility in keeping the classroom clean.

- Have student pictures posted somewhere in the room.

- Use the power of soft music in the classroom as students are working or reading. Music is a powerful way to help students feel at home and focused in a classroom.

- In elementary school, ask parents and caregivers to send a picture of their student doing something they love to tape next to their name in their cubby.

- Words and messages posted in the room should be in a positive tone. For example, instead of a sign saying, "Do not go in this back room," it could instead read, "Please respect this back room is only for adults."

During my first two years of teaching, my classroom didn't feel like a second home to either myself or my students. I didn't have any pictures of students posted, little student work was displayed, and the desks were in rows. Graffiti from students was drawn all over the desks and bulletin boards, and I honestly couldn't keep up with cleaning it off every day. I also had bright fluorescent lighting, no plants, torn books, and gum stuck in more desk corners than I could even count. It was clear that the students didn't treat our classroom like a home, and neither did I.

Your Turn

1. How do you think your students most often feel in your classroom? Is there something you can do about the room environment to change this?

   _____
   _____
   _____
   _____
   _____
   _____
   _____
   _____
   _____
   _____
   _____

2. How do you feel in your classroom? Why is this?

   _____
   _____
   _____
   _____
   _____
   _____
   _____
   _____
   _____

Real Conversation With an Eighth-Grade Student

Student: Ms. Pariser, what do you call pasta that is not real?

Me: I don't know.

Student: An impasta!

Me: [laughs loudly]

Student [to another student]: See, that's how you know they are getting old, when they laugh at that.

Student [to me]: It was just a social experiment.

PART 2
FORMING POSITIVE RELATIONSHIPS WITH YOUR STUDENTS

What Doesn't Help Form a Positive Relationship With a Student

My eighth-grade English teacher put a very talkative boy in the closet to get him to stop talking, and forgot about him. The boy went to sleep and woke at 6:00 p.m. when he heard the janitor cleaning the room.

—Ellen, Age 69

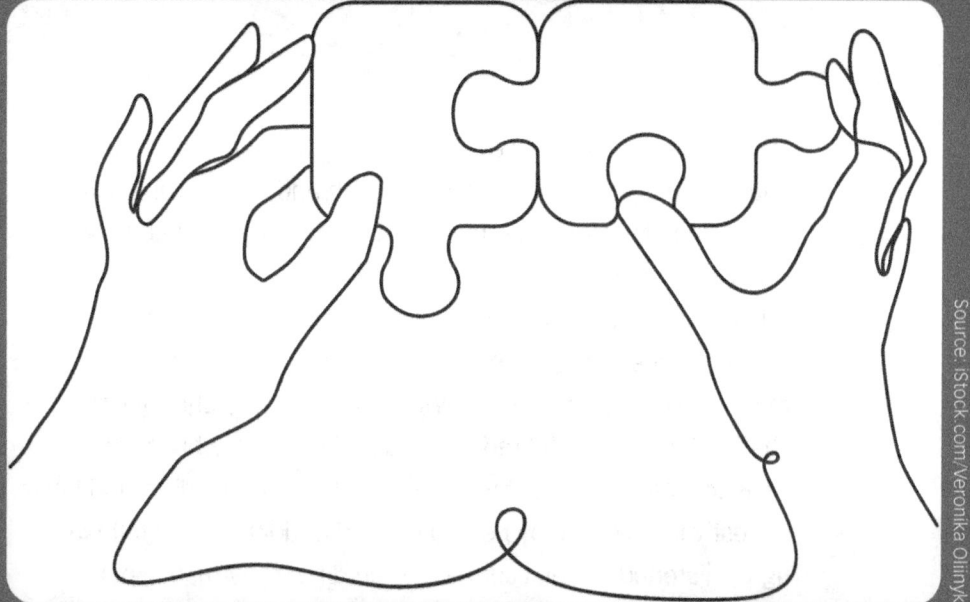

Source: iStock.com/Veronika Oliinyk

How does forming positive relationships with your students relate to classroom management?

Connection is the strongest form of classroom management, but it's virtually impossible to have a strong connection with every one of your students. There just aren't enough hours in the day. In a realistic sense, positive relationships lead to a more pleasant classroom environment all year long and a more powerful learning and teaching experience for you and the students. Investing in building positive relationships with students means understanding off-task behavior and knowing how to intervene appropriately to empower students. It means they will be excited to come to your class and look forward to seeing *you*. Some days this may not be the case, however, and that's okay. Don't take it personally; it's usually not personal.

I REMEMBER WHEN...

I remember my first day of finally having my own classroom. I was both nervous and excited. It was March and I was taking over a first-grade class for a teacher who had moved out of state. When I was walking to pick up the class, a parent came up to me and asked, "Are you the new teacher in Room 3?" "Yes, I am!"

   She proceeded to tell me that her son Fred was in my class and that I was not to let him get away with anything. She told me that I had to be strict with Fred or he would become a big behavior issue for me. This parent was very loud and demanding, and I was honestly intimidated by her. So instead of doing what I felt was right, I listened to her. I spoke to Fred differently than I spoke to the rest of the class. I asked other kids nicely to do things, but with Fred I used my firm "I mean business" teacher voice. I gave Fred time-outs, he missed recess, and I didn't let him get away with anything, just like his mom had requested. But the problem was, Fred, in turn, didn't like me. His behavior actually got worse, and what I was doing obviously wasn't working. I nervously called Fred's mother in for a meeting and told her I had tried her way and it just did not fit with my personality. I suggested that we try positive means to change Fred's behavior. I started using sticker charts, tickets, rewards, and, most of all, just complimenting Fred on the things he was doing right. She was very adamant that those things would never work with Fred, but she agreed to let me try. It didn't happen overnight, but Fred's behavior began to turn around. He realized that I liked him and cared about him and began to try. You know the saying, "You'll get more with sugar than with salt?" Well it's true, and I learned it first-hand with Fred.

—Erika Perez
21 years' experience
Jefferson Elementary IB
STEAM Magnet School
San Diego, CA

Recognize Your Power and Use It Positively

· ·

> You can tell when a teacher trusts you because they listen to you. I actually do more work in their classes because I know they want me to succeed.
>
> —Penny, Grade 9

There's a quote that used to hang in the back of my private teacher cabinet. It was actually the message I pulled from a fortune cookie after a delicious meal. It resonated with me so deeply that I retyped it and printed it out in twelve-point font, large enough for me to read but small enough for a student not to see if he or she accidentally opened up the cabinet (which sometimes happened). It read:

"A teacher holds the power to single-handedly change the atmosphere of a classroom."

I felt as if I had discovered the secret to life. *That's a lot of power to have!* I thought to myself. I would be lying if I told you that I utilized that quote every single day, but it still is in my thoughts constantly today. I follow this credo. We teachers are the *emotional leaders* in the classroom.

Think of a presentation you have had to sit through. Audience members or students tend to take on the energy of the presenter. Have you ever felt energized after a presentation because the lead presenter was smiling, stimulating, uplifting with words and tone, and thought-provoking? Now think of the opposite. Have you ever felt drained after a monotone, long-winded, and boring presenter? We have the power to control the mood of the class. My goal is usually to make the students smile and laugh at the beginning of each class. I do this by praising behaviors I like to see, telling a funny story, starting with an inspirational quote, or just smiling in general. Don't be afraid of not being able to get them focused and ready to learn. I believe this is what stops some educators from letting the class start with inspiration rather than intimidation.

In my first few years of teaching middle school, I spent the first five or ten minutes of class asking Kiko to stop fidgeting or Xavier to stop banging on the desk. By the time I started the lesson, I was already frustrated and exhausted! Pretty soon I changed tactics. Instead, before I started each lesson I tried to remember to glance at a simple reminder I had pasted to my teacher station to remind me that my mood and my energy will radiate to the class. My reminder was a tiny strip of paper with one word on it: *positive*. In fact, I glanced at it so much that even years later it's emblazoned on my memory: The word written in purple pen on a yellow sticky note folded in half and secured to my teaching station with clear tape. I placed it where I would see it many times throughout a lesson. That tiny strip of paper helped many days when I needed the reminder for the sake of the class. We all need our reminders from time to time. I knew if I could be positive even if I felt differently inside some days, learning would be ten thousand times easier for the students. Occasionally in my smaller classes I would tell a joke, often one from a Laffy Taffy wrapper or something simple I picked up somewhere. For example, after all of our serious work was finished and we had a minute or two in the class, I might say something like the following:

Me: Okay, we have an extra minute left of class and I have some new material.

Class [whining]: Oh, Ms. Pariser, not again! [smiling]

Me: How do you make a tissue dance? Anyone? Anyone?

[Students would scream out answers]

Me [screaming back with excitement]: Put a little boogie in it!

Some students would look disgusted and some would laugh, but either way the sound of joy was in the classroom. In ten seconds I got half the class laughing. The positive vibe was becoming conditioned into their heads. I was always careful to know which classes this would work for, and it was often the smaller ones.

Easier said than done, right? Making the toughest inner-city kids smile before you start teaching them is one example of using your power for good. On any given day we could spend the first five or ten minutes, or even the whole period, focusing on the negative. It's just easier to do. "Samika, why don't you have a pencil?" "Celia, turn around." Before you know it you'll have ten more behavior problems that you didn't have before. Why? Where was your attention? That's where the students will focus as well. I've always thought the positive is so much harder to focus on, but it is worth it. Isn't that true in life?

Tips for Focusing on the Positive

- **Praise the positive from the moment they step into your room.** According to author Amy Rees Anderson (2015), *"A person who feels appreciated will always do more than expected."* So I spend the first three to four minutes of each period solely on positively reinforcing specific student behavior, saying things such as, "Julie, *thank you* for getting started silently on the board work." What happens when I say this? Other students will scramble to take out their planners. They want recognition, and everybody loves to be appreciated. Or I might say, "I *really appreciate* how Table #3 is all sitting down. I like how Melanie's table is about to refocus." What happens? Students will scramble to sit down. Melanie's table will agree and refocus. It's a self-fulfilling statement. The trick is to never be condescending or sarcastic. Be genuine. Positive dialogue can be done with both grade school and tough high school students successfully. Nobody is too old to receive positive attention, including ourselves. We all want the same things: love, attention, and feeling like we belong.

  Think about a teacher instead saying, "Orman, can't you see how Table #3 is all sitting? Why can't you do that?" That teacher would be trying to reach the same goal (seated students), right? But not only did this teacher embarrass Orman, she also set a negative tone in the classroom and set herself up for failure for that lesson—with everyone. Who wants to teach or learn in that kind of environment?

  The funny thing about this trick is that you have to be specific in what you praise. Think of what you'd like your class to do and then praise the individuals who are doing that. It works. Two years ago I decided I wanted students to clap for each other. It made the learning different, more supportive, and fun. I started the next year by saying, "That was a beautiful answer, it would have been so nice if somebody had clapped." Lo and behold, somebody did clap for the next answer. Usually as a joke, but they were still smiling. Before the end of the period, after I had constantly praised that specific clapping behavior, high school students—yes, high school students—were all clapping for each other when they answered. That may be a little too much for you, but perhaps not. You'd be surprised how fun it can make learning.

- **Know that the mind is more open when it is happy.** The most successful companies know this. Google lets its employees bring their dogs to work and has pool tables in the break room. This

(Continued)

(Continued)

successful company knows that when the mind is happy, innovation flows. Think of how you feel when you are scared, sad, or angry. Are you open to learning? Now think of how your mind feels when you are peaceful and comfortable. The mind is a sponge. Yes, students will be quieter if you yell, but I always think of this as their mind's doors slamming shut. Keep your tone gentle; talk *to* the students and not at them. Talking *to* the students means you are talking to connect with them. Talking *at* a student means you are talking to silence them. This is sometimes more difficult to do in a larger classroom, where you have to make sure everybody hears you. Keep your mind always on the goal: The students must learn. You want to keep their minds open. A happy student is a good producer of quality thinking and work

Once a positive classroom environment has been established, it can continue throughout the school year. The positive attitude will be conditioned. Sometimes school is the only place a student will receive praise! In some rare cases, you could be a loving adult they do not have outside of school. If the class does slip into a negative tone for a few days, all you have to do is ask, "How do we get our positive classroom back?" Perhaps you brainstorm with your class or perhaps you use your own ideas. Usually it just takes a few small key adjustments because the students already are confident they know how to be positive. However, once a class crosses to what I call "the point of little or no return," it takes one heck of a teacher to get them back. It is doable, however!

- **Sit a few happy students in the center of the classroom.** Every class has a different personality. They take on energy. In the beginning of the year, before its personality has surfaced yet, the class will typically follow the student who appears to be a leader. Every group of people looks for a leader. You actually can decide which student you want to lead the class. You want the students who smile, respect and help others with their words and actions, and eagerly raise their hands to become the natural leaders in each class. You can make this happen. (See Best Practice #6 for more on purposeful seating charts.)

I learned this trick one year when I could not figure out why one of my classes had suddenly switched from happy to grumpy, moody, and overall blah. There was one particular girl who I had recently switched to the center of the room when it all started. I switched her seat because she was talking too much to her friend on the side of the room. She wore heavy black eyeliner, and her mood seemed to match her dark makeup every day. I felt like she was not getting enough attention, so I put her right in front of me. Big mistake. My life as a teacher became very difficult for the next few weeks until I figured out what was going on. She had a presence and demeanor that other students watched and emulated. Students, like any other people—or animals for that matter—tend to mimic what they see.

Soon, I had students to her left talking back to me. *What the heck!?* I thought. How is she telegraphing her negative attitude? Ahh! It all clicked! Just as you have the power to spread your mood all around the classroom, so do the students in the center of the room.

Now, do not make the mistake of sitting all of the positive students in the center. You'll have a heck of a time trying to control the other areas. Just sit two or three students who raise their hand and are smiley in the center and you'll be surprised how their energy will create a positive mood for your whole classroom. See Best Practice #6 for how to seat the happy and engaged students and also the grumpy students. A smile is contagious and it just works!

Remember:

- You are the emotional leader of the classroom.
- Your energy will radiate out into the classroom.
- If needed, keep a visual reminder that reminds you that you are the energetic leader of your classroom somewhere where you will see it often.
- What you focus on will thrive in the classroom.
- Do not seat negative students in the center of your classroom.

Your Turn

1. What behaviors or habits do you want your students to engage in in your classroom? Have you been praising the student who engages in these habits genuinely? Think to yourself when you can praise these specific habits or behaviors in class. During the first few weeks, you may need to write yourself a reminder to allot the praise either on your desk or in your lesson plans.

　　_____
　　_____
　　_____
　　_____
　　_____
　　_____
　　_____
　　_____

2. How can you make your students happy? Can you use one of your strengths for this? List three things you can do or say in the near future to put a smile on your students' faces.

　　_____
　　_____
　　_____
　　_____
　　_____
　　_____
　　_____
　　_____

Celebrate Mistakes as Learning Opportunities

I used to spend the first week of school making sure the kids were quiet, obedient, and knew my rules. Now I don't have rules. We have class expectations, and I spend time teaching them, but I spend a lot more time teaching the students how to *get over their fear of making a mistake* when sharing out or presenting. Allowing for mistakes to be made is much different from how many of us were taught growing up. A friend once told me of a horrifying memory from fifth grade when she raised her hand to answer a question incorrectly and had to suffer the embarrassing laughter of her classmates. She remains fearful of raising her hand in a class-like setting to this day. Mistakes, handled improperly, can be scarring. However, by using mistakes as learning opportunities, teachers are able to arrive at the correct answers while achieving a more comprehensive and enduring learning process. We build student confidence, self-esteem, and self-worth when we redirect and encourage.

Students come to me each year with the notion that being quiet is better than talking and making a mistake. This frustrates me year after year. By the second week my students usually understand that I want to hear their voices—I need to hear what they have learned so I can guide them if necessary. I don't get angry or frustrated with a wrong answer. A wrong answer is just one step closer to the right answer. Let's look at a couple of examples of teachers handling incorrect answers.

Scenario A

Teacher: What do you think is the theme of this story?

Student 1: Animals?

Teacher: Really? *Really?* After three theme lessons you think the theme is animals? Have you been paying attention? That's wrong.

I assume a lot of teacher wait time would be created after this response because the teacher just instilled fear in students not to share unless they are certain they are right. This means the teacher will really only be able to tell what a few of the students are thinking. Let's look at the same example from another teacher.

Scenario B

Teacher: What do you think is the theme of this story?

Student 1: Animals?

Teacher: Okay, I see where you're going—who can help her out a bit?

Student 2: Well, it's about animals but more about humans, too.

Teacher: Okay, we have good stuff here to work with. So now what do you guys think the theme is? Remember what *theme* means?

Student 3: Man versus nature!

Teacher: Exactly.

I don't agree with everything in this video, but sharing stories can build relationships.

It's really hard to unlearn failure. When kids get the idea in their head that they failed at something, they carry that with them. Be somebody in their life that shows them mistakes are part of growth. It takes an extreme amount of patience and practice to do this, but it is well worth the payoff. Who doesn't want a classroom of students who aren't afraid to answer?

SAFE MISTAKE-MAKING ENVIRONMENTS	UNSAFE MISTAKE-MAKING ENVIRONMENTS
Teacher uses incorrect answers to guide class to the correct answers.	Teacher says, "No, that's wrong."
Students know not to shame a student for giving a wrong answer.	Students in class laugh or ridicule when student gives a wrong answer.
Many hands are raised for each question asked. Students are eager to try.	Students are afraid to raise hands.
Teacher asks classmates to help the student out when an incorrect answer is shared.	Teacher gets frustrated easily when an incorrect answer is shared.

Your Turn

1. Think about a class where you felt safe making a mistake. How did the teacher or instructor create this environment?

   _____
   _____
   _____

2. How did this maximize the learning for you and the other students? Why did you feel more comfortable raising your hand to share out?

   _____
   _____
   _____

3. Now answer #1–2 for a class where you were fearful to make a mistake.

   _____
   _____
   _____

4. What type of classroom do you want? With a partner, practice your responses as a teacher when a student makes a mistake. Ask your partner how they felt when you responded the way you did.

   _____
   _____
   _____
   _____

Strengthen Inclusion and Belonging for All Students

We will have students with IEPs (individualized education plans) in most of our classrooms. Students have these plans for a variety of reasons. IEPs are made so students can get the additional support they need to meet the same expectations as the other students. Sometimes students are placed in our classrooms with highly detailed IEPs to meet social goals. These are students who may be in a special class for most or part of the day; these classrooms are often called DCD (developmental cognitive disability) classrooms and they exist in almost every school. Students in DCD classrooms may have serious intellectual disabilities, have suffered brain injury or strokes, be nonverbal, or have other cognitive disabilities. Often, some of the students are in wheelchairs or have mobility limits. The beautiful thing is that they are placed in general education classrooms for perhaps one or a few classes or one elective purely to meet social goals, and the amount of time is individualized for each student.

If you are lucky enough to have these students in your gen ed class for a period of time, our job as teachers is to make them feel included in our classroom community. This is where social-emotional learning comes in. The students coming from a DCD classroom have the opportunity to emotionally grow and connect with students who are mainly gen ed. In turn, the gen ed students have the opportunity to collaborate with empathy and understanding with students who are a bit different than them. This relationship might not grow naturally. It's our job to facilitate that connection and collaboration with love, guidance, empowerment, acceptance, and knowledge.

How do we do this? Here are some suggestions:

- In the beginning of the year, have classroom conversations or teach mini-lessons about how not everyone is the same but we are all equal. Explain that some people need extra help.

- Students from the DCD room should participate and be included in absolutely everything the rest of the class is doing. The way they are able to participate might look different, however, so provide modifications and prepare other students.

- If a student has a one-on-one aide that comes with them to class, have a dedicated space for the aide in your classroom so they feel a part of the class as well. This usually works best if they are sitting next to the student or students they support but always in a group with gen ed students as well.

- If the student is in a wheelchair, make sure they have enough space to get in and out of the classroom easily. Consider this in your overall classroom design so you don't have to move things around later to accommodate them.

- These students should not be assigned seats in the back of your class or all together without any gen ed students in their groups or at their tables. This sends a message to the rest of your class that they are not really a part of your class community and can make the DCD students feel like an afterthought. Place them in the front and on the side, with gen ed students all around.

- They should always be placed near a few gen ed students to start forming social bonds. When independent work time comes and the DCD students need extra academic support from their one-on-one aides, that's the time to pull them together. They then go back to their normal seats near gen ed students when that time is over.

- Try your best to mix in some of the gen ed students at their tables or in their groups. If there is one aide in the room assisting two or three students, it's best to place those students in the same area (but not all at the same table so they can meet their social goals with other students) so the adult can help all of them without running around the room. This also gives the DCD students the opportunity to socialize and work with the other students. This is the entire point of inclusion.

If we don't take time to really include special needs student in our community, the other students will either distance themselves from them or, in the worst cases, bullying may occur. Yes, these students may look and act differently, but it's important to keep in mind that students today are much more open-minded about inclusion than they were even five years ago. Disabilities are being normalized in today's world, and our classrooms communities can keep up. Often students just need a little guidance from us. Students may have questions and be unsure whom to ask, so they might make assumptions themselves—and we don't want that. Take time to learn more about the special abilities and disabilities of any students in your class and allow open conversation and questions from other students. Instead of focusing on the weaknesses or cognitive deficits of the special needs student, let your other students know what that student is interested in outside of the classroom. This is where you can use the help of the one-on-one aide. They spend a lot of time with this student and can provide good information for teachers and peers. Yes, you will receive the IEP for the student, but ask the aide questions about the student's personality, interests, and talents.

Questions you can ask include the following:

- What are the student's strengths? Do they love to laugh? Are they really friendly and social?

- If necessary (especially if the student is nonverbal or has limited speech) ask the one-on-one adult how the student prefers to be greeted. So this could look like teaching them to say, "Good morning, Cairo, high five?" in younger elementary grades.

- What are their vocal abilities? Can they hear well? Do they see as well as the other students? Are they sensitive to loud sounds?

Then, when the included students are working with the gen ed students, you can casually share some of what you've learned when it's appropriate. You might say to Jamal (a gen ed student), "I see you have a Dungeons & Dragons sticker on your binder. Did you know Kent (a DCD student who sits at Jamal's table) loves playing Dungeons & Dragons on his computer at home?" And boom—a connection is made. That's really it. Students are all very loving deep down and want to be friends, but sometimes they might not know how to start. It's equally important that the included students feel accepted and that the rest of the class knows how to socialize and work with people who might look or act differently than them. Students are more curious than anything, and empowering them will help create a community of learners.

Your Turn

1. In your opinion, why are healthy inclusion practices equally important for gen ed students and DCD students?

   _____
   _____
   _____
   _____
   _____
   _____

2. Let's imagine that healthy inclusion practices were taught and practiced in a classroom. How would this affect the students' lives in tomorrow's world?

   _____
   _____
   _____
   _____
   _____
   _____

3. What questions linger in your mind about teaching and practicing healthy inclusion practices in the classroom?

   _____
   _____
   _____
   _____
   _____
   _____

Stick With the Students Who Challenge Us the Most

I am amazed how you never gave up on me.

—Timothy, known to others as a "bad" kid,
Grade 9, in a letter to his teacher on the last day of school

There isn't a teacher alive who hasn't dealt with a challenging student. I remember my first year. I thought administration was playing a joke on me when I was handed my roster. *There are no good kids in my class!* I thought. (Disclaimer: I would never use the term *good kid* now that I know better! This was my first year of teaching, when I thought much differently about many aspects of teaching.) Why would they give the most inexperienced teacher in the school all the most challenging kids? Were they trying to weed me out? How was I supposed to use anything I had learned in my college classes with this group?

There was one student in particular who I'll call Dennis. He looked a little older than the other sixth graders. He watched me for a few weeks before he started acting up. It was like he was more confident and aggressive than the others. Each day he had a little more attitude than the day before. I didn't understand what was going on because the neighboring teacher did not have the same issues as I did with this student. I remember a specific day when Dennis had a basketball in his hand as he lined up for my class. He bounced it and looked at me.

Me: Don't bounce that ball or I'll take it.

Dennis: [smiles] [bounces ball]

I walked over and reached to take the basketball, but Dennis gracefully swooped it behind his back. The kid had skills. Now I'd dug my own hole. I couldn't reach for the ball again without really jeopardizing my job, and he had won the battle. I retreated, fuming, and he bounced it again. The other kids laughed. I thought, *Now I am supposed to start my lesson? Really?*

Thankfully, this doesn't happen anymore. There's a way to not get yourself in this situation. We've all learned—some, like myself, the hard way.

First of all, with the tough kids, they are used to being disciplined and scolded, not valued or even liked. This is sadly what they are comfortable with. Do you want to be the same as every other teacher, or do you want to be kinder and more respectful than the others? These students will respect you more for the latter if you still stay firm with your classroom structure.

The bottom line is that the challenging kids want to be treated like everybody else. They want to be spoken to like everyone else; they want to be considered as smart as everyone else. So why don't they act like everyone else? This is where you have to be the adult and start the learning process of how to connect with them. First, treat them like every other student. That will answer 99 percent of your questions about them. Students misbehave for one of four reasons (or a combination of these reasons):

1. They want power.
2. They feel inadequate.
3. They want to get even.
4. They want attention that they are not getting elsewhere.

If you can pinpoint the main reason for a student's misbehavior, you can find a solution that works. Remember, *they don't know why they are misbehaving,* they just do sometimes. It's our job to figure it out and help them become successful. Let's run back through the same scenario with Dennis. First of all, I challenged him from the beginning. I challenged his reputation in front of the class. Of course he wasn't going to back down and stop bouncing the ball. Here's how I would handle this situation today if Dennis was bouncing a ball as the class was lining up:

Me: Hey, Dennis, I didn't know you played basketball. Are you on the team?

Dennis: No.

Me: Do me a favor please [always have the students do *you* a favor—the wording just works] and let's hold off and not bounce the ball right now. I really appreciate it. I don't mind holding the ball for you if it makes it easier.

Speak to students with this much respect. That is how I speak to my students now, and it is the same for most other successful teachers. Most of the time the student will oblige if you respect them, set your boundaries (I let Dennis know bouncing a ball was not acceptable at that time), and are willing to meet them halfway (I was willing to hold the ball for Dennis). At no time would this student feel threatened or demeaned, but you achieve the same or better results. Try not to use your teacher power if you do not have to. Teacher power should be saved for those special situations where it would be most useful. The kids who challenge us aren't used to being respected and might very well act differently for you if you treat them differently than other teachers have in the past.

My beliefs about children's behavior have changed over the years. I no longer believe there are any "bad" kids, as I did my first year. I referred to the more challenging kids with this term because I was frustrated that I could not get through to them. I later found that these students were the ones who shaped my teaching career. They were the ones who challenged me, the ones I worked the hardest for, the ones who touched my heart, and the ones who came back years later to visit. These are the students who make or break teachers.

More Tips for Teaching Challenging Students

- Give them their space when they need it.

- Find at least one quality you like about them.

- Ask them to help you with something that you can't quite understand. For example, ask them to help with something on the computer, if that's a skill you know they have. This lets them show you a strength and helps them to feel valuable.

- Find out one thing they are interested in outside of school. If a student likes cars, pick up a car magazine and let them know you thought they might be interested in it. If they like skateboarding, ask them to bring in a picture of them skating and tell them you'd love to hang it in the classroom to show off their skills. Show them you care about them.

- Ask them questions about what they do after school and on the weekends.

- Don't take students' misbehaviors personally. It's usually not about us. Realize this. They are going through something, and they are children or teenagers.

- Do not hold a grudge. Start every day optimistic about their behavior.

- Find their strengths and let them use their strengths in the classroom. If you don't do this, sometimes a strength can cause the most trouble in the classroom. Think of the student who is a wonderful articulator but is always silenced. That student will find a time to talk, whether you give it to them or not. Give them room to shine.

- Don't make everything a fight. Ask them to do what you want them to do quietly and privately; don't demand they do it publicly. They need to save face in front of the class. Otherwise, they will challenge you. Do you want to take on this unnecessary power struggle?

Your Turn

1. When was the last time you used your teacher power in your classroom? Was it necessary or not? Why?

   _____
   _____
   _____
   _____
   _____
   _____

2. Think of the toughest student in each of your classes. What are they interested in? How can you find out this information?

   _____
   _____
   _____
   _____
   _____
   _____

3. Think of the toughest student in each of your classes. What are their academic strengths? How can you use this to help the class?

   _____
   _____
   _____
   _____
   _____
   _____

Best Practice #12

Become a Teacher Detective to Discover Why Students Aren't Performing Well Academically

When a student doesn't do work in your class, *it's usually not personal.* However, it can feel personal to us since we put countless hours into our lesson planning. Let me break it down for you. I spent a few months frustrated that my students never had organized binders. They had papers out of order and spilling out of the sides. Our school policy was that each classroom teacher had to make sure students had organized binders. The first time I asked students to take out their binders, I almost had a heart attack. I exclaimed, "What? This is what you consider clean?!" I yelled, I scolded, I threatened detention, but still the binders remained messy. This was about the same time I was getting my master's degree in educational technology at San Diego State University, and we were studying a concept that I will explain below. Suddenly, it clicked. The students just needed time. Teachers were giving them papers at rocket speed and not giving them time in class to put them in the correct sections. They knew *how* to clean out the binders, and they *wanted* to have neater binders, they just were not given time to do the organizing. It was such a simple answer to the problem: They needed time. We all have these moments in teaching when a simple solution

This video looks into figuring out why students aren't performing academically.

takes longer than it should to discover. Let me speed up the process for you to save some time.

I've come to believe that laziness only explains why students do not do work 33.3 percent of the time. There are actually two other reasons. I used *Analyzing Performance Problems* by Mager and Pipe (1997), a text that discusses why people might not perform a task when asked or assigned. Basically, it states there are a few reasons a human being will not do something when asked or instructed to. In the classroom we can almost always narrow it down to one of three reasons as to why students aren't performing. Ready? Drum roll, please. The three reasons are lack of skills/knowledge, motivation, or resources. And here are some suggestions for how to overcome each:

- **Skills/knowledge.** If a lack of skills/knowledge is the performance barrier, the student does not have the skill or knowledge to complete the task. A learning disability such as a reading disability or a processing disability may fall into this category. In this case, the teacher can either reteach the material in a mini-lesson or tutoring session, or pair the student with a more knowledgeable peer for a specific task. Or perhaps the work is just too difficult. For example, if a student who really wants to earn an *A* on a paper does not know how to compose a proper concluding paragraph, she is lacking the necessary skills and knowledge to be successful. She needs a refresher or full lesson on how to compose the paper.

- **Motivation.** If motivation is the performance barrier, the person does not have a reason motivating enough to do the work or task. As teachers, we can easily mistake this performance barrier for laziness. However, the formula for motivation is value times confidence. Think $V \times C$. So, if one of the variables is 0, the product is 0. Students have to find value in what they are doing and know they can do it, even if it takes some help. *Value* can be defined as seeing something as important or mattering. This can be for many different reasons. For example, a student who wants to play in the soccer game after school knows he has to complete an assignment to do so. The student sees the assignment as mattering for this reason. Or a student could see value in a Spanish assignment because she wants to take AP Spanish next year and knows that she needs to learn her verbs to do so. Both of these cases add value to an assignment for that student.

  In this case, the teacher could assign a grade, add on a competitive factor to the project, or speak to the class about the purpose of the task. Hint: Extrinsic motivation is always easier to use to get students motivated, but intrinsic motivation is a thousand times more powerful. Extrinsic motivation often leads to intrinsic. Think of extrinsic motivation as training wheels to intrinsic motivation.

Extrinsic motivation can sometimes be a barrier, however. For example, a student might know how to compose a paper but just doesn't care to finish it because good grades are not a driving motivator, or a student might not need the grade for some reason. As educators, especially middle and high school teachers, we have to remember that students have so many factors going on in their nonacademic lives.

> Extrinsic motivation is always easier to use to get students motivated, but intrinsic motivation is a thousand times more powerful.

Get them to want to please you. Sometimes we are a parent substitute. Our job is to teach them how to balance these factors (significant others, family drama, friend drama, etc.) to stay motivated in school.

- Resources. If a lack of resources is the performance barrier, the person does not have the time or resources to complete the work or task. Help here as much as you can. First determine which resources are lacking and consider how you could provide those resources or enlist help to do so. For example, if you notice a child doesn't have time at home to complete homework, can you (and colleagues, if necessary) help them find time during the day to focus on homework assignments? Or if you notice a child repeatedly comes to class seeming tired, discuss with them privately what might be helpful in getting more rest; in this case it might be worth enlisting the school social worker or counselor too.

Basically, in most cases students either do not know how to do a task, do not have a reason valuable enough to them to do it (intrinsic or extrinsic motivation), or do not have the time or materials to do it. It can also be some combination of these three reasons, but there is usually one driving force.

Wow, really? That is it. With this knowledge, as a teacher you can usually "fix" the problem and get students back to work. Many times they will not understand why they are not working or be able to articulate their needs, but you can now use this information to correctly diagnose the issue. Let's look at an example.

Scenario #1: "Lazy" Gary

Gary is sitting at his desk with a paper in front of him, not working. He has a pencil in his hand, and he seemed to understand the lesson when the teacher explained it, but he still is not working. The teacher goes over and says if he does not start working, he will have to stay after school. Gary gets angry and says he cannot stay after school. He says he hates this stupid project. The teacher calls his home, the project does not get completed, and Gary and the teacher are angry with each other.

Okay, take a breath. Now let's look at this scenario from another standpoint.

Scenario #2: "Lazy" Gary (a Closer Look)

Gary is sitting at his desk with a paper in front of him, not working. He has a pencil in his hand, and he seemed to understand the lesson when the teacher explained it, but he still is not working. The teacher goes over and asks what he needs. Gary says he doesn't know. The teacher asks if he needs help getting started. Gary says maybe. The teacher and Gary come up with the answer to the first question of the lesson together. Gary smiles, and after two more problems finds he can do the rest on his own.

It is not always this picture-perfect, but you get the idea. What was the difference between the two scenarios? The teacher did the detective work. Here's what went on in her head: *I know the barrier is not motivation because Gary really wants the grade, I know he has a pencil, time, and paper to work, so it must be skills/knowledge. I wonder if he just needs a little help.* Also, in the first example, the teacher angered Gary. An angry student will almost never ask for help.

If you want to take it one step further, this theory can be applied anywhere (even with colleagues). Next time you hear your not-so-pleasant-at-6 a.m.-on-no-coffee colleague complain, "Why can't teachers learn to use this copy machine?" you can now try to determine if this is an issue of skills/knowledge (they do not know how to work the thousand buttons), motivation (there is no reason to learn how the machine works), or resources (there is not any paper in the machine, or any time to learn how it works) You will be surprised how this problem-solving thinking can change your career into one of a teacher detective. Be careful about sharing this knowledge with other adults, however; it can seem a little pretentious if you do not vent with them about how nothing is fixable. Sometimes people simply want and need to vent, and you can just listen. But use this information in your classroom and see the results!

Why do students work for some teachers and not as much for others? The teachers they work for have tapped into performance-barrier thinking, perhaps on a subconscious level. If they know this information to some extent, they will make sure the students have the time and materials to work, know how to teach the content so the students understand it (skills/knowledge), and know how to provide students with either (or both) extrinsic or intrinsic motivation in their classrooms.

So are students lazy? Perhaps sometimes, but now you know this is only because they are not either intrinsically or extrinsically motivated for some reason. Be the detective. Figure out how to fix the problem, or at least start with having compassion. Students rarely can diagnose themselves. Add an element of competition, use grades as a factor, or explain the purpose of the assignment (and it better be meaningful).

You hold this power. Use it wisely and see the results. I found in my years of teaching that figuring out how to eliminate barriers to facilitate the amount of energy the students put into their work was exhilarating problem-solving.

PERFORMANCE BARRIER	WHAT DOES IT LOOK LIKE IN THE CLASSROOM?	STRATEGIES TO INTERVENE AS A TEACHER
Resources	Student is "frozen" and not working but not asking for help. Student is overly talkative during work time. Student is sleeping during class time.	Privately ask student what student needs to begin. Reach out to parents to make sure student has necessary materials for class. Privately ask student how much sleep they are getting at night and if they are eating breakfast. Have a one-on-one student conference. Introduce a system where students can check out paper, pencils, or other needed supplies in your classroom. Hold a time management mini-lesson.
Skills/knowledge	Student is "frozen" and not working but not asking for help. Student is overly talkative during work time. Student is not participating in lesson.	Pull student into a small group instruction with an adult in the room. Ask your coteacher to reteach the concept in a different way in a mini-lesson. You reteach the concept in a mini-lesson. Have students reteach each other difficult concepts in small student-led groups Have student lead a small group of struggling students in reteaching the concept. If student has an IEP, and the skills/knowledge barrier is hindering the student from succeeding in your class, contact the case manager or school psychologist for strategies to work with student academically. Sign student up for tutoring. Increase collaboration in your lessons. Increase informal checks for understanding in your lessons.

(Continued)

(Continued)

PERFORMANCE BARRIER	WHAT DOES IT LOOK LIKE IN THE CLASSROOM?	STRATEGIES TO INTERVENE AS A TEACHER
Motivation (Value times confidence; neither variable can be 0)	Student is "frozen" and not working but also not raising hand. Student is overly talkative during work time. Student is sleeping during class time. Student exhibits difficulty concentrating or a lack of engagement.	Add a competitive aspect to the lesson, unit, or project (value). Let the students know you believe in their success (confidence). Ask students to praise each other after a day of groupwork (confidence). Praise students for participating (confidence). Create a behavior/work contract for student if issue is consistent (value). Institute a full-class behavior modification system (value). Have a one-on-one conference with student to build confidence in task (confidence). Reach out to parent about lack of motivation (value). Explain to the student privately how the assignment fits into the bigger picture. (value). Be sure to keep students updated regularly on their current class grade (value). Try a project- or problem-based unit in your classroom (value).

Note: There can be more than one barrier, but the key is to find the driving barrier and intervene accordingly.

Your Turn

1. Think of a student who never seems motivated. Now, with the new knowledge you have, is motivation that student's biggest barrier to performance, or is it one of the other two? Remember that it can be a mixture of barriers, but usually one is the biggest issue. Target the biggest and use the chart above to brainstorm ways to give the student the support they need to overcome it.

   _____
   _____
   _____
   _____

2. Based on what you have learned about performance problems, what does this student need the most to be successful based on their biggest barrier? What actions do you need to take to make this happen?

   _____
   _____
   _____
   _____

3. Do the same with another student that others have misdiagnosed as being a problem student. What different steps might you need to take to help this student?

   _____
   _____
   _____
   _____

Focus on the Positive and Create Positive Students

> This is the happiest family ever!
>
> —Emily, Grade 8 [describing her English classroom experience]

The first two weeks of any school year are wonderful. Everything is fresh, your classroom is spotless, you stay on top of your workload, and you have the one stack of papers from your first assignment graded. All of the students are quieter in the classroom because they do not know each other fully yet, and they are eagerly waiting for your next lesson.

Around the third week of school, something interesting usually happens. A few students in the class start to test your limits. Don't worry, they will do so gently at first. This is the nature of human beings. We all do it. The third week of school will try your patience, most likely. The key to this week and the weeks following is to focus on the positive. Students who are testing the rules should experience the consequences you have put in place, privately if possible. But overall, keep the energy in the room positive.

One of the most powerful ways to keep the vibe of the classroom positive is with your words and demeanor. Always look as if you are in control, smile, and keep the pacing going! Would an actor stop a show for one distraction? Probably not . . . although an amateur actor might. See the comparison? Have your consequences in place (Week 1 works the best to set your class expectations and clear consequences) and follow through and use them when needed, but as a tool, not a weapon. Assign the consequences quickly and privately, and use "I" statements. Be calm, not angry. Stay in control. The teaching and momentum are more important.

Here are two different ways to speak to the class on Week 3:

Positive Ms. Patterson: I just love how quietly you came into the room. You really know how to follow directions. Almost everybody has their book out and ready to read. Once the last two students get their books out we'll be ready. Amazing, guys!

Negative Mr. Netherland: You came into the room all right, but look at what we aren't doing! Two people don't have their books out? How do you not know this on the third week of school? Remember you're [insert grade here] graders. You should know this by now.

It's pretty obvious which teacher is going to get students to follow directions and feel good during class. Remember the mind is open when students feel good. Doesn't that last negative example just put a pit in your stomach?

We know that teachers who have strong teacher-to-student relationships have fewer behavior issues in their classes. In *Five to Thrive: Answers to Your Biggest Questions About Creating a Dynamic Classroom* (2022), I looked into this further, noting the following:

> As Karpinski (2021) writes, "Relationship researchers have shown that successful intimate relationships need about five positive-support interactions for each critical-challenging one. Tom Rath, senior scientist at Gallup, says we should target about 80 percent of our interaction time to be in positive areas—talking about successes and strengths—and only 20 percent to be in areas for improvement or difficulties." (p. 64)

The bottom line is that in order to have healthy relationships with our students and cultivate positive classrooms, we have to be mindful about what we are saying to our students. Are we criticizing more or praising more? It makes a huge difference.

> A tense teacher will usually have a tense class. A happy, upbeat, and positive teacher will often have an upbeat and happy class. Energy is way more contagious than most of us think, and it starts with us—the words and tone we use with our students have an immense impact on the classroom.

Focusing on the negative creates a snowball effect in the classroom. As soon as you do this, the students who thrive on negativity or normalize it due to circumstances at home or with friends will multiply the negativity. They will also have a negative tone. Listen to them next time. It's pretty astounding. When you have an overly dominant positive tone, the positive students in the class will speak up, they will smile, and they will raise their hands to answer. What will happen is that the students who are used to being negative will stay quiet for a little while. This tone is foreign to them. They will eventually have to adapt. They will eventually be conditioned to be positive in your presence. You may notice a vast difference between their hallway demeanor and their classroom demeanor. They may continue the negative tone with friends and/or family (although hopefully they can empower themselves to change this as well), but they will be positive in your classroom.

Listen to yourself the next time you speak. Which teacher are you? If you catch yourself being a Negative Mr. Netherland, change in that moment! We all make mistakes—teachers and students alike. The best teachers just know how to self-correct and move forward.

Your Turn

1. When was the last time you lost your cool during a class? Describe what happened. Was this because of one student or was the whole class off task?

   _____
   _____
   _____
   _____
   _____
   _____
   _____
   _____
   _____
   _____

2. What was the impact on the rest of the class period?

   _____
   _____
   _____
   _____
   _____
   _____
   _____
   _____
   _____
   _____

Dig Deeper With Connection Kids

> It sucks when teachers don't trust me. It makes me question if they think I'm a good person.
>
> —Jocelyn, Grade 9

Alan was in my third-period English class. The first time I had met him was actually when he was in seventh grade. I was covering a colleague's science class when Alan got up without permission, walked to the door, whipped his long hair out of his face and spit out the door without reservation. He could read the appalled look on my face as he glanced my direction without concern and said loudly for all to hear, "I have a 504B plan, I get breaks, look it up." He then walked out the door with swagger. I stood in shock, not sure what to do. I had been "schooled" by a twelve-year-old boy.

The following year, on the first day of school Alan walked into my eighth-grade class and sat down. He didn't remember who I was, but I sure remembered him. He shouted out without permission, put his feet up on the desk when he wanted to relax, and occasionally either fell asleep in class or had trouble staying in his seat. Other teachers expressed the same concern, even in the first week of school.

In most classes, you will have (cough) a student who presents a challenge. Perhaps you have several students who fit this bill. Either way, you have many ways to address this. I by no means believe any student is "bad." This is how they are thought of and described by most. I like to think of them as connection kids. These are students that, before they will learn from you, need to feel heard and understood, like you, and know that you like things about them as human beings (not just as students). They are often challenging in the beginning of the school year because they do not have a connection with you yet. I get excited when I spot them in class at the beginning of the year. In my head I'm mentally rubbing my hands together and thinking, *Ha! Let the work begin.*

You can spot them, too. Look for the student who yells out, the student who is disrespectful to another without realizing it, etc. They are screaming for help. The trick is to catch them early. You know the students I'm talking about: They make careless decisions and have little self-control. There is a whole list of reasons as to why one child may be more difficult to teach than others. Let's call this student "the child with challenging behaviors," keeping in mind that the challenging child *wants* to be known as the good child. It's true. Deep down all students want to be known as the good student. For the naughty student, something just went wrong down the line somewhere. Every student has a light that shines brightly, and it's our job to find that light. Sometimes we have to ask questions to get there.

How to spot a connection kid:

- The student who is usually a behavior management issue for substitute teachers (this is because they have no relationship with the substitute)

- The student who has a behavior management issue very early in the school year (because they do not have a relationship with the teacher yet)

Tips to Keep in Mind With Connection Kids

- Children who challenge want equality. They want to be treated just like every other student. The fastest way for you to lose their respect or trust is by saying their name more than others or in a different tone than others, or disciplining them directly and in front of the class. This will be a showdown even the most experienced teacher can lose. Speak to these children in the same tone and volume that you use with the other students. Have the disciplinary conversations with them privately. They will show better behavior.

- *Show* students with challenging behaviors you are not going to give up on them, but don't hold their hand. Encourage them to take responsibility for their behavior. The secret is to show them that you

(Continued)

(Continued)

are not going anywhere and neither is your support. Challenging children almost always have instability in their family lives. Show them with your actions that you are a constant factor in their lives. Even if they mess up, you will hold them accountable and expect the best for next time. Ask them, "What could you do differently next time?" Build their thinking skills and show them you are listening. Actions mean much more than words to these students.

- Expect them to do well. Students know whether you believe in them or not. They know which teachers think they are intelligent. They will perform the best for these teachers. Believe in them. This is something you have to do internally. Do not think, *Oh, I hope Sarah doesn't blow it again on this test.* Instead think, *I know she will do better this time.* What you think will come out in your words, energy, and actions towards the child.

- The best practice I've found that works with students like this is finding out what interests them. You can even print out articles on that subject for them to read. When you find out what interests them and you take an interest in that as well, *they translate that into you caring about them and they see a way to connect with you.* Often with connection kids, you have to connect with them nonacademically first, before learning can happen. Just telling them what to do can cause them to spiral downhill quickly.

- It's important to ask ourselves, *Have I laughed with this child about anything?* Think about it: In our personal lives, how do we know we are liked by others? We probably know this because they smile when they are around us, or we laugh often together. Connection kids may need this from you before they start working for you. At least give them a smile . . . come on, you can do it!

Alan used to bring a skateboard into class. Although our school had a policy to check skateboards in before entering our campus, Alan somehow bypassed this system. He wanted to hold on to his board. I realized that I should use his interest in skateboarding to get him interested in reading. I started asking casual questions about which skaters he liked, where he skated, etc. I asked if he had any pictures of him doing cool skate tricks or videos I could watch. He started showing me pictures of him doing tricks after the class ended. He was actually really talented! I wanted to find out everything I could about his interest.

I began to print out articles about famous skaters that he read during independent reading time. He no longer slept during this time; he was actually reading. He asked me for more skating articles and started showing me videos of skate tricks he had mastered on the weekends or after school. This became our normal routine. I even snuck some current events in there about skate legislations, etc.

Shortly after this, he started taking notes in class and working with others during groupwork time. The other students started asking him about skateboarding, and he felt like he belonged more in the classroom. With his permission, I printed out a picture of him doing a skateboarding trick and hung it on our student wall. He was sheepish, and at first he felt embarrassed. I convinced him that others would like to see how talented he was. The other kids asked him to sign the picture. When our wall was full, I hung the picture next to my desk. He noticed and continued to complete work in class.

His academic grade went up, he was more engaged in class, and he felt connected to our classroom. At the same time, I also placed him on an eight-week behavior contract (see Best Practice #17) that helped redirect many of his off-task behaviors, such as shouting out and not staying in his seat. Yes, he still took his breaks, but he took them with permission, and he also completed classroom and worked well in a group most days.

Another connection kid I had when I taught ninth grade in a public school was a girl we'll call Colleen. Colleen loved makeup and fashion. In fact, she loved it even more than academics because she would do her makeup and hair during every class. I started saving my copies of *Vogue* and brought them in to her every week to take home and read. I didn't give them to her with any expectation of her owing me anything. I just quietly put a magazine on her desk before class and it was there waiting for her when she arrived. She knew I remembered every week. She would beam and yell, "Thanks, Ms. Pariser!" She then started to try her best to complete her work and participate during class. I knew she liked fashion and I respected that. Colleen took a little less work than Alan, but a version of the same best practice was used: Find out what they're into and take an interest by asking them questions. *Listen genuinely* to what they say. Then ask more questions. Eventually, try bringing them articles or items that show you are genuinely invested in their interest. Their interest will be validated.

When you do this for students they feel like you "get" them.
Remember:

- The connection kid wants to be trusted by adults.

- The connection kid wants to feel like they belong in your classroom.

- The connection kid wants to be known as "good" deep down.

- The connection kid wants to be understood.

- The connection kid is used to not feeling heard or understood.

- The connection kid wants to be valued by their classmates academically as well as socially.

- The connection kid will quickly lose trust if your words do not match your actions.

- Find out what interests a connection kid and attempt to connect through that.
- Tiny favors or recognition go a long way with connection kids.
- The connection kid is screaming for connection but doesn't always know how to initiate it.
- Connection kids who are low achieving academically often make up for lacking in academic ability by being heard and seen socially. If you can help them succeed and become engaged academically, they have less of a need to be heard in other ways.
- Connection kids who are high achieving academically are often just bored academically. Challenge them.

Your Turn

Think back to a connection kid you have had or worked with in a classroom. Look at the tips for how to handle these students above.

1. Which of these strategies did you try? How did it work?

   _____
   _____
   _____
   _____
   _____
   _____

2. Were any of these strategies not used?

   _____
   _____
   _____
   _____
   _____

3. Think of a student in one of your classes that exhibits problematic behavior. Do you know what interests them? What do you notice about what they wear, how they spend their time, or what they talk about that can help you discover what interests them?

   _____
   _____
   _____
   _____
   _____
   _____

Reward Students

> I think that my actions deserve a reward.
>
> —Dom, Grade 8

Every student loves to be rewarded, but many aren't as outspoken as Dom. If you think your students don't deserve rewards, you might not be giving them opportunities to succeed. Some teachers will threaten to withhold rewards from the entire class to gain power and a sense of authority. Be careful not to fall into this easy trap. If you do this, the students will think you do not want them to earn a reward, and that's not what we want. We need them to see that we believe in them and think they can achieve. The students should always feel that we want them to get rewarded.

Emphasize student successes. Give them a chance. The most valuable reward is one that they have to work for. Students love to be rewarded in groups or with their friends. Make sure the reward is fitting for how they performed, for how hard they worked. Make them compete against each other to earn the reward. Your classroom will have an energy to it, and students will be focused as they are competing for the prize—or, in teacher terms, they will be doing their work and learning. There is some controversy surrounding extrinsic prizes for students, but I always believe that an extrinsic prize is the perfect soil to grow intrinsic motivation. As they work for the extrinsic prize, students will feel successful and confident, which is the perfect environment to nurture intrinsic development. For ideas on how to reward students, search for behavior modification systems to see what you find. These are the same rewards I use with behavior contracts (see Best Practice #17 for information on behavior contracts).

Tips and Ideas for Extrinsic Rewards

Here are some rewards that have worked for me:

- Whole class gets technology time during lunch
- Individual student (or student and a friend) gets technology time during lunch
- Microwave popcorn (so easy if you have a microwave)
- Whole class watches *America's Funniest Home Video* episode during lunch
- Individual student (or student and a friend) watches *American's Funniest Home Video* episode during lunch
- Bookmarks
- Teacher's assistant for a day
- Field trip
- Greeter privilege for a guest speaker
- Cool pencils/school supplies
- Popsicles (easier to clean up than ice cream/frozen yogurt)
- Popsicle party with a friend (They just sit and eat popsicles, but they love it.)
- A surprise reward always works really well (see Best Practice #52: Surprise!). Have an item or two under a box with a question mark on it.
- Lunch with the teacher (This works well in elementary school.)

Note: Any reward that can be celebrated with a friend of choice makes it much more enticing for students.

Your Turn

1. What are your thoughts on extrinsic rewards to foster intrinsic motivation?

2. Did you ever have a project in middle or high school that had a competitive edge? Did that make you work harder? Why or why not?

3. Brainstorm some additional rewards that would be fitting for your grade level or classroom.

Motivating Students in Elementary, Middle, and High School and How That Might Look Different

You'll have a hard time finding a teacher who doesn't wish for a class of students who are all intrinsically motivated. However, often motivation has to start with extrinsic factors that can, over time, foster intrinsic motivation. For some students, intrinsic motivation comes naturally, but for others it is a trait that grows and develops over a school year. Sometimes we need to give a little boost to help students develop habits that they'll carry with them through grades. Most of the rewards noted in Best Practice #15 work with older students, too, but here are some special considerations.

Elementary School Motivational Tips

- Praise, praise, praise.
- Give helpful and direct feedback often.
- Hold class celebrations.
- Invite parents and caregivers into the class to read to the class or carry out other activities (see Best Practice #37 for other ideas on how to incorporate families into the classroom).

- Have show-and-tell days where students bring in an object, toy, or picture that is important to them and talk to the class about it.
- Invite students to bring in something from their home culture to teach and share with the class.
- Send out a weekly newsletter to parents and caregivers detailing upcoming events, class happenings, and what you are working on academically the following week so families can be empowered and talk to their kids about school. The newsletter can look the same each week; you just change out some of the content. Parent and caregiver involvement and student motivation go hand and hand, especially in the younger grades.

Middle and High School Motivational Tips

- Plan curriculum that directly relates to the world around them.
- Praise, praise, praise.
- Provide authentic audiences for projects.
- Know the interests of each student.
- Demonstrate that you truly believe in every child's future.

Your Turn

1. What methods have you tried that worked well to foster student motivation in elementary, middle, or high school? Why do you think these methods worked?

   _____
   _____
   _____
   _____
   _____

2. Conversely, was there a time you tried something to foster motivation that did not work? Why do you think it didn't work, and what could you do differently next time?

   _____
   _____
   _____
   _____
   _____

3. Do you think motivation is an innate skill or something that can be nurtured and formed through time?

   _____
   _____
   _____
   _____
   _____
   _____

Consider Behavior Contracts

What do we do when it seems a student has lost all hope, doesn't have the social skill set to stay motivated, creates a constant class disruption, or seems defiant or just shut down? How do you motivate them? Do you have a student with whom you have the same conversation regarding an unwanted behavior over and over, yet you see no change in behavior? You may need to use a behavior contract to redirect behavior. According to Intervention Central (n.d.), a behavior contract is "a simple positive reinforcement intervention that is widely used by teachers to change student behavior." I wish I had had formal training about behavior contracts in my first few years teaching.

As a general rule, the earlier you start a student on a behavior contract, the more successful the results. I suggest starting a student on a behavior contract in the first month of school, if possible. A behavior contract's success is all about the pitch. By *pitch*, I mean how you speak to the student about starting the contract.

> Behavior contracts are most effective for students in second grade and above as they may not be developmentally appropriate for younger kids.

Unwanted behaviors that you're trying to redirect might include, but are not limited to, the following:

- Excessive talking
- Shouting out at inappropriate times
- Not staying in seat
- Making fun of others
- Rudeness/defiance to teachers or other adults in class
- Not following instructions the first time asked

These are the major actions that most teachers say interrupt a lesson. A behavior contract can and will redirect these behaviors. Such compacts are used to redirect and extinguish unwanted behaviors in order to continue with the learning.

The trick with behavior contracts is they are temporary and focus on specific, observable, and measurable behaviors, not just on "being good." Also, *they only focus on three desired behaviors unique to that particular student.* You can see Jamica's behavior contract in Figure 17.1 and Figure 17.2.

It's better for the child if the behavior contract is used with every teacher that child has, but the adults all have to work together to make sure it is signed daily. Sometimes it's only possible to logistically have a behavior contract for your class. Perhaps the success the student experiences there will bleed into their other classes. The key to success with behavior contracts is giving the student opportunities to feel they are achieving the desired behaviors on the contract.

How do you choose which students need a behavior contract? A student should be put on a behavior contract when your classroom consequences are repeatedly not working for that student and the unwanted behaviors are holding back the learning of the class.

Mistakes and Misconceptions

The most common mistake I see teachers make is complaining about the behavior but not using a contract and just hoping the behavior will go away. Although that would be so much easier, 99 percent of the time this won't be the case. The earlier a behavior contract is implemented, the better, but it's really never too late to start a student on one. I once developed a behavior contract with a student for the last eight weeks of school, and my life was so much easier after he redirected his negative and distracting behavior. I wish I had done it sooner.

A common misconception is that behavior contracts are taxing on the teachers. Yes, they will take a little time, but the payoffs are worth it times a million. Your class will most likely turn into the only—or at least the first—class where the student redirects their behavior.

Another common misconception about behavior contracts is that they are only for students with IEPs. In reality, any student can benefit from a behavior contract. A behavior contract is separate from an IEP and made by the teacher, not the case manager. I suggest you only have up to three behavior contracts (one or two is optimal) in each class, for your own stability. It's too much work for the teacher to have more than that. Choose your top student or two who set(s) off the rest of the class with unwanted behavior.

I've also heard teachers say their whole class is on a contract. I guess that could be the case, but it's highly unlikely. Behavior contracts are private contracts with select students *who need help reaching your normal class expectations*. The help they usually need is *motivation* to follow the class expectations. Think of the contracts as behavior training wheels for a select few.

Creating a Behavior Contract

A child has to truly believe you want them to succeed, and you have to believe they can meet the goals of their contract. That's the only way a behavior contract will work. You have to be on their side. This may take a little change in perspective on your part before making the contract.

A behavior contract should be co-created with the student in order for it to have the best chance of working. The font can be chosen together, the picture can be chosen together, the desired behaviors should be chosen together, and, most importantly, the rewards should be chosen together. This way the students take ownership. Otherwise you're just handing them a piece of paper.

It's helpful if you can print the contract on a colored sheet of paper so the student can find it easily in their binder. It could look something like the contract in Figure 17.1 and Figure 17.2. This is the contract passed down to me that was created by my mentor, Dr. Orletta Nguyen, and which I have used for my most challenging students, year after year. It works better than any other contract I've tried to use. This is just a simple template she created on Microsoft Word, and it is a mixture of many of the behavior contracts out there.

If the student has an IEP, one of the many great aspects of the contract is that there are percentages for behaviors that can be brought into IEP meetings if need be and if the desired behaviors align with the IEP goals. For rewards, I find many boys like food and friends as the reward. Girls are a bit trickier with rewards they desire, so you may have to give them a few choices. The prizes should gradually grow larger every week. Keep in mind rewards can be experiences and privileges, not always "stuff." (See Best Practices #15 and #16 for a list of reward ideas). If you have a student on a contract for more than four weeks, on Week 5 they still start on a low-level prize, the same as Week 1.

Figure 17.1 Front Side of Behavior Contract

Jamica's ENGLISH CLASS
Contract

Week of _____
      (date)

Week 1 GOAL Percent to reach reward: 60% = 9 boxes marked with a 3, 4, or 5

	Monday	Tuesday	Wednesday	Thursday	Friday
Be polite to all adults in room with words and actions	5				
Follow directions the first time asked	4				
Stay focused without sound disruptions during instruction time	5				

*A LOST CONTRACT RESULTS IN A 1 FOR THAT ENTIRE DAY

5 = 80–100%   4 = 60–80%   3 = 40–60%   2 = 20–40%   1 = 0–20%

Source: Behavior contract created by Dr. Orletta Nguyen.

Figure 17.2 Back Side of Behavior Contract

I, _____, agree to the following contract. If I am successful I will receive the weekly prize. If I am unsuccessful, I will receive a negative phone call home. I will give this contract to Ms. Pariser at the END of every class to sign.

   PRIZES!!

WEEK 1: Technology time during lunch with candy
WEEK 2: Technology time during lunch with candy AND popcorn
WEEK 3: Technology time during lunch with friend with candy, popcorn, and soda
WEEK 4: Technology time during lunch with two friends with candy and popcorn

Source: Behavior contract created by Dr. Orletta Nguyen.

Every Monday give the student a nice new contract. In Week 1 have the student work towards 60 percent of the fifteen boxes being marked with a 3, 4, or 5. Then Week 2 should be about 70 percent. Week 3 should be about 80 percent, and Week 4 should be about 90 percent. You're gradually changing behavior because that's how forming new habits works. You go over what reward the student is working for and the three desired behaviors. The student hands the contract to you at the end of each class period, and both of you talk about how they did that day for each desired behavior. Most of the time the student will be able to accurately self-assess what they did well and how they can improve the next day. This is empowering to a student. This takes about thirty seconds, maybe less. You hand the contract back to the student; they are in charge of it.

Pitching Behavior Contracts

The way you start a student on a behavior contract can make a huge difference. Are you a talented salesperson? This is the skill that will help you with a contract. I will share a script below that can help.

Let's go back to the student contract shown in the figures on the previous page. Here's what I did to start this student on a contract. First, I asked her to stop by my room during lunch. You want to pitch a behavior contract when there aren't other students in the room. This is the most important aspect of a behavior contract: the sale. The reality is, you want this student to change their behaviors. You want them to *want* to follow the contract. At this point this student asked if she was in trouble. I responded, "Actually, no, it's a good meeting!" She was curious about the meeting all morning. This is what you want. If you have a paraprofessional or another teacher in that class, it's helpful if they can be there as well so all adults in the room are on the same page with the behavior contract. I had my coteacher there as well.

You'll need a solid twenty minutes to have this launch meeting. In this meeting you will not only "sell" the student on wanting to follow a contract but also co-create the contract with them using a template. Have the template pulled up on your computer ready to personalize with the student and also—this is very important—*have the three desired behaviors you want already in your head or written down somewhere you can glance at them*. You have control of what they are, but you want the student to think they chose them too. So, for this example student, we wanted her desired behaviors to be to

- respect all adults in class,
- follow directions the first time asked (this one I love because it can cover so much), and
- stay focused during instructional time without any sound disruptions to stop the lesson.

These goals are measurable, observable, and stated in the positive.

Also, have weekly rewards jotted down that you think the student may like. Try saying something like this:

Teacher: How are you liking our class?

Student: Good.

Teacher: Well, I have an idea. You know how you used to be doing really well in class and had a *B+* average? That was really nice and I felt like you were enjoying class more. Didn't you like that time?

Student: Yes. [Guaranteed, she'll still be wondering if she's in trouble.]

Teacher: I had an idea on how you can focus more in class. However, I can't do this for everyone, so please don't tell others about it; I don't want them to get jealous and everyone will want this. Do you want to hear about it? [Basically, if she tells everybody about her contract, other students will want the contract, too, and you'll be giving rewards to the entire class. Other students won't perceive it as fair, even though it is because this specific child just needs a *temporary accommodation to reach the same behavior expectations as the other students.*]

Student: Sure.

Teacher: It's called a behavior contract. Have you ever seen one of these before?

Student: Oh yeah, I've been on a contract before. I hate them.

It's fine if the student says this. At this point, a student that you choose to put on a contract may have been on one before. If they have, you can say this:

Teacher: Oh no, yeah, I know about those other contracts. This one is different. You'll love it. I chose you for this because I think you'll really appreciate it. The reason I picked you is because I noticed your behavior has been slipping and I'd really like to see you feel more a part of our classroom and feel like you're learning something. And I think you can improve your grades, too. There are so many students that beg to be on these every year. I just can't do it for everybody. Want to hear about it?

You have to show enthusiasm about the contract. Make the student think it's an opportunity. Think of yourself like a car salesman. Your demeanor can't convey to the child that they are in trouble and this is the last resort. They have to feel special that you chose them for the contract. The student may still be a bit confused, but they are often curious at this point. This is where you want them. You now have one of your most difficult students on board.

Now pull up your computer. It's better if the contract is already ready to show them so you won't be scrambling around. If you have a document camera, you can project it as you personalize it. Students really love this. Start with letting them pick the font (any font is fine) that they like and ask what type of things they like (dance, football, soccer, even street art is fine). Put a little picture of this interest on their contract. You'll use the same contract every week, so let them take their time picking a picture of their favorite singer, football player, etc. I have had many contracts with a picture of Ronaldo kicking a goal. Now they are excited. At this point, explain the rewards first.

Teacher: So each day you are graded on three things. Just three! What do you think would be the best thing to change so you can focus more in class?

Student: Maybe my seat?

Teacher: No, I think your seat is actually fine. Hmmm . . . let's think. What about how you speak to our coteacher, Ms. Wish, sometimes? Do you think maybe you could be a little kinder with your words?

Student: Oh, yeah. Maybe that would be good if we changed that.

Teacher: So do you think that could be one of the things we rate every day?

Student: Yes.

You do this until you get the three behaviors you originally wanted, but the students will think they actually made the decisions so will own the behaviors more. It's fabulous. Spend time going over the rewards and be excited when you talk about them. Then say:

Teacher: There might be a week that you don't make it. I hate when that happens, but because I'm putting in so much with the rewards, we do have to have consequences if you don't make your contract points one week.

Student: Okay.

Go over the consequences and let the student know you really want them to get the reward every week. They have to truly believe this. Have the student sign the contract and shake hands (you just made a sale). Congratulations—you just got your sanity back! The contract should start that day or the next. So if you want to start a contract on a Monday, you should have the meeting on a Friday or Monday morning before class. It's all about the sale.

For consequences, use what will be most effective for that particular student. Here are some ideas:

- You inform their sports or extracurricular activity coach about their misbehavior at the end of the week only if they do not make the contract goal.

- You place a parent phone call home at the end of the week if they do not make the contract goal.

- You give them a lunch or after-school twenty-minute detention. Make sure that a detention doesn't turn into a counseling session or even a homework makeup session. For detentions, my mentor showed me the trick of setting a timer and not allowing the student to socialize with you or anybody else for that time. If they start to talk, just walk over and stop the timer without saying anything. They will groan. Then restart the timer again when they stop socializing with you or the other student(s) in the room. Unfortunately, we need them to feel uncomfortable for a short amount of time so they will not want that consequence again and will work harder for the behavior contract goals the next week.

One of the secrets of a successful behavior contract is *the student has to make their goal the first week for it to be most successful*. They need that taste of success. Really work with them to believe they can reach it, and they probably will. If they do not succeed the first week, they might give up on it. Then you're back to square one because they won't want to do the contract anymore and they most likely won't follow your classroom expectations based on their behavior history.

If they don't reach their goal in the weeks after Week 1, then they receive the consequence and start over on that goal the following week. They work for that goal until they make it—and they will.

If you have pushback from other teachers who say you are "bribing" students to do well, know that's not the case. Other teachers knew I was doing something different because even children with the most severe behavior problems were displaying excellent behavior in my class. Because students felt successful in my class, they were more comfortable in my classroom and also with me as a teacher, and our relationship was healthier. This leads to increased learning. You are using extrinsic motivation to foster intrinsic motivation. Your school psychologist would agree with the theory behind this contract. This is a temporary scaffold to redirect desired behaviors to maximize learning. If you take the student off of the contract after four weeks, they may very well continue with the great behavior because they've conditioned themselves to act appropriately in your classroom. Some students need eight weeks of a contract, and some need even longer. When you feel it's time to take the student off of the contract, make it a celebration. Reward them with lunch with you and tell them how proud you are of them.

Tips for Effective Behavior Contracts

- An unwanted behavior will most likely not just go away without intervention. It will most likely get worse.
- A behavior contract's success is all about the pitch and consistency.
- The earlier the better with a behavior contract.
- A behavior contract takes a bit more front work from the teacher, but the payoff is well worth it in the long run.
- Behavior contracts are not just for students on IEPs.
- Choose behavior contracts for students with whom your classroom consequences are repeatedly not working.
- Behavior contracts are co-created between the teacher and the student.
- Behavior contracts should focus on three specific, measurable, and observable behaviors.
- Behavior contract desired behaviors should always be framed in positive words.
- Only have up to three students in each period on a behavior contract. Otherwise it's too much work for the teacher.
- Behavior contracts are temporary scaffolds for the student.
- An entire class should not be on a behavior contract. Instead, a class could be on a behavior modification system. A behavior contract is for your most challenging students.
- A student on a behavior contract has to believe you really want them to succeed for it to work.

Your Turn

1. Have you ever used a behavior contract with a student? Did it work? Why or why not?

   _____
   _____
   _____
   _____
   _____

2. What new ideas about behavior contracts did you learn from this section?

   _____
   _____
   _____
   _____

3. Imagine that you have a student you are going to put on a behavior contract. Describe what this meeting would look like.

   a. When and where would you have the "pitch meeting?"

   b. How much of the contract would you have finished before the meeting?

   c. How much time would you allot for the meeting?

   d. How would you pitch it so the student wants to participate in the contract?

   _____
   _____
   _____
   _____
   _____

Real Conversation With a High School Student

Student [to a teacher a few days before final grades are due]:
Teacher, can you round my *C+* to an *A*?

PART 3
ENGAGEMENT AND INSTRUCTION

Desperate Times Call for Desperate Measures

I had this teacher in fourth or fifth grade, she was an elderly teacher that didn't have a very strong voice. She used to keep this glass paperweight on her desk. I remember it was shaped like a hockey puck, the perfect shape to hold in the hand. For some reason, her desk was made of metal. She used to pick up this hockey puck paperweight and slam it down on her metal desk over and over again to get our attention.

—Michael, Age 57

Source: iStock.com/Vitalii Barida

How do engagement and instruction relate to classroom management?

Engagement and instruction are at the core of classroom management. If you can plan instruction that is rigorous, engaging, collaborative, and connected to the real world, your behavior problems will start to disappear. I used to spend countless hours being reactive to classroom management. This is a slippery slope. Once I flipped how I was using my time, my classroom behavior issues decreased dramatically. Planning quality instruction is the most effective, proactive way to have strong classroom management.

I REMEMBER WHEN...

I remember when I first started teaching at an alternative high school in South Carolina. I completed my student teaching in another alternative school in Minnesota, but it was nothing like this one. This school was for students who had been expelled from traditional high school. There were regular fights on campus (some that would happen in classrooms, which was dangerous for teachers), drugs being both sold and used on campus, rival gang members made to be together in the same classroom, etc. I had multiple students who would start in the middle of the year, straight from a stint in a juvenile detention center. I even had more than one student arrested for murder while I was working there. (One student was actually arrested in my classroom on Monday morning for a murder the night before.) Needless to say, teaching conditions were difficult, as most of the students absolutely did not want to be in school one iota.

Feeling unsure what the best approach was, I thought back to college when I had read Aristotle's *Metaphysics*. I recalled how Aristotle talked about how every single person, by nature, has a desire to know and to learn. With that as my motivation, I turned all of my efforts to instruction tactics and lesson planning. I tried to make each lesson as engaging, interactive, and hands-on as I possibly could. Good grades, a diploma, or even cool prizes were no motivation for these students. I had to appeal to their intrinsic desire to learn and be curious about the world, all while keeping their attention on learning and not on each other.

I quickly found that a well-planned-out lesson was the key to successful classroom behavior management. I relied on all of the principles of pedagogy I had learned in college to keep the students focused and interested for each and every one of the fifty minutes of class. Not only did the students learn, but they also enjoyed class and found it to be a calm and peaceful respite from their unimaginably difficult home lives and the culture of violence and poverty they were born into. I ended up being named Teacher of the Year my second year at the school and was one of very few, if any, teachers who never had any serious behavior issues in my classroom. This was all thanks to a focus on lesson planning and instruction.

Watch Jeff Kirschbaum, a twenty-year veteran teacher in San Diego, tell his story.

Jeff Kirschbaum
15 years' experience
The Academy of Our Lady of Peace
San Diego, CA

Make Learning Powerfully Authentic and Make It Transferable

> Thank you for helping me by changing my thinking.
>
> —Vicky, Grade 9

What is the role of a teacher? Is a teacher a distributor of knowledge or an inspirer? I always liked to be more of the latter. Students almost worship teachers who can make learning fun and interesting. Make the learning relevant to their lives. Make the content into something they *want* to learn rather than something they *have* to learn. The best way I learned how to do this was to work with projects. When planning a project I asked myself, *Where will they need to use this knowledge or skill in the real world?* This question forced me to make the learning real. Then I planned my project accordingly so the learning was relevant and exciting.

For example, one time I wanted my students to experience a piece of classic literature. I was becoming annoyed with the fact that they were being fed "inner-city youth" books because people assumed that's what they could relate to. I chose *Of Mice and Men* by John Steinbeck even though I was cautioned that the students might not be interested in two hillbillies during the Great Depression. I thought, *How do I get my ninth graders to want to read this book?*

To start, I looked to the real world. I thought about how the book is banned in many schools. I took that angle and printed out reasons why the book is sometimes banned but left its title out of the write-up. I had a sheet of arguments both for and against the ban. After reading the short critique, the students were in. They were sold. I told them I had gotten special permission to read the book with them (I mean, I *did* have to clear it with my supervisor). They were honored and chomping at the bit to know what the book was.

"When are we reading? What is it!?" That was all I heard the next day in the hallways. I gave them a few vague clues like, "One of the characters is mentally challenged, and I'm certain the class will disagree on what they think of the ending!"

The students who guessed from the vague clues were sworn to secrecy (I knew they would tell—it was part of the fun) and they could barely stop from screaming out the title. The next day I had copies of *Of Mice and Men* in the center of the room, in a wrapped box (to add another element of surprise). I had a sign on the box that read, "What could be in here?" The students came in and all eyes were on the box. Some tried to poke it. When class started, I ripped open the box and I couldn't stop them from grabbing at the books and opening to the first page. This enthusiasm was much different from the nonengagement and chaos of the first class, remember? We began to read. I played an audiobook. I'm a strong believer in using audio for class novels as it is good for auditory learners, incorporates character voices, models perfect pacing, and gives you a break. I stopped the book at the exciting parts where something was just about to happen. When I pressed stop, students would scream,"*No! Five more minutes!*" I mean, really? High school students acted like this? Yes, really!

Now here's where I brought the book to life. As we were reading the novel, I also had them read short nonfiction articles that related directly to serious issues in the book. I made sure they saw both sides of the issue by giving them two different articles on back-to-back days. For example, one day we would read a pro-euthanasia article and the next we would read an article or firsthand account arguing against it. This led to critical thinking, heated in-class discussions, deep questioning, and pushing each other's thinking. This all resulted in higher engagement and, yep, way fewer—if any—behavior issues. The highly controversial topics we studied alongside *Of Mice and Men* were euthanasia, the death penalty, and lobotomies.

When we finished listening to the book I asked them one question: Did George make the right decision to end his best friend's life? They were torn and upset. We had a class discussion and they were told they had to choose a side by the next day. The class split in half. I didn't tell them what side I was on so as not to bias opinion and to add an element of surprise again. While we were reading the novel, we also read and dissected nonfiction articles about court cases involving the mentally challenged, asylums, and lobotomies to make their arguments real.

Think about it: If a student felt George had made the wrong decision by ending Lennie's life, the student had to be ready to speak about the condition of asylums during that time period. This also allowed us to cover more standards (shhhhh!).

They were then asked to write a position paper or persuasive essay defending their side. There's your persuasive essay composition in those, oh yeah, dry standards. After they wrote their paper, they still weren't sure what was coming next but knew something else was on the way. Students were then placed on debate teams and told they would go head-to-head to see which team would win a debate about whether or not George Milton made the right decision. They were taught how to debate with passion, how to write note cards, how to cite, how to use textual evidence, and how to hold a formal debate. Team members were also told there would be surprise guest judges at the debate. The guest judges were students from other grades who had read the book the previous year. Of course, you could also invite parents and other adults at your school to be judges, *American Idol*–style. These debates were usually the highlight of my year. From start to finish, it was a seven-to-eight-week unit.

Enthusiasm, intense rage, rigor, and unbridled passion were unleashed from the students all for a . . . book. Wow! This can and will happen when you bring learning to life and make it real. You can be an inspirer.

Tips to Get Students Engaged

- Add an element of surprise to your units or lessons. You want them to be thinking and talking about your class, even when they are not inside your classroom.
- Add a competitive edge to your projects.
- Let students work in groups or partnerships for projects.
- Add an element of student choice in your projects.
- Connect your units to the real world.
- Invite parents to see the final projects.
- Invite students from other grades to see or judge the final presentations of learning.

Your Turn

1. Think of a project you have done with your class that went extremely well. What elements of the project contributed to that? Could you have made it even better?

   _____
   _____
   _____
   _____
   _____

2. Think of a project you have done that maybe didn't go as well as expected. Why was this? Was there an element of it that was missing?

   _____
   _____
   _____
   _____
   _____

3. Now think of a project you are planning in the near future. How can you make it exciting and real for your students? Competition? Guest speakers? Working in groups?

   _____
   _____
   _____
   _____
   _____

Learn and Grow Using Trusted Sources

Remember, the most effective, engaging, and powerful teaching is being done every day all around the world. Research to find an idea better than yours or one that can help you. A majority of great teaching relies heavily on research about what methods work best. As dry as research books on teaching may be, they are extremely worth reading. Instead of constantly being reactive in the classroom, books on teaching methodology can actually show you how to prevent misbehaviors and the nonunderstanding of concepts in the first place. So, when you have time to catch your breath—probably in about your second or third year of teaching—pick up a few teaching methodology books. Here are some of my favorites:

- *Differentiating Instruction in the Regular Classroom: How to Reach and Teach All Learners* (2012) by Diane Heacox, Ed.D.
- *The First Years Matter: Becoming an Effective Teacher: A Mentoring Guide for Novice Teachers* (2017) by Carol Radford
- *Mentoring in Action: Guiding, Sharing, and Reflecting With Novice Teachers* (2017) by Carol Radford
- *Letters to a Young Teacher* (2007) by Jonathan Kozol
- *Culturally Responsive Teaching and the Brain: Promoting Authentic Engagement and Rigor Among Culturally and Linguistically Diverse Students* (2015) by Zaretta Hammond

- *Positive Discipline in the Classroom: Developing Mutual Respect, Cooperation, and Responsibility in Your Classroom* (2013) by Jane Nelson
- *Mindset* (2016) by C.S. Dweck
- *The Learning Challenge: How to Guide Your Students Through the Learning Pit to Achieve Deeper Understanding* (2017) by James Nottingham
- *Best Practice: Bringing Standards to Life in America's Classrooms* (4th ed., 2012) by Steve Zemelman
- *Answers to Your Biggest Questions About Creating a Dynamic Classroom* (2022) by Serena Pariser and Victoria Lentfer
- *The Will to Learn: Cultivating Student Motivation Without Losing Your Own* (2023) by Dave Stuart Jr.

However, if you find yourself without time to read a book, we now have the luxury of education-themed podcasts where you can get bite-sized chunks of information for teachers. What's great about podcasts is that you can multitask with them. I like to listen to education podcasts as I clean my kitchen, for example. Here are some I recommend (in no particular order):

- *The Staff Room Podcast*
- *The Shake Up Learning Show*
- *Teachers on Fire*
- *The Cult of Pedagogy Podcast*
- *Teacher Saves World!*
- *Teacher to Teacher: Sharing Our Wisdom*

And, of course, being a part of educational professional organizations will keep you afloat and connected with what's going on in your field. These organizations usually hold one conference a year where you can meet other trusted professionals in your field. I suggest you try to belong to at least one. Hey, maybe your administration would even send a group of teachers from your school to a conference! Here are a few organizations I recommend:

- AMLE (Association for Middle Level Education)
- ISTE (International Society of Technology in Education)
- NASET (National Association of Special Education Teachers)
- ASCD (Association of Supervision and Curriculum Development)

- NEA (National Education Association)
- NCTE (National Council for Teachers of English)
- NCTM (National Council for Teachers of Math)
- NCSS (National Council for the Social Studies)
- NSTA (National Science Teachers Association)

Think of teaching as you would cooking. The best chefs are those who are not afraid to try new dishes. They've probably messed up a thousand times getting where they are, but they've used their blunders to perfect their craft. The more I read the research or books on teaching, the more I kick myself for not having read them earlier. The time you invest in the research will save you loads of exhaustion, frustration, and energy later.

The research works. Just think that everything you are trying to do has been done successfully somewhere else. Why not read about it?

Your Turn

1. What teaching books or podcasts have benefited your teaching or knowledge of education?

   _____
   _____
   _____
   _____
   _____

2. What educational organizations are you a part of? How has this benefited your classroom?

   _____
   _____
   _____
   _____
   _____

3. How are you staying abreast of current trends and research in your field?

   _____
   _____
   _____
   _____
   _____

4. Do you consider yourself to have a growth mindset? Why or why not?

   _____
   _____
   _____
   _____
   _____

Pick up the Pace

In addition to the common practice of using a timer to pace your lessons, you can also use a timer projected on a document camera for chunked portions of independent work for students to self-monitor their own pace. A timer projected for students to see can also help with classroom management by empowering students to stay on task for independent reading time.

A very common educator mistake is teaching too slowly. By this I mean spending too much time on one activity before moving on. It's simple: Pick up the pace. Today, teachers are competing with television, social media, video games, YouTube videos, and music that all seem to move at a zillion miles per hour. How are we supposed to keep students engaged if we are going only one mile per hour? Keep the students on their toes; they will give you the gift of their attention.

> Keep the students on their toes; they will give you the gift of their attention.

Here are some tricks to keep your pacing up. One of the most successful ways to keep up the pace is by planning your pace. By planning, I mean actually writing the minutes you'll allot to each part of your lesson on your lesson plan. Pacing is like goal-setting: If you do not plan your goals in life, life plans them for you. If you do not plan your pace, the class plans it for you. Chunk, or break up, the lesson on your lesson plan. Use only twenty-minute increments at the longest for middle school, and thirty to forty minutes for high school. Set a timer. If the timer goes off, move on. You have most likely lost the students' attention or are about to. Use your best judgment, though. If the class is still engaged, keep going, but watch for glazed eyes and other signs of disinterest. They will be falling off the wagon, so to speak, shortly after.

Below is an example of a simple thirty-five-minute plan for a chunked lesson for elementary or middle school.

Example of *Chunking* and Planning *Pace* in a Lesson

Minutes	Lesson objective:
	Given a collection of poems, students will analyze personification by explaining and illustrating personification in poems on a graphic organizer.
5	Anticipatory set: Watch the short two-minute clip from *Beauty and the Beast* that includes many examples of personification. Ask students to jot down their response to the following question: What did you notice the objects doing in the movie that they can't do in real life? Answers might mention the dancing teacups or laughing water. Share out responses with a neighbor, then the whole class.
5	Model: Share a model poem with personification. Explain and illustrate why it contains personification in boxes. Explain how the objects in the Disney clip were personified.
10	Guided: After reading a second poem with the class using choral response (students repeat lines after teacher) at seats, students sit in groups at tables to analyze that poem. The poem is printed on a sheet with boxes next to the words to record information. One box on the sheet asks students to sketch a picture illustrating personification in the poem. In another box students are asked to write a mini-paragraph of three to five lines describing the personification in the poem.
10	Independent: On the other side of the sheet is a third and final poem with the same boxes next to the words. The students analyze the poem and complete this sheet independently.
5	Closure: On exit slips, write down three other examples of personification.

Your Turn

1. I challenge you to use a timer next time you teach. Keep track of how long your students are in one learning modality. Then reflect: Was any chunk or part of the lesson more than twenty minutes (for middle school) or thirty-five minutes (for high school)? This may lead to engagement issues, which can quickly lead to classroom management issues. Use a timer when you teach on the first few instances to time each chunk of the lesson to get yourself situated to the new pace.

Use Arm's Length Voice

Here we will discuss not the students' voices but the teacher's voice. If you are talking to a student one-on-one, that should be the only student who hears you. *If you are talking to the whole class, the whole class should hear you.* As teachers we need to be smart about our voice control. This is a common mistake, but it is one with such an easy fix.

Think about being in a public library working on a paper or reading a book. Think how you feel when someone starts talking at a normal volume level to their friend. Remember that frustrating and upsetting feeling you get in your head? My thoughts usually sound like this: *Really? Do you not see me working right here?* This is how our students feel when you speak at what seems like a normal volume when you are working with them one-on-one. *Keep your voice at arm's length when speaking one-on-one or even to a group that is sitting around you, like in small group instruction or station learning.* This means if you hold your arm out, your voice shouldn't be heard more than that distance away from you. It's about three feet. It is also helpful to kneel next to the student to whom you are speaking to get their full attention without disrupting the overall flow.

Another good rule of thumb is that if you are redirecting a student, speak to them quietly and in private. It can look like you calmly walking over to their desk and whispering, "Do you need help with something?" It shouldn't look like you saying loudly in front of the entire class, "Sarah, why are you talking?" This not only disrupts concentration and focus for the rest of the students but it's also pretty embarrassing for Sarah. Remember, we are always working to empower students, not break them down.

Keep in mind: Other students out of arm's length of you shouldn't hear what you're saying so they can stay on task.

Your Turn

1. How can it benefit student learning to use an arm's length voice when speaking to one student?

   _____
   _____
   _____
   _____
   _____
   _____

2. When speaking to a small group of students, how can it benefit the class to have only that group hear your voice?

   _____
   _____
   _____
   _____
   _____
   _____

3. Have you ever been in a coffee shop or library and heard a loud talker at the next table or chair? How did that make you feel? How did that affect what you were reading or studying?

   _____
   _____
   _____
   _____
   _____
   _____

Use Technology in Lessons to Enhance, Not Replace

Students may be savvier with technology than we are. Most likely they will eventually be working in jobs that require strong technology skills. However, many of our students tally countless hours of screen time at home and on the weekends, so they don't need to be staring at a screen during our entire class period too. Learning should be a social activity, even with technology use.

> Learning should be a social activity, even with technology use.

We have to remember that employers are looking for strong communicators and collaborators. So, when incorporating technology into lessons, think about how the tech can enhance communication and collaboration instead of replacing it. For example, working within Google Docs instead of in paper notebooks can offer students easier options for peer feedback or groupwork. And there are many ways tech platforms and tools can enhance engagement without removing social interaction.

There's a difference between what we're used to and what the generations we are teaching in our K–12 classrooms are used to—and growing into. We've used technology to consume information. The students in our classroom will have to be able to use technology to create. We should keep this question in our thoughts as we are deciding on technology uses in the classroom: *Will using this technology help this student succeed in tomorrow's world?*

Since technology uses and popular apps are constantly changing and improving, I encourage you to find some trusted sources who are using technology and advising teachers how to make the most of it. Below I've listed a few resources that can be helpful in keeping up with technology, but there are many more out there.

> Ask a few students to be helpers the day you use technology to assist you with minor technological glitches. Choose students who are naturally good with technology. If you have a second adult in the room, you could also ask them for help. You will want to make sure you aren't tied up with too many minor glitches that take you away from teaching a lesson, and this also empowers those students to feel valued and helps you see them through an asset-based lens.

- https://www.iste.org/explore: ISTE (International Society for Science and Technology) blog. Here you can find tips on the latest and greatest in technology use in the classroom.

- https://classtechtips.com/about-monica/: Monica Burns is an author, consultant, and thought leader in the field of education technology. Her blog focuses on educational technology.

- https://www.edutopia.org/technology-integration: Edutopia, a widely popular foundation dedicated to transforming preK–12 education, offers suggestions for implementing technology into your classroom.

Ways Technology Can Enhance a Lesson

HOW TECHNOLOGY CAN ENHANCE A LESSON	WHAT THAT LOOKS LIKE IN A CLASSROOM
Provide an authentic audience for students	Students can write e-mail letters to local community members about issues in the community for a letter-writing unit. Or students could e-mail community members with a solution to a societal problem after a research unit.
Incorporate technology in station learning	Technology can act as the teacher for one station as students could be asked to watch a short video together on a laptop and then complete a reflection or answer questions.
Add a high amount of visual stimulation to a lesson	Photos or short videos can be used in a lesson to enhance a concept or help make it more concrete. Presentation-making tools can also help create visually engaging slides to accompany a lesson.
Create shared documents among the class to create a sense of community	Padlet or Google Drive can be used to create one class document of students' hypotheses about what might happen in an experiment.

(Continued)

(Continued)

HOW TECHNOLOGY CAN ENHANCE A LESSON	WHAT THAT LOOKS LIKE IN A CLASSROOM
Use instant polls in lessons	Adding student polls into lessons can dramatically increase engagement in a lesson.
Give feedback in real time	Live documents can be shared with the teacher as students are working using platforms such as Google Slides or Google Docs. The teacher can check in at any time and add feedback as the students are working.
Use open-source AI to help create mentor texts or samples to use in instruction	Open-source AI sites such as ChatGPT and Google Bard can help streamline your prep time. It's not that they will do the work entirely for you, but you can use what open-source AI generates and make it better, change it a bit for your learners, and make it feel comfortable for you. For example, you can use open-source AI to create examples of good (or not-so-good) writing, or use it in a lesson about checking sources. Or show students how to use tools such as Wordtune or Grammarly to revise sentences they've already written.

When using technology in a classroom it's also important that we teach these concepts:

- recovering accidentally deleted material,
- vetting and citing sources, and
- avoiding plagiarism.

Your Turn

1. How have you preserved an aspect of socialization and collaboration with students when using technology in the classroom? If you haven't done this yet, how could you?

   _____
   _____
   _____
   _____
   _____
   _____

2. When is it ever easier and faster just to have students use pencil and paper for an activity?

   _____
   _____
   _____
   _____
   _____
   _____

3. What are your favorite apps to use in the classroom?

   _____
   _____
   _____
   _____
   _____
   _____

Be One or Two Steps Ahead of the Class

Let's use our imagination for a moment. You just received a call from a friend inviting you to dinner this week. You show up and your friend's house is a mess and dinner is not cooked. Your friend is frantic and looks a little annoyed. You wonder if you did something wrong. Should you help or stay out of her way? You enter sheepishly and try to make light of the situation. Your experience has been lessened and your friend obviously is not ready to entertain, mentally or otherwise.

Now relate this scenario to a teacher who is not prepared. Yes, we've all been there once or twice. I remember when I was teaching a class my first year and I came to class worn out and tired. I felt like my life was a pile of papers waiting to be corrected. I laid textbooks on the desks, put an assignment on the board, and thought the students owed it to me to do their work. After all, didn't I put in long hours for them? As Julia Roberts stated perfectly in *Pretty Woman*, "Big mistake. Big. Huge!" Your students will work only as hard in class as you do on the lesson. When my students came in, they saw the books and groaned. One or two students opened them. The class soon turned into me repeating over and over again like a broken record, "Stop . . . don't . . . what! . . . no!" Being unprepared as teachers leads to being stressed teachers who have less patience, snap at students, and feel overwhelmed in general. Prepared teachers are more patient, calmer, happier, and more confident as they are teaching. This leads to more student engagement and fewer classroom management issues. Who doesn't want that?

If you do have to do textbook work, try this: Let the students know you spent some time finding an exercise that is important to their learning or interesting for a specific reason. You can go over the lesson with the whole class and then pull a group of struggling learners to a side table or another part of the room to get extra help from you as the rest of the class works independently. This shows you did put some thought into your teaching. Don't insult your dinner party guests by cooking frozen pizza, and don't make the mistake I did by insulting your class by putting a page number, or webpage, or a subject to Google on the board and praying for quiet. Teachers, that's a dangerous path. We've all felt like doing it sometimes, but if this becomes a habit the students will start to think, *This teacher is never prepared. She doesn't care about us or our learning.* As my principal used to say, "Do your homework." Be prepared.

Now imagine you are invited to the same friend's house for dinner. You walk in and smell dinner almost ready, and appetizers are on the table. Name cards are even on the table for a fun icebreaker. You can see how excited your friend is to entertain that evening. You have your contribution in your hand (your host was one step ahead of you and let you know what to bring), and you know this will be a wonderful evening. This is what a student feels like when a teacher is prepared, mentally and physically. The classroom is set *and* the teacher is obviously mentally "put together."

I used to have the classroom completely set up, but I spent so much time and energy doing this I never took a few minutes to prepare *mentally* some mornings. This also leads to disaster. Take a few minutes before your class in the mornings or afternoons to mentally prepare, get calm, energize, and be ready to host your class! If you want to go the extra mile—or need to (as I did for three years)—do a mental run-through of your lesson each morning or even after school the day before. I would place my lesson plan in front of me, lock the door, turn off my cell phone, and practice my lesson. This pointed out issues such as, "Oh, I will need markers on the desk for that. Wait, I need notes on the chart for that." The rehearsal made me much more confident when I was actually teaching the lesson, ensured that all the materials were ready, and made me always prepared. I felt the students knew I cared and was prepared. This takes only a few minutes. I recommend it in your first few years of teaching until it becomes natural and effortless to you. Think of yourself as a performer doing a dress rehearsal.

Tips for Demonstrating to Students That You Are Mentally Prepared

- If they are in groups or working with partners, have baskets or bins on the tables with materials they will need for the day. You can even include the worksheets they will need that day so you can avoid downtime as you pass them out. A rookie mistake is spending too much time passing out papers. I have noticed the time spent passing out materials and/or papers is one of the most frequent

(Continued)

(Continued)

times the students begin to lose engagement. Students will become disinterested and start having side conversations. Don't let this happen!

- You can have the notes written beforehand depending on how you do your delivery. A prepared PowerPoint or digital presentation also works. Then you can just write side notes, visuals, etc., as you are speaking to keep momentum.

- Know how long each part of the lesson is and use a timer. Show the students you are both on a schedule. Students will take as long as you give them more often than not. The times should be reasonable and made public (project the timer for the class if your technology allows, announce the time remaining often, write time remaining on the board, etc.).

- Tell the students what they will be learning that day and why they will be learning it at the very beginning of the lesson. Make the learning relevant. Be brief, clear, and motivating.

- Have the lesson materials you will need in your teaching area, wherever that may be, so you will not have to say, "Wait, where did I put that?" Think of your teaching materials as props for your lessons.

Your Turn

1. Make a T-chart of two different lessons you have taught. On the left, describe a lesson where you were unprepared. On the right, describe a lesson where you were prepared. Next to each, describe how you felt while teaching that lesson.

   _____
   _____
   _____
   _____
   _____
   _____
   _____

2. Now jot down how the students reacted to each lesson.

   _____
   _____
   _____
   _____
   _____
   _____
   _____

3. Only you know what works best for you. How can you make sure your lessons are prepared every morning for students to learn?

   _____
   _____
   _____
   _____
   _____
   _____
   _____

Keep Everything Contextualized (Including SEL Lessons) and Do Projects!

....

> We all learn from each other.
>
> —Mary, Grade 8

My first few years teaching I felt like I was drowning. I was barely keeping my head above water. I was planning lessons late the night before and would come to work exhausted, short fused, and dragging my feet. I couldn't think about what the students were going to do even a week in advance because I was too busy making phone calls home, grading papers, and dealing with the mental exhaustion and frustration that comes with disciplining and yelling all day. I remember putting textbooks on the desk, assigning a page, and wondering why the students weren't engaged. *Kids just don't want to learn,* I thought daily. Sometimes I made worksheets and hoped that would keep them busy the whole period. They wouldn't listen to me anyway, so I thought maybe if they saw it in print it would help. I was more a police officer than a teacher, patrolling the room for noise and misbehavior. I just wanted them quiet and learning.

Looking back, what would have helped me immensely is if I had taken the time to plan projects from start to finish. I could have then launched the project and let the students become more empowered learners while I took on more of a facilitator role. We live and we learn.

Project-based learning is powerful. Period. Have you ever felt like I did my first few years? Perhaps you too have gone through the motions without passion, excitement, or purpose. Was it after a breakup, after you suffered a loss, or during a transitionary phase of your life when the larger picture was unclear? One of the most important things we must remember is that students are human beings too. They get angry, they get scared, they get demotivated—and for most of the same reasons we do in life. Most importantly, they need a larger purpose for what they are doing. They don't want to just complete a worksheet.

I know you can relate. Think of how excited or motivated you were when planning a fun trip or vacation. You probably got many tasks done quickly and put thought and care into the planning. Everything you were doing was for a specific purpose. You knew the outcome. You saw the bigger picture. Your motivation was contextualized.

Students think the same way. Think of the final project as their vacation. Do they know what they are working toward? Will they be building something, showing off something to parents or the community, debating against classmates, or presenting something to classmates or other classes even? What's the overall goal of the unit? Once the goal has been established, they will understand how the learning is contextualized and will be motivated to work more diligently. Your job will quickly slide into the role of the facilitator, guiding the students to their goal of the finished project. An added bonus is that behavior issues will severely decrease and students will become (dare I say it) inspired.

Before you launch a unit, take some time to develop the bigger picture and describe that picture to your students right away. Inform them of what they will they be doing, creating, performing, or competing for in this unit. It's really your judgment call as to when you reveal this information, but ideally it should be done within the first week. Don't just tell them what the end project is, also let them know *why* they are learning this content. This does take a little extra time in the beginning of a unit, but it will dramatically help with engagement and student satisfaction throughout the entire rest of the unit. It will ultimately lead to your greater satisfaction as an educator. Engaged students lead to a satisfied teacher.

Problem-based learning works the same way. The difference is that the students are asked to *solve a problem* as their overall goal and the learning is contextualized. This is different from the students' overall goal to *create something* in project-based learning. Depending on your task, you can decide if your unit is more geared toward project- or problem-based learning.

With project or problem-based learning,

- behavior issues significantly decrease,
- students become more empowered and inspired to learn,
- your role becomes more of a facilitator than a leader,
- more planning up front from the teacher is needed,
- learning becomes contextualized in "the bigger picture,"
- students are asked to create something or solve a problem, and
- the usual unit time period is two to eight weeks.

Here is an example of a unit of study where students know the larger picture. You begin by saying,

> Students, today we are going to be starting our class novel. Why are we reading this particular book? This novel will help us understand the world of [insert answer here]. The more we read, the more likely we will develop a love of reading that will help us in high school and beyond. After we read the novel, we will get to do so many things with it! First, we will have class discussions throughout. Then we will get to decide how we feel about the ending of the novel. After we read the book, we are going to be doing an exciting class project, so be sure to pay attention to the different characters and all of the details of the book.

Let's see what the students just heard. They just heard they are going to be held accountable as the class is reading the novel. They also heard that you are looking out for their best interests. You also kept part of the project a surprise so they could not argue and say the project was boring or stupid. They also know you have something larger planned. You have them hooked. Think of it as someone telling you that you just won a trip to a surprise tropical location and to start planning. If you add the element of surprise into the mix, this will not only keep your students motivated but they will not be able to argue against the project. The trick is to be as excited as you want them to be. They are going to be looking at you for clues to see how cool the project is. You are the salesperson for this project.

Contextualizing Social-Emotional Learning Lessons

In almost every classroom in the past few years we have been asked to do social-emotional learning (SEL). It's not just the counselor's job anymore.

A powerful way to incorporate SEL is to relate it to what you are teaching. One of the simplest ways to do this is talking about the social-emotional aspects of a book you are reading with the class. You could ask questions such as, "How do you think the character felt when that happened to them? What emotions do you think they are going through?" Also, if students are working in groups for a project it's so simple to have them reflect on how they used empathy or perhaps even peaceful conflict resolution skills to get through a slight hiccup. This brings SEL to life. Work with your colleagues to integrate themes from your school's SEL curriculum every day; this gives the SEL work more meaning and relevance to students and also engages their emotions in the content-area learning.

Your Turn

1. Can you remember a time when you weren't sure why you were doing an assignment or didn't see the larger picture? How did that make you feel?

   _____
   _____
   _____
   _____

2. Did you ever do a project or unit in your schooling that you still remember really enjoying? What made it enjoyable? How can you transfer this to your own teaching?

   _____
   _____
   _____
   _____

3. Do you agree that contextualized learning maximizes performance? Why or why not?

   _____
   _____
   _____
   _____

4. How can you make learning contextualized, engaging, and stimulating?

   _____
   _____
   _____
   _____

Tap Into Students' Curiosity With Problem-Based Learning

> Thank you for having me in your class this year. You are by far the best teacher ever. You are my hero. You rescued me from having a very shy and lonely life. You are funny and always give good advice. You have inspired me to be creative and open-minded. Thank you very much.
>
> —Roy, Grade 9

One of the reasons Roy felt this way about our class is because we did projects that tapped into students' curiosity. The same can happen for all of our students if we give them agency, freedom to think, and the opportunity to tap into the questions they probably already have.

Students are curious about current events and issues they see in the world around them—and they have tremendous access because of today's social media and news cycles. Naturally they have questions, but too often they might not have a place to get the answers.

The students sitting in our classrooms are going to be in positions of agency to fix some of the societal issues in our world that our generation and the ones before have created. That's a lot to swallow. This means when our instruction taps into students' curiosity and, more importantly, gives them the opportunity to get informed and create elegant solutions, we have hope for our future.

Also, yes, behavior management issues will likely drastically reduce and often even disappear in problem-based units because you are tapping into one of the most powerful types of engagement: emotional engagement. (See Best Practice #35 for more on emotional engagement.) You are harnessing their curiosity and their passion or anger about an issue. They will get to collaborate, learn to work productively in groups, and build student agency as they create and present solutions. A unit like this can also connect your classroom to the community.

I had few classroom management issues during these types of units because the students were too engaged with learning, challenging each other, and having discussions about their honest opinions with their groups. I probably could have left the classroom for long time periods and they wouldn't have noticed! It was beautiful. I went home with way more energy during this unit, and I was impressed and moved by the level of critical thinking and the deep questions expressed by the students. In this section I want to share one problem-based unit that I did with both eighth graders and ninth graders that tapped into their curiosity. You can tweak it to meet the needs of your own students. I titled the unit (I titled all of my units) "Solving a Societal Issue."

Setting Up a Problem-Based Unit: Student Buy-In, Rationale, and Student Grouping

1. Give students a sheet with an outline of the project and a paragraph or two on the rationale of the project and how they will be empowered to create a solution. You could start the rationale with something like, "There is so much beauty in the world around us, such as [list some examples], but some issues still exist. Students often have answers that adults haven't yet thought of, and this project will give you an opportunity to research, think, and create elegant solutions, and then to share those solutions." Let them know the steps of the project, what they will be creating, when their work will be due, and how their work will be graded. This empowers the students.

2. Consider showing a short clip from YouTube. Scan the QR code to see an example of a short video that might hook the class and create buy-in for your unit. Think about age or grade level when choosing a video.

Watch a quick animated video about young people solving global issues together.

3. Now, project or show topics they can choose from. I've provided a list below, organized for elementary or middle/high school students. Note: For more controversial topics, depending on your community, you might want to have parents sign a waiver allowing their students to do the project. Also, let your administrator and colleagues know your plans.

4. Have students individually choose the top three topics they are interested in from the lists below. This can easily be done through a Google Form or just on a sticky note. You want to group the students based on interest and passion, not just with the people they want to work with. On the form ask students if they really think this issue is a problem. This will increase engagement, boost productivity and curiosity, and limit classroom management issues. I would do this the day you launch the project and show the film. Give them at least ten minutes to choose in a quiet environment where they can really think deeply about it. I would also give students the opportunity to choose a topic that's not on the list if there's one that sparks their curiosity. For example, I once had a student in foster care want to research what he thought was a broken system. Two other students joined him, and it was one of the most well-done presentations because he was so curious and had a personal connection with an issue many didn't know much about, including myself.

UPPER ELEMENTARY/ MIDDLE SCHOOL TOPICS	UPPER MIDDLE SCHOOL AND HIGH SCHOOL TOPICS
Screen addiction	Cancel culture
Homelessness	High school drop-outs
U.S. fast-food craze	School violence
Obesity	Global warming
Pollution	Abortion illegal in certain states
Social media bullying	Global pandemics
Animal shelter overpopulation	Lack of face-to-face interaction and isolation
Deforestation of rainforests	Ageism
Lack of understanding of recycling benefits to the environment	Lack of understanding of handicapped or mentally disabled individuals
Animal abuse and/or neglect	Racism
Climate-related weather disasters	Hate groups
	Xenophobia
	LGBTQ/trans discrimination
	Teen depression
	Teen anxiety
	AI possibly disrupting the job market
	School-to-prison pipeline
	U.S. foster care system
	Anti-Semitism
	Employment and social acceptance of individuals recently released from prison

5. Create groups based on interest, three to six to a group, and tell them to be ready to go the next day. Have students sit with their groups and you can get started!

Steps for a Successful Problem-Based Unit

Step #1: Before you get started, kids will need the following from you:

- an outline of items you want to see in the final presentation,
- a rubric for how their initial paper and final presentation will be graded,
- a graphic organizer to help keep track of research facts,
- a to-do checklist with dates for completion to help empower your students to keep on track with their deadlines, and
- suggestions for roles within each group so that everyone plays an important part. Your students can assign roles to each other or volunteer for a role.

You'll want students to clearly state what the problem is they're researching, why it's a problem, and what has been done already to try to solve it. They will meet with the teacher briefly to get their topic approved before they dive into the research together.

It's a good idea to teach mini-lessons guiding them through where to get information, how to find credible sources and avoid fake news, what options are available for creating presentations, how to make professional presentations, etc. Plan periodic check-ins with each group to answer questions, to ensure everyone understands the goals and steps, and to make sure each student is participating. (Check-ins may carry a grade or a simple check mark for completion. Explain all of these things in the beginning so everyone understands.)

Step #2: After the presentation or paper is created, now comes the really fun part. They are not done yet, and you haven't given them a final grade. You then do a mini-lesson empowering them to develop a creative solution that the world hasn't tried yet or add on to what the world is already trying to do. They then have to create some sort of visual to explain their solution and why they think it would work. This could be on an ending slide, an artistic canvas, etc. This is where there should be tons of group collaboration, pushing each other's thinking, and critical and creative thinking. They create this as a group. You could give them a graphic organizer to guide their thinking.

Step #3: Each group presents their project to the class. To make it really engaging and ambitious, you could invite community members to watch as well, or other adults around your school. It's important that after each presentation you allow the audience (your class) to ask questions and let the group answer. They are now the experts. It's equally powerful to let the group presenting call on the students while you take a back seat. The students can also raise their hands to praise the group, and that's equally powerful. You can stay out of it. After the presentation, you can give them their final grade based on the rubric. It's up to you if you want to give each group member the same grade or not.

Step #4: (Note: I actually never had time to do this part, but I would if I could do the unit today). The group then collectively writes an e-mail or a letter to somebody in the community that is in a position of power, asking them to consider their idea. This teaches business letter writing. This is where they have an authentic audience. If you have time, they could even make a quick movie to send. You would probably have the letters e-mailed to you so you could print them out, but have students address the envelopes. Show them how to find the addresses online and make sure they put your classroom name in the return address section so they can receive a response. You might be surprised how many responses you get.

Step #5: Spend a day or two reflecting on the unit with questions. This will neatly tie up the unit.

This unit should probably take about four to six weeks from beginning to end (taking up part of each class period but not necessarily the entire period). From a teacher's point of view, you won't really have graded much until the end of the unit. You taught quick mini-lessons here and there, but it was more about checking in with each group and prompting them with things to consider more deeply about their topic. Tapping into students' curiosity this way can help you create units where you'll come home with more energy, the student engagement in your class will soar, a community of learners will be strengthened, and students can be inspired to take stances and be active on issues that are affecting our world. And—*wink wink*—your behavior management issues will start to vanish during these units. Isn't that what this book is all about?

Best Practice #26

Rely on Formative Assessment to Drive Instruction

An effective teacher does way more than just check for understanding once at the very end of the lesson. That was a mistake I made in the beginning of my teaching career. I would teach a lesson without any formative assessment throughout, then become frustrated that more than half of the class failed the weekly or biweekly assessment. I would point fingers at the students when in fact I should have checked their understanding multiple times throughout the lesson. It pains me just to think of teaching like this now.

So, what is formative assessment? Think of it as a quick snapshot of how much the students are learning. In simple terms, it means checking for understanding along the way instead of waiting for the big test at the end of a lesson or unit. Rather, the effective teacher does a few checks throughout the lesson. What can this look like? In our third book, *Five to Thrive: Answers to Your Biggest Questions About Creating a Dynamic Classroom* (2022), my co-author and I gave a few suggestions (see Figure 26.1).

Once you check for assessment, what you do afterward is where the magic lives and instruction can be driven. Here are some rules of thumb:

Five powerful ways to do formative assessment to drive instruction and check for understanding

- If more than half the class doesn't seem to understand a concept, consider reteaching the concept in a different way the next day.
- If more than half the class doesn't seem to understand, consider having a group of four to six nonunderstanding students be retaught the concept by a student or two who understands. This can easily be done using information from exit slips.

- If only a few students do not understand the concept, they can work with a peer or with you to understand.
- When doing Thumbs-Up/Thumbs-Down from above, before the students move to independent work, ask the students who had their thumbs sideways or down to quickly come to an area of the room so you can reteach the concept in a small group. When they understand, they can leave. This particular strategy can be very effective.

> It's important we stay humble and open enough to realize that if most of the class doesn't understand a concept after it is taught, it's up to us to figure out what we might have missed in our teaching or lesson.

Figure 26.1 Engaging Ways to Check for Understanding

Thumbs-Up/Thumbs-Down

Example: Ask students to tell you if they understand what they are supposed to do for the next fifteen minutes by giving you a thumbs-up ("I understand"), thumbs-down ("I don't understand"), or thumb to the side ("I'm unsure"). When you start the activity, ask the students who didn't have their thumbs up to come to your desk so you can re-explain the directions. (Please note, this is a great quick assessment, but do not rely solely on the data it produces; students will often put their thumbs up so they are not "found out" for not understanding the material. This is good for checking understanding of directions, but not necessarily for comprehension of content.)

Whiteboards

Example: Students each have a small whiteboard. You ask questions about what was just taught and each student writes their answer on the whiteboard and holds it up.

Exit Tickets

Example: Students answer questions about the concept taught that day and hand them in to the teacher before they exit the classroom. Students who didn't fully understand can be pulled into a small group the next day to be retaught or to practice a concept.

Source: Pariser and Lentfer (2022).

Your Turn

1. What types of formative assessment have you used or do you want to use in your classroom?

   _____
   _____
   _____
   _____
   _____
   _____

2. How would you use this data to drive instruction?

   _____
   _____
   _____
   _____
   _____
   _____

3. How does using formative assessment to drive instruction directly affect classroom management?

   _____
   _____
   _____
   _____
   _____
   _____

Be a Warm Demander to Challenge and Support Students

> I loved your class the most. It was the most challenging of my classes to keep up in. You gave me the extra support I needed, and I knew someone believed in me.
>
> —Karen, Grade 9

In our 2022 book, *Answers to Your Biggest Questions About Creating a Dynamic Classroom*, my co-author and I discussed the concept of a warm demander teacher. This type of teacher has been proven to be the most effective in the classroom. Let's take a closer look at what exactly is a warm demander.

In the words of Delpit (2013), "Warm demander teachers expect great things from their students, convince them of their own brilliance, and help them reach their potential in a disciplined, structured environment" (p.77). Further, "Teachers with a warm demander approach expect a lot from each student but also support them in getting there. They expect students to take risks, and at the same time create a safe space for students to do so. They embrace student mistakes and see them as learning opportunities." (Pariser & Lentfer, 2022, p. 47).

Consider Goldilocks from *Goldilocks and the Three Bears*. She couldn't sleep in the bed that was too hard, or the bed that was too soft. She had to find one that was just right. Some students are like Goldilocks. They may not respect a teacher that is too easy, nor do they like one that's too difficult. The goal is to be just right. To do this, first challenge them, then support them where needed and encourage them as they experience success. Let them know a lesson will be challenging, but show them how you will help them.

Let's look at a specific example. Say you are teaching poetry. An easy teacher may have students conduct their own research on poetry. Perhaps this teacher would make it more fun by letting them share with each other or some other enjoyable but low-rigor activity. Fun, but what is the purpose? A teacher who is too difficult, on the other hand, may say, "Write a two-page narrative poem. This will be graded. You have the computer to help you." Note: If this is where your students are, then that is a different story.

A warm demander teacher would have a challenging lesson presented in clear parts, manageable to students. First, she would show students models of narrative poems. Then, she would likely break down the elements of a narrative poem quickly. The key is not to give too much help or you will belittle the students' abilities or give them an excuse to be lazy. The class could then brainstorm possible topics of narrative poems. Finally, the teacher could explain how the assignment will be graded (referring back to the great examples that were shown in the modeling of poetry when the lesson began) and allow time for the students to work on the project. She might also pull aside a group of struggling learners for additional help as the other students write and have access to computers for help. See the difference?

This teacher will earn respect because the students are challenged and given the help that they need—but not *too* much help. The students are also instructed on the grading process and will feel like they *need* the teacher's help because the assignment is difficult and they would like a high score. Ultimately, you'd like to see your class rely less and less on you as the school year goes on. The hope is that by the end of the year, your students will be able to perform, learn, and converse as a community of learners *without* you. It's then you know you've inspired a change greater than yourself. You will succeed and will no doubt be respected if you achieve this. However, until that time comes, challenge them. Make them need you just enough, and be sure to support them. They will grow with your nourishment.

Remove scaffolds throughout the year. For example, with groupwork you may choose early in the year to assign each group member a role on how to contribute to the group. This is a scaffold to effective collaboration. By the end of the year, your students shouldn't need these roles assigned and will hopefully be able to work in a group effectively. Expect them to work more independently with better results as the year progresses. This means you give them less academic support and set the expectation that they perform at a consistently higher level. If they falter, be there to give them the support they need. Keep doing this and they will grow.

Remember the following:

- If your class is too easy, your students will cruise through and your connection with them will be weaker because they won't need you for support. Students may feel like they are missing out on learning what they should.

- If your class is too difficult without support, students will become frustrated and distant and feel like they aren't heard.

- The goal is to have challenging curriculum with supports such as collaboration, engaging projects, small group instruction, checks for understandings, and best practices to engage and challenge students throughout the learning journey. Challenged and supported students feel respected.

Listen to this informative, down-to-earth podcast on the warm demander teaching style.

Your Turn

1. What are the qualities of an instructor who is too difficult? How can this make a student feel? What about an instructor who is too easy?

   _____
   _____
   _____
   _____
   _____
   _____

2. What are some specific teaching strategies, practices, and habits a warm demander teacher would employ? How would this make a student feel?

   _____
   _____
   _____
   _____
   _____
   _____

3. What type of instructor do you see yourself as now? How do you want to see yourself in the future? Are there gray areas?

   _____
   _____
   _____
   _____
   _____
   _____

Lean Into Learning Activities That Are More Engaging, Fun, and Collaborative Rather Than Relying on Direct Instruction

In 2018 author Heather Wolport-Gawron debunked a common misconception that engagement doesn't always equal fun. This is discussed in her book *Just Ask Us: Kids Speak Out on Engagement*. Wolport-Gawron surveyed over one thousand K–12 students nationwide and asked them what they specifically want in a lesson—what engages them. Interestingly, what the students reported matched up with what the data suggest is beneficial to student engagement and teacher satisfaction.

The students surveyed reported that they wanted teachers to do the following:

- Let us work together.
- Make learning more visual and utilize technology.
- Connect what we learn to the real world.
- Let us move around.

Watch teachers implement engaging learning activities in their classroom.

- Give us choices.
- Show us you're human too.
- Help us create something with what we've learned.
- Teach us something in a new way.
- Mix things up.

What does all this actually mean? Let's break it down.

WHAT STUDENTS REPORTED REALLY WANTING IN A LESSON	WHAT THIS ACTUALLY LOOKS LIKE IN YOUR CLASSROOM
Let us work together.	This could be groupwork, partner work, a friendly competition in class, having a class earn badges or level up together (a class thermometer could be used to keep track of progress), or having students contribute to shared documents as much as possible to build a sense of community. It's important that all students participate and contribute when working together. Roles to help facilitate this are covered in more detail in Best Practice #33: Make Groupwork Work.
Make learning more visual and utilize technology.	You could use photos, cartoons, or other visual formats to explain a concept.
Connect what we learn to the real world.	You could utilize project-based learning and invite authentic audiences (other grades in a school, community members, etc.) to project presentations.
Let us move around.	This could include things such as class debates, stations, carousel learning, movement activities, or providing unique seats where students can move their bodies a bit while they work.
Give us choices.	You could try structured choice or ability-tiered student choice where students choose the tier comfortable to them, Allow students to choose how they would like to do a project or give students choices on project topics.
Show us you're human too.	Use humor in lessons, share certain elements of your life, and be honest if you mess up.
Help us create something with what we've learned.	Incorporate creating something in every unit (drawings, gadgets, inventions, trifolds, storybooks, etc.).
Teach us something in a new way.	This could mean teaching in ways other than direct instruction.
Mix things up.	Use different engagement styles in a lesson, do fun experiments, act out skits, or use comedy sketches to illustrate a concept. (For more on engagement styles, see Best Practices #35.)

Here are some lesson activities you can try in your class tomorrow that can really spice up the lesson while increasing learning and engagement.

> Students want to know who you are as a human being. Don't be afraid to smile and laugh sometimes while you are teaching. They'll be more connected to both the content *and* you.

NAME OF ACTIVITY	WHAT IT LOOKS LIKE IN A CLASSROOM	PURPOSE(S)
Socratic Seminar	Students sit in a circle, read a text, and prepare with written notes. Then the teacher facilitates by asking open-ended questions to guide a student discussion.	• Gain a deeper understanding of a text • Empower students to use their voice • Teaches active listening skills
Class Brainstorms	Class thinks aloud together about a concept and ideas are recorded for everybody to see. Brainstorm can be revisited at the end of the class to show how much students learned about a concept in one class period.	• Values student voice by writing all thoughts down during a collective brainstorm • Gives teacher knowledge about what students already know about a concept before it is taught
Carousel Activity	Different questions are hung around the room on chart paper and each student has a marker. Students add their input on the chart and rotate when they hear a sound, such as a bell, a fun song, or even just the teacher saying "Rotate" loudly.	• Gets students moving • Can be an engaging way to share information the whole class can use; for example, a question might be, "What are powerful transitions that can be used in an essay?" • Can be an engaging way to answer questions such as, "What do you think about. . . . ?"
Station Learning	Stations are set up around the room and usually numbered. Stations can be led by a teacher, coteacher, or student; be self-instructed; or involve technology. Student groups of four to six practice different concepts at once. Groups rotate to the next station when a timer goes off.	• Gets students moving • Students can work collaboratively in each station • Keeps student attention longer as each station is a bit different • Keeps students task-switching at a healthy pace because when they move, they switch tasks
Jigsaw	Student groups each take a part of a text to dissect, then they come back together and teach their part to the entire class.	• Summarizes a longer text or document when it is not necessary for every student to read the entire text
Inner-Outer Discussion	Similar to a Socratic Seminar, but the outside circle is sitting with their backs turned away from the inner circle and listening intently to take notes.	• Gain a deeper understanding of a text • Empowers students to use their voice • Teaches active listening skills

(Continued)

(Continued)

NAME OF ACTIVITY	WHAT IT LOOKS LIKE IN A CLASSROOM	PURPOSE(S)
Gallery Walks	Hang up student work—drawings, poems, etc.—then students walk around the room silently to view each other's work. They can put praise or comments on sticky notes next to the work. This can be done walking around the desks. (Be sure to teach students about constructive comments to avoid negative or insulting notes, and ask students to write their name next to their positive comments to help create a community of learners.)	• Helps create a community of learners • Students get to see everybody's work efficiently and with little effort from the teacher • Students are all moving around the classroom
Class Debates	Class debates a concept you are teaching that has two sides.	• Teaches active listening • Students are exploring real-world issues • Students are practicing compassionate listening • Students' voices are heard • Students can become more engaged in a concept they are learning
Parallel Instruction	Two adults are each teaching a concept the same way at the same time to half the class in heterogeneous groups. It usually works best if the teachers are facing away from each other on opposite sides of the room so the voices don't carry over one another.	• Students are taught in smaller groups, usually leading to more interaction between the instructor and the students
Small Group Instruction	Students are with an adult and usually being retaught a concept or provided extra support on a concept.	• This is a powerful method for students who have fallen behind, need extra support, or could benefit from a concept being taught in a different way
Worksheet Cut Up	Cut up your worksheet and place each section at a station. Have the students walk around to complete the worksheet to get movement into the lesson.	• Gets students moving and adds a layer of creativity and collaboration
Reciprocal Teaching	Students get the opportunity to be the teachers with a small group of classmates. The teacher sets students up for success by modeling how to guide group discussions with reading comprehension strategies.	• Empowers students by giving them opportunities to lead • Students become aware of their own cognitive processes while reading a text • Promotes student reading comprehension

Your Turn

1. What is one activity you have not tried from the above chart that piques your interest?

　

2. Could this activity help your students with a concept they are are currently learning?

　

3. How would you set behavior expectations before doing one of these activities to set your students up for success?

Take Risks in Your Lessons

Great teaching is all about risk-taking. My greatest memories as a teacher are when I took the biggest risks. By risks, I mean planning something more than what you have seen the students do or could even imagine them doing. When you take risks, you have to visualize what success will look like. Then you teach and inspire your students to rise to your vision. When you take risks there are two things that can happen: Your students will fly or they will fall. Here's the secret: They almost always fly. You have to teach them the skills they need, inspire them, believe in them, and then let go. They will fly. The biggest risk-taking usually took place at the end of the year for my class. That's when they were ready.

The first time my students really flew I'm not sure if I'd slept the whole month before. I kept wondering what would happen if they didn't perform. It was the last project of the year with my eighth-grade class. They were in groups, and each group was assigned a concept that we had learned throughout the year. They had to create a poem to perform with props, movement, and gestures in a spoken word manner. I thought about whom to invite and decided on a younger grade. My students panicked. They didn't think they were ready. I let them practice a bit more, and they started to build up their confidence. They were looking great! My mentor suggested I go big, really big. She asked why I wasn't inviting the whole school. I hadn't even thought of that. So I did.

I sent out an Evite to make it a formal event. Classes RSVP'd one after another, and so did administration. Each administrative member received a private invitation. As a class, we checked the Evite every day on the document camera. The students knew the pressure was on, big time.

To say the class was engaged was an understatement. They knew this was bigger than me or even us now. The day of the performance, the entire auditorium filled with parents, administration, students, and teachers. My students looked like deer in headlights as they watched class after class come down. They couldn't believe everyone came to see them. They rocked the stage! Although they were a bit terrified at first, it showed them they were worthy of attention. They received a standing ovation and were beaming from ear to ear afterward. They were the talk of the school! I could sleep again. They had flown.

Another time I took a risk was when a student in my class broke a class computer. I had at least three options: (1) to pretend it didn't happen and move on, (2) to have a very harsh talk with everyone about computer care, or (3) to make this situation into a life lesson and take advantage of a teachable moment. I chose the hardest but most powerful option: the third. My rationale was that only one student had misbehaved. I knew who I thought it was. I knew he wouldn't confess, and I knew that I could not really prove he did it. My goal was that I wanted the class to understand the severity of the situation and I wanted them to understand learning is priority one. I wanted to discuss how we could work together to move on. I wanted to build a community.

I pulled them in a tight circle of chairs the next day and told them what had happened. I explained that our class could have its laptop privileges taken away. They all started pointing fingers. I stopped them. I said I didn't have an answer and I needed their help (this was half true). I knew that in all honesty I could have privately sorted this out with our technology department since this sometimes happens. However, my gut instinct was to turn this into a learning experience. We brainstormed for a few minutes as a class about how to raise the money to fix the computer. We came up (or I should say *they* actually came up) with the idea of a car wash. We made signs during lunch, and I pulled a few strings and got permission to hold a car wash at our school on a Saturday. I was a little fearful that nobody would show up, so I assigned shifts. The morning of the car wash came early. I didn't see any students. I took a deep breath and had faith that they would come. One by one, students arrived with a smile. Soon many of my students had shown up, and one even brought their dog. I saw a caring side of this "tough" class that I had never seen before. The students raised over $300 that morning and felt more connected to each other. The class became a cohesive family. The message became clear: We will help each other out during this school year. They had each other's backs. I took a risk, believed in the students, and hoped for the best. (Keep in mind, if you are more comfortable taking smaller risks at first, refer back to the Part 1 opener (blue page) with the history teacher and her colleague. That was a risk, too, that resulted in powerful learning for the students!)

Your Turn

1. What message do you send your students when you take risks with them?

   _____
   _____
   _____
   _____
   _____
   _____

2. What is the worst that can happen if a risk flops?

   _____
   _____
   _____
   _____
   _____

3. What message do you send your students if you do not take risks with them?

   _____
   _____
   _____
   _____
   _____
   _____

Prepare Ahead for When You Just Can't Be There

....

As a child's teacher, you often see them more than you will see some of your own friends. And chances are they see you more often than even most of their friends. Let's face it: They will grow comfortable seeing you every day. More than anything, children learn to trust reliable adults. One of the most effective ways to earn trust is to be reliable and consistent. However, we also know that life happens. So how do we miss a day of school without losing our students' trust?

First, don't miss too many days, but know when you might need a personal day to recharge. A students' world revolves around themselves. They are not adults yet. So they may not grasp the concept that adults get sick, people get married, kids have doctor appointments, etc., and some days you may not be able to be at school.

If you've set up classroom expectations well and practiced them from Day 1, students need only to be reminded that those expectations still stand, even if you're not in the room.

Here are some other tips for preparing for a day you can't be in school:

- Have seating charts on your desk so the substitute teacher can refer to students by name.
- Leave two to three names of students who can help with any questions about the day, routines, etc.

- Have some activities ready for the absences.
- Be sure to leave an organized desk for the substitute and leave materials for the lesson in one spot.

Planned Absences

If you have a planned absence, an effective method to reinforce the trust with your students is to have a talk with them the last five minutes the day before you are going to be away, even if it is only for a day. Let them know you are sorry. One or two students may joke and applaud, but most will wholeheartedly appreciate that you valued them enough to share that you will not be there. Share with them why you will not be there (if it is student-appropriate). Sharing should be limited, purposeful, and honest. Let them know you will be back the next day, if that's the case. If it's a personal day, you don't need to share that. You can simply say, "I won't be here tomorrow, but I will be back the next day."

Here is an example of what you might say:

> Students, I want to speak with you seriously for five minutes, and I need your attention. My best friend is getting married this Saturday and the wedding is in Virginia. I have been invited to the wedding and have to take a flight tomorrow morning. Unfortunately, I will not be here tomorrow, but I will be back on Monday. Now, let's talk about how we respect a guest teacher. What type of behaviors do I expect when a guest is in the room?

You may get some students asking questions here about the actual wedding, and that's all right. Personalize it. Show them you are a human, not some teacher just ditching them. They will end up appreciating you more for this.

Some of my former students remember four years ago when I flew to Virginia to be in a friend's wedding. They remember this because I told them about how she and I became friends and why it was important that I went. When I returned I also told them a funny story about an incident that happened at the wedding. They enjoyed being a part of my life for a second. If I had not had this conversation, I would have been just another teacher who missed another day. A conversation such as this will not only empower the students with knowledge but also show them you value their learning and their trust.

Unplanned Absences

It happens. We get sick unexpectedly, or our car breaks down. Have a letter ready either on your desk or that you can e-mail to the sub that states what type of behavior you expect your students will display and indicate anything specific that they need to know about your classroom routines. This can be something you write during the first week of school that stays at the ready for emergencies.

The main idea is to treat the students with respect and as if they are part of your family. Teacher absences can be a shock for students and throw off those who really need consistency and structure. Make your face a familiar one they will see every day.

Your Turn

1. What are you really telling the students when you let them know in advance that you will not be there?

   _____
   _____
   _____
   _____
   _____
   _____

2. How do you think this makes the students feel?

   _____
   _____
   _____
   _____
   _____
   _____

3. How could this prevent classroom management issues with the substitute and empower students when you are not there?

   _____
   _____
   _____
   _____
   _____
   _____

Implement Creative Discipline

Something miraculous happens when you start to get comfortable and confident: The students pick up on the vibe that you have their best interests and learning at the forefront of your mind. This means if you take a few minutes to handle a discipline issue with the class, they listen and take it seriously. Every once in a while something a student does disrupts the values of the entire class and the learning environment.

Because I do full class discipline so rarely, the students know it's a pretty big deal. However, most discipline and redirection can and should be handled privately and quickly between you and the student. Praise, on the other hand, can always be public.

In one of my later years teaching, I recall three times when I put my foot down to help facilitate a better learning environment.

The first time was when the students were saying no to me in the middle of the year after I asked them to do something that was beneficial to their education. Now, students usually listened very well to my instructions, but if one student starts to challenge, it can spread like wildfire. This happened rarely, but once when it did I made it very clear to that student privately that this was not going to continue, and I called the parents to discuss what had happened.[1] I knew if I let the challenge go unmet, I would have one heck of a year with students deciding when they would follow directions.

---

[1] High school teachers have conflicting views on whether and when to involve parents. I usually do if the student needs the extra support, especially in the ninth or tenth grade. High school students can get very defensive when parents are in the middle. Be careful not to take the problem to the next level. The biggest win is when you can empower the students to change on their own. Use your gut to decide whether or not to call parents.

I want my students to know they cannot be defiant but that we have a positive relationship where they can express their feelings in a respectful and articulate manner without being judged or scolded. It is always necessary that they be heard. You don't always have to act on it if they misspeak. You are teaching them the respectful way to speak, not waiting for them to make a mistake. My guide was always if the disrespect or malice was intentional, that was an issue. If it was unintentional, they were learning, and I taught them how to correct their words or actions. They knew there was a time, place, and way to phrase their concerns and that I would listen. Defiance and open communication are two different things.

In this instance, the students were being defiant and holding up learning. Two strikes! I extinguished that fire quickly: *I made it very clear to the students that saying no was not an option they had at the time, that what I was doing was best for their learning, and that I would listen to any concerns after class.* I told them the learning was going to continue and that choosing to work with their friends was not an option they had that day, although they would have it in the future. I said all this with a very stern and serious face and did not lose control of my emotions.

At the end of class, I left five minutes to recap with the students why I was disappointed in their behavior. I let them tell me, not the other way around. They recapped that I was upset because they were outwardly defiant, which stops learning in a classroom. I made it very clear how much I valued their education and that it wasn't fair to others to not have a solid day's learning because their classmates choose to be defiant to the teacher. It's important that the class understands specifically why you became frustrated or they may repeat the same mistake again. Before the recap, a few of the students thought I was disappointed because they wanted to work with their friends, which was not the case. The reason you are frustrated should always be about them and their best interests.

The second time I put my foot down was when a few students were rude to me one week. This was absolutely not going to fly in my classroom. I overexaggerated my reaction and raised my voice that day. I made it clear I was not angry that they were overly talkative that day, but that I was angry at the tone and demeanor they were using toward me. I used an "I" message:

> I want to be very clear why I am frustrated with not only a few students but the class as a whole. I value respect. I always try my hardest to give you the most respect I can. You are making a conscious choice to be rude. I need you to understand this is not the correct choice and turn it around. Am I angry that you were too talkative today? Not really. Although it is not acceptable, it happens sometimes. That's just how a class works. However, you do not have to be rude. I need you to understand the mistake you made and stop it, now.

Then I was deliberately quiet the rest of the class (I had to fake that part since I have an extremely forgiving heart by nature) and let them know how much I valued respectful and polite words and actions toward the teacher. After that, they understood. My students then became extremely polite and exceeded my wildest expectations.

The third time happened when we had an issue with stealing. Personally, I've always felt that this is one of the worst things that can happen in a classroom. If you catch it when it's small, it prevents it from becoming a larger issue. This has happened a few times in my career, and I now know that *deciding* how to react is a superpower that comes with years of teaching.

When push comes to shove, the bottom line is our job is to protect the safety, morale, and learning of our students. But you can be creative in how you get your point across.

> *Deciding* how to react is a superpower that comes with years of teaching.

When a gifted box of chocolates went missing in my classroom, I decided to blow up the situation to prove a point. I taped off the exact spot where the chocolates had been with an outline, similar to a body sketching the police would do. I put yellow police tape around the front of the room where the chocolates once sat. I had a few miniature bright orange cones I placed around the area. I also had a chart up with the words "Why the chocolates?" on it in large writing (an idea from a college tutor in my room who helped with creative ideas). I had the chart flipped around, however, so the students wouldn't be able to see what was written on it when they entered. I took all the chairs from the desks and put them in front of the "crime scene."

I had a very serious look on my face as the students entered and sat silently in the chairs and stared at the strange scene in front of them. I had a prelude up that asked them how they would feel if somebody they trusted took something from them. They all responded in writing about how hurt and betrayed they would feel. I then (still seriously) explained that I felt the same way. I let them know that up until now, I had trusted the class. I also said that it was really important to me that they felt like their materials and belongings were safe as well (remember it's not you versus the class). Then, when they "got it," I flipped the chart over and they giggled.

I explained with a somber tone that I had called the FBI to do a thorough investigation of the crime scene, but I needed information. I said the culprit could confess anonymously and my goal was to restore trust and safety back into the class. I thought I knew who did it before we started the "investigation." However, during the talk, as the rest of the class was giggling about making such a big deal over chocolates, a different boy in the front row had his arms crossed, could not stop shaking his foot, and was red-faced. I could feel his discomfort. *Interesting,* I thought. I had all the information I needed. I spoke to the boy privately after that. He would not confess, but I knew. I took down the crime scene, and the boy was never a discipline issue after that, as he had been prior. He knew it was *my* classroom. I also heard him say to his friend once, "I'm an honest man now." I knew I wasn't going to get the chocolates back, but I decided to use the incident to help me win over the class.

Would I have done this if something of value had been taken? No. The reason nothing of value has been taken from my classroom since my second year is because I stop the little crimes—the missing markers, etc. Little crimes usually lead to bigger crimes.

Today, nothing is locked up in my classroom. This is a decision I make to let the students know I completely trust them. They notice. You are welcome to make your own decision regarding this. I still completely trust my students. Would another teacher have handled the chocolate theft differently? I would assume most likely yes. However, I went with my gut. I felt very safe afterward. I knew who had taken the chocolates and have not had even a marker disappear since.

Trust your instincts on how to monitor behavior creatively, or run your ideas by another teacher first. Just remember that teaching is like a dance; everyone has their own style, rhythm, and flow. Different teachers value different aspects of the craft. Try something and know if doesn't work, it's okay. Take risks and let yourself mess up. That's the only way to learn. It's just a mistake, and you will try something else next time. Don't be afraid to be creative. Your students will appreciate it more than traditional behavior management. I solved the chocolate mystery in just fifteen minutes without ever having to raise my voice. What would you have done?

Your Turn

1. What can you absolutely not tolerate in the classroom? Things that are not tolerated should not be specific behaviors but things that jeopardize a value system. How do you let your students know this with your actions and words?

   _____
   _____
   _____
   _____
   _____
   _____

2. Have you told your students how disciplinary issues negatively affect learning? How can you explain this in a tactful way that puts their learning first?

   _____
   _____
   _____
   _____
   _____
   _____

3. Think of the last time you had to discipline a full class. Would this have been an opportune time for creative discipline? Why or why not?

   _____
   _____
   _____
   _____
   _____
   _____
   _____

Vary Levels of Noise in the Classroom

Noise level is extremely tricky to get right when you first start teaching. I'm a firm believer that a class that's always so quiet you can hear a pin drop is a red flag . . . and a class that's always full of screaming and noise is also a red flag. As teachers, we should have a balance and be able to control the noise level based on the learning activity we are doing. Some days it may be very quiet, and other days it could be buzzing with energy, excitement, and laughter.

One of my biggest failures as a student teacher was attempting to get control of the noise level of a classroom. I had a class of twenty-five eighth graders. I asked them to stop talking and be silent to take a test. They didn't. I raised my voice, thinking it would help if I was louder than they were. It didn't and just added to the chaos. In frustration and desperation I yelled out, *"This isn't silent! Do you guys even know what silence sounds like!?"* One sly student, with a devilish grin on her face, replied, "Why don't you just tape our mouths shut?" This excited the rest of the class, who started shouting, "Yeah, yeah! Do that!" I replied that I really couldn't tape their mouths. They then had the clever idea for me to just give them the tape and they would do it.

I decided to go to the extreme and give in. I walked up and down the aisles and gave them each a piece of Scotch tape. I said half-jokingly (I was also making the mistake of trying to be their friend), "Use this tape—I want you to hear what silence sounds like!" The kids were having a field day. They taped up their mouths, waving their hands in the air and forcing humming sounds out of their nose. Some even screamed through the tape what sounded like "Help me!" as if they were being held hostage.

This all happened, yes, right as my supervisor walked in with a community guest.

Now, there are many times a teacher worries if they are doing the right thing. As soon as I saw my supervisor's face, it was not a question: I had messed up. She asked me at the meeting she summoned me to later that day if I had been doing an experiment. I knew very well that putting tape on my students' mouths was not in my lesson plan, but I said yes, knowing that I had to figure out how to control noise without any office supplies. I'm thankful I was not dismissed from my student teaching position that day. And I can now offer alternative suggestions for controlling noise levels.

Alternative Tips and Ideas for Controlling Noise Level

- Get a box fan. This is a quirky trick, but it works. I always keep a fan somewhere nearby that I can turn on when students are working or taking a summative assessment and the room needs to be silent. The louder the fan, the better. There is something soothing about the sound that keeps students working, quiet, and calm. I turn the fan on discreetly and point it toward the wall so they do not feel the breeze (this is key because many will complain if you start blasting them with air). The white noise of the box fan also drowns out the chair squeaks, heel clicks, and other odd distracting noises that can break the silence.

    A closer look at different ways to incorporate music into a classroom.

- Music can be a powerful tool in the classroom. Playing softer music can help students focus during reading time, and more upbeat music can really add some energy into a collaborative or fun activity. See the QR in the margin for more on using music to help achieve the noise level you want in a classroom.

- If the room should be silent, then the teacher shouldn't talk either. Instead of verbally responding every time a student breaks the silence, just put your finger to your mouth to signal the noise level that you want. Every time you talk, unfortunately, *you* are breaking the silence, which is hurting the classroom noise level. A look and a few silent signals can do wonders to maintain the calm, quiet classroom that some students need to perform.

- Develop a class signal, such as raising a hand, that students can use to let you know they need assistance. To keep your class silent (during testing for example), you could say, "We know that

(Continued)

(Continued)

    some learners need a silent environment to do their very best. Let's respect each other and keep the entire class silent the entire time. I really appreciate how you respect each other's learning needs. I am sure your fellow classmates will appreciate the quiet time as well. If you need anything, please raise your hand and I will help you." This shows the class why they should remain silent: You are putting the needs of the entire class first. It also shows you are willing to help individuals if needed. Any student requiring help can simply raise their hand and you will answer them quietly and discretely (remember your arm's length voice here). During testing, turn that voice into an even quieter one. You are meeting *all* students' needs in the classroom.

- If you are playing a game, let the students get loud—not out of control, just fun-loud where you can literally hear the buzz of excitement. Let the students' energy and enthusiasm fill the room. That's what makes a game fun! Give the students guidelines or set some limits, such as the following:

    o Do not argue with each other or the referee (teacher).

    o Do cheer on your team.

    o Remember that this game will help your learning.

    You can put the guidelines on the board before you begin so you can have a written reminder to point to if they accidentally break a rule, which they very well may do if they are that excited. (Just remember that you as the teacher are always in control.) Have you ever been to a really quiet football game? Exactly. Games, especially competitive ones, are more fun with a little noise.

- If the students are working on an assignment, let them ask each other questions. I explain the expected noise level to my class like this, "As you work on this assignment, the only talking I should hear is a whisper to your neighbor if you have a question. I want to make sure you have the help you may need. Other than that, please remain focused on the assignment." A few students may need reminders, so give them a look or motion with your hand that they should be writing. Be careful not to overreact to a little bit of noise. When we overreact, it tells the students that we are not in control. We are not presenting calm and controlled leadership. We should always give off the image that we are in control.

Your Turn

1. Think back to your favorite class. Did your teacher allow you to talk or even get a little loud? Did you feel like that teacher had control of the classroom?

   _____
   _____
   _____
   _____
   _____
   _____

2. How do your students know what noise level is acceptable during certain activities?

   _____
   _____
   _____
   _____
   _____
   _____

3. What is your personal opinion of noise level? How can voices help a classroom?

   _____
   _____
   _____
   _____
   _____
   _____

Make Groupwork Work

> We work as a group. It feels nice to have freedom.
>
> —Zac, Grade 8

Groupwork can be your biggest ally or your worst nightmare. If you ask students, they will almost always respond that they love working in groups. This may be because:

- They like the social aspect of working with other students.
- They receive the help they need without having to ask you.
- It's easier to do an assignment with help from other students.

From a teacher's point of view, groupwork is beneficial because:

- Students can learn social skills while working together academically.
- Students will ask you fewer questions because they have each other to help.
- Students will need to be able to work with others, including those who are different from them, in tomorrow's world.

However, groupwork can go sour very quickly. I find that every class is different. Some classes work very well together from the start. Others need extra scaffolding and support with groupwork, and that's okay. Groupwork is more than just pushing desks together.

Tips for Making Groupwork Work

- **Consider how you want to group the students.** There are many ways to group students. Think about the goal you want them to accomplish. Is the assignment harder than what they could do on their own? If so, do heterogeneous grouping. This means that you will have students of different skill levels working together. This way, each group has a mini-teacher to help them. Otherwise, all the students performing at lower levels will sink together. This is a nightmare for everybody. You could also let the students work in pairs or in groups of three. Groups of four to six are the usually most productive, however, and the larger size gives them more power to perform.

- **Arrange group seats before students enter classroom.** Arrange the desks and chairs for how the groups will work before the students walk into the room. Groupwork success might depend on how well the desks are arranged. If one desk is pushed to the side, that student may subconsciously feel as if they are not part of the group. Perhaps even give a group the option of sitting on a carpeted floor in a hip or comfy corner of the room. I usually don't ever force a student to sit on the floor, however. That just seems cruel (some girls feel uncomfortable sitting on the floor in skirts, it hurts some larger students' legs, etc.). But if you give them *the option*, one or two groups will usually jump at the opportunity, even in high school.

- **Give each student a role.** Make sure everyone is carrying their own weight. To ensure this, you might assign roles to the group members. For example, one student could be the motivator. Another student could be the recorder. A third could be the acknowledger to make sure everyone is participating. You can also assign a group leader that reports to you. I like to let the groups pick the leader. That is an organic way for students to be empowered by other students. You can also have an encourager, which is someone who cheers the group on as they are working. I used to call this the cheer person, and the students absolutely loved this role and had a lot of fun with it. You could also have an includer role. That person makes sure everybody is participating and encourages those that are not. I've also had groups where I didn't assign roles to let the students' natural strengths surface organically. It's really all about what your tasks are, what age you're working with, and what you feel your students are capable of.

- **Provide both written and verbal instructions.** Groups will usually only fall apart if they do not know what to do or are not held accountable. Make sure there are written as well as spoken directions to the groups. Desks are usually arranged all around the

(Continued)

(Continued)

room with groupwork, so it's a good idea to have a set of written directions or procedures for each group of students.

- **Explain the daily point system.** If needed, you can give students a participation grade or points each day. Before they start the groupwork, clearly go over the written rubric of how they will be graded. A rubric with examples will prevent arguments. Be sure to actually go over and teach the rubric before the assignment. If you quickly score them in class (if the participation grade is based on work produced and behavior) and they see the points immediately and in writing, this is very effective in either maintaining the stellar behavior and work completion for the next day or empowering them to change their behavior the next day in their groups.

One strategy that you can use in any K–12 classroom to make sure every student feels included is to have your student pick partners or groups to work with. However, *this can also be one of the most revealing times that students can feel left out of the class.* If you are going to let students choose groups, there's a tactic you can use to make sure everybody feels included. When there's a student that isn't chosen for a group, it's usually because they don't work well in a team and the other students know this. The student, however, rarely self-identifies this deficit and simply thinks nobody likes to work with them. They rationalize this exclusion as, "I like to work alone." It's okay for a student to work alone for some tasks, but in the world today we need students to also know how to work in teams and get a job done.

When I have one of these students in my class, I usually ask them the day before which student they work well with in the classroom. You might be surprised who they say. It's usually different from who the teacher thinks. I'll do this in casual conversation.

Let's say, for example, Amira is the student who is never picked for groups. Amira tells me that she works well with Darin. So I'll show a note to Darin asking, "Will you ask Amira to be in your group when I have the class choose groups today?" I'll hold the note there for a few seconds, wait until the student says yes (and they always do), then *I'll crumple the note up and throw it away so Amira never sees it.* When I announce the choosing of groups, Darin walks over to Amira and asks her to be in his group. Amira will most likely be sheepish and shy. She'll say sure and maybe shrug her shoulders like she doesn't care. Don't look over at this point. Amira will look at you to see if you had anything to do with it. Do your "teacher things" for a few minutes and let them get settled into a group together. Now Amira is in a group and feels included and flattered. Since she feels she belongs, she will probably participate more than she usually does and do so with confidence. You also most likely will not have any behavior issues from Amira while she is in the group since she now feels like she is valued. Darin feels good about himself as well, so it's a win-win.

If you don't have time to have the conversation the day before, you can skip a step and pick a good role model in the class and ask them to invite the student into their group when groups are chosen. Explain to the role model student that it would make the other student feel accepted. This adds a layer of empathy training. If you are asking another student to choose someone for a group, as I did with Darin, I suggest writing the request because kids hear everything and it's most powerful when the students don't know we actually set it up. That way everybody feels like they belong and are empowered. I've used this strategy in elementary, middle, and even high school effectively.

Your Turn

1. What roles could you give each member of a group for a project?

   _____
   _____
   _____

2. What is the benefit of choosing groups? What is the benefit of assigning groups? When is one more beneficial than the other?

   _____
   _____
   _____

3. What data could you use to assign heterogeneous groups? How can this help every group succeed academically?

   _____
   _____
   _____

4. Is there a student who is never picked for groups and who probably feels excluded from the classroom community? How do they react during groupwork in your class? Would you want to try the strategy above? Why or why not?

   _____
   _____
   _____

5. What social skills are students learning when they are working in a group?

   _____
   _____
   _____

Let Their Creative Juices Flow

Creativity engages students. Creativity also frustrates traditional teachers because it is not the way we most likely learned while growing up. It forces teachers to think outside of the box. The key to engaging students is allowing creativity to flow while supporting students in the learning.

Have you ever seen Ken Robinson's TED Talk, "Do Schools Kill Creativity?" It's a powerful talk that explains the importance of creativity in the classroom. I highly recommend you watch it together with a few colleagues, if you haven't seen it already.

Creativity best shows up in well-planned lessons. When you bring creativity into your lessons, you will often engage the reluctant students, since they are not restricted in their learning.

> ### Tips for Infusing Creativity Into Lessons
>
> - For projects, give students choices (some more creative than others) on how to present their final project.
> - Use multiple engagement styles in your lessons to allow creativity in students (see Best Practice #35).
> - When students show creativity, praise them so other students see you value this in your classroom.
>
> *(Continued)*

(Continued)

- If a student has an idea to add to your unit or lesson, speak with them during class or ask them to stay after class to discuss the idea. Students often have the most creative ideas. Explain to them why or why not their idea will work so you encourage creative thinking in the future from that student.

- Give students options for how to present their final projects, but grade them all using the same rubric expectations. Options could include a skit, a song, a video, a podcast, a talk show format Q&A, a newscast, a documentary, a digital presentation, or even a form of art.

- Use your resources. Search online, ask a friend, or even use social media to ask for a creative input on a lesson or unit. I find X has a large group of dedicated professionals in the teaching world. I've sought creative input many times on social media and have given advice to many educators in turn.

Your Turn

1. What are your thoughts on the value and importance of creativity in a lesson?

   _____
   _____
   _____
   _____
   _____
   _____

2. In your opinion, does creativity decrease or increase academic rigor? Explain your answer. Try to give specific examples for your thoughts.

   _____
   _____
   _____
   _____
   _____
   _____

3. What is the most creative project/unit/lesson you've ever come across? How did the students respond to it? How much did the students learn?

   _____
   _____
   _____
   _____
   _____
   _____

Best Practice #35

Teach Every Different Type of Learner

> I enjoy this class because it's very interactive.
>
> —Sarah, Grade 9
> [an intrapersonal learner, ironically]

This video shows how to use multiple engagement styles throughout your lesson.

Wouldn't it be simpler if everyone could learn and become engaged the same way and amount from just a worksheet, a lecture, or a digital presentation? Unfortunately, the world isn't like this and neither is the classroom. Not everyone is the same type of learner. Students learn in many different ways. An experienced teacher knows this and will add tasks for different engagement styles into a lesson to accommodate all learners in the classroom.

I remember my first job interview. It was for a prestigious high school in a suburb of Philadelphia. They told me to create a thirty-minute lesson on anything in the language arts content I wanted. They told me that my audience was eleventh graders. However, my real audience during the interview was six administration members. I thought long and hard about what I wanted to teach, but I didn't spend as much time thinking about *how* I was going to teach it. This was a rookie mistake.

I decided to do a lesson on Shakespeare's works. I entered the room with a transparency (yes, transparencies were still a thing back then) bulleting his plays. I lectured for twenty minutes on his life from index cards. I was shaking. I went through his life, answered a few questions from my fake student audience, and had them independently complete a worksheet on what I had taught them oh so well. I wasn't hired. Big surprise.

Upon reflection, I realized that, like many new teachers, I was showing the class how smart I was. I was distributing my knowledge. Let's fast-forward seven years and see how I would do it all over again.

I would probably start by asking the class what they already knew about Shakespeare and jotting down what they said on the board or screen to show them that what they say is important. Then I would show an engaging three-to-five-minute video introducing Shakespeare and ask them to add to our list on a sticky note as they are watching. I would then ask the class what they learned from the short clip. I might ask them to jot it down for kinesthetic learners. (You could also use a K-W-L chart.) We would share out and create a class bank of collective prior knowledge to continually refer back to. Then I would pass out a timeline with a few of Shakespeare's works and life events filled in and a few left blank for them to find in resources and articles I provided for them. They could work in groups or with partners.

Later, they would write a summary of what they had learned, and I would do a short recap of Shakespeare's life and work using their knowledge to summarize and to make sure we were all on the same page. At the lesson closure, I would ask each student to share with a partner what they had learned about Shakespeare from today's lesson. Finally, we would share out and add to the class bank. Together we would cross out information from the prior list that we had learned was not true. They would visually see what they had learned in just one period.

Do you see the difference between this lesson and the one I actually taught? This is just one of dozens of ways to teach this concept and cater to different engagement styles. All different types of learners would be engaged and learning. Unless the students were linguistic or auditory learners, the first lesson would not suit them. You would lose engagement with more than half the class, or they would pretend to pay attention but not comprehend as much as they could another way.

I'm sure you all have heard of or studied Gardner's theory of multiple intelligences. There's a bit of discussion now about whether they are actually intelligences or engagement styles. Let's call them engagement styles. It works. Once I started adding more than one type of engagement style in my lesson, more and more students were engaged in the same content, but for different reasons.

The multiple intelligences theory is not just for elementary or middle school teachers. High school students are still the same types of learners. They will most likely be these types of learners their whole life. According to Howard Gardner, there are eight types of ways people learn (Edutopia, 2016):

1. **Bodily-kinesthetic** learners are engaged in learning best when some movement is incorporated into the learning. Bodily-kinesthetic students learn the best by *doing*.

Ways to incorporate this type of learning into a lesson:

- Total physical response (students move their body to the learning)
- Activities where students move around the room
- Pantomime
- Charades
- Scavenger hunts
- Exercise

2. **Visual-spatial** learners are people who learn best when they see the content.

Ways to incorporate this type of learning into a lesson:

- Short clips of videos (I never go longer than five minutes)
- Pictures
- Draw a visual of the learning
- Realia
- Graphic organizers
- Make a map
- Posters and displays
- Create a mental image

3. **Musical** learners are people who learn best when content is in sounds, tones, or rhythms. Musical learners are also quick to spot patterns in tones and rhythms.

Ways to incorporate this type of learning into a lesson:

- Playing a song that goes with the lesson
- Having students compose a song or jingle with the content
- Creating a cheer with the content
- Tapping out a rhythm or cadence to the learning
- Playing sounds that go with the lesson (your iPhone has sound apps or you can download off the computer)

4. **Logical-mathematical** learners are people who learn best with logical and scientific thinking and deductive reasoning.

Ways to incorporate this type of learning into a lesson:

- Solve a problem using numbers or mathematics
- Create a timeline
- Analogies
- Brain teasers
- Scientific experiments
- Construct a graph
- Compare and contrast

5. **Naturalistic** learners are similar to kinesthetic learners. They love the outdoors and learn best when they can feel, touch, and hold items. Naturalistic learners have an innate appreciation for the world around them.

Ways to incorporate this type of learning into a lesson:

- Go on nature hikes.
- Bring realia such as rocks, plants, or flowers in from nature to incorporate into a lesson.
- Give these students an outdoor area to read/complete work.
- Identify and classify nature.
- Take students outside to be inspired by nature when they are creating art or writing poetry.
- Listen to audio of nature sounds. (You could play this in the background as they are working or reading.)

6. **Linguistic** learners are people who learn best with words, either written or spoken.

Ways to incorporate this type of learning into a lesson:

- Socratic Seminars
- Classroom debates
- Lectures
- Group conversations
- Written responses

7. **Interpersonal** learners are people who learn best with and from others. These students also read others' emotions very well and communicate and respond appropriately. Interpersonal learners enjoy the social aspect to learning.

Ways to incorporate this type of learning into a lesson:

- Partner work
- Conducting a student survey
- Tutor a classmate
- Group discussions
- Students teaching students
- Groupwork

8. **Intrapersonal** learners are people who learn best by themselves and know themselves as learners very well. Intrapersonal learners are often independent.

Ways to incorporate this type of learning into a lesson:

- Independent work
- Worksheets
- Personal goal-setting
- Diary or journal entries about the learning
- Self-evaluations

I'd like to add one more engagement style: **emotional engagement**. I believe this to be the most engaging learning type. If you can get your students emotionally hooked or passionate about a concept (one that is preferably two-sided), their engagement will soar through the roof, critical thinking will be at an all-time high, and behavior management issues will likely disappear. The following are some instances when I've used this type of engagement:

- When the class read *Of Mice and Men* by John Steinbeck: Did George make the right decision to end his best friend's life? We had an entire mock trial and students played lawyers on both sides.
- When the class read *Monster* by Walter Dean Myers: Was the main character guilty or innocent? We also took a field trip to the local courthouse as they were reading the novel.
- When I taught a unit in which they had to solve a societal issue that they saw in the world around them.

In all of these units, students became heated in their discussions, empathetic, passionate, and curious. They often changed their minds on their position, which showed they were listening to their classmates and thinking critically. This is what emotional engagement looks like.

If I have to sit through a lecture without any visuals, I space out after fifteen minutes. I need to see stuff. I'm a visual learner. Before I learned about the multiple intelligences theory I used to just think I wasn't smart because I couldn't retain as much by listening. It's not true. Don't let your students think this about themselves. Our students need us to respect their preferred way of learning. A great way to do this is to give your students a multiple intelligences survey or quiz at the beginning of the year. Google "multiple intelligence quiz" and you'll find one. Explain to your class that this testing is solely to help teach them effectively. This will help ease tension and also encourage parental support, since they will know you are looking out for their students' best interests. It is also empowering if the students know what type of learner they are and can advocate for themselves. Also, you will have this information to use with your lesson plans. Students can be more than one type of learner. For example, a student could be equally dominant in both visual and musical learning.

So how do you use this information in a real lesson? My most engaging lesson plans always have at least three engagement styles in them. Go through your lesson and list where you can use each engagement style if you need to. It will pay off in the long run. If you can include more than three, wonderful. The more styles, the better. If you go through a lesson and you only have one or two engagement styles included, beware! Including as many engagement styles as possible will help more students in your classroom and ultimately lead to fewer behavior problems and more focused learners.

Below is an example of a simple lesson plan with at least three different engagement styles.

Example of Lesson Plan With Different Engagement Styles

Lesson objective: Given notes and a sorting activity, students are to apply knowledge of fiction versus nonfiction.

MINUTES		ENGAGEMENT STYLE
5 minutes	**Anticipatory set:**	Interpersonal
	Ask: Why do people read books? Students jot down a response, turn and talk, and then share out with the class. (Ask about textbooks if they don't say "to learn facts.")	
5 minutes	**Model:** Show two piles of books, one fiction and one nonfiction. Have class textbook in the nonfiction pile. Do a think aloud of characteristics of each pile. Ask students to share out characteristics of each pile. Make a chart to add to input.	Visual

(Continued)

(Continued)

MINUTES		ENGAGEMENT STYLE
10 minutes	**Input (notes and teacher explanation):** There are two general forms of writing. <table><tr><td>Fiction</td><td>Nonfiction</td></tr><tr><td>"fake"</td><td>"real"</td></tr><tr><td>meant to entertain</td><td>meant to give or relay information and facts</td></tr><tr><td>has a sequence of events/plot</td><td>nothing made up</td></tr><tr><td>made up or created by author</td><td>"how to" books</td></tr><tr><td>can be based on an actual event</td><td>science books</td></tr><tr><td></td><td>history books</td></tr><tr><td>may have pictures to paint a picture</td><td>biographies</td></tr><tr><td></td><td>usually has pictures to show information</td></tr></table>	Linguistic
5 minutes	**Quick sorting activity in their table groups:** Sort big piles of books into fiction or nonfiction and put a sticky note on top with the purpose of each type.	Kinesthetic
15 minutes	**Independent reading:** As students are reading a book, ask them to think about whether their book is fiction or nonfiction and why. Have them write down their response and the title and author of the book on a sticky note. Have two pieces of chart paper or two areas of the room, one labeled fiction and one labeled nonfiction. Students either place their sticky on the appropriate chart paper or get up and place it in the appropriate area of the room for other students to see. Give students a bit of time to read their classmates' sticky notes.	Intrapersonal and kinesthetic
5 minutes	**Closure** Turn and talk: What are the two main types of books and why do people read each type? Share out answers.	Interpersonal

Your Turn

1. Print out or reflect back to a lesson you have taught that went either poorly or just so-so.

   _____
   _____
   _____
   _____

2. Label where you appealed to each type of engagement style. The more the better, but you don't necessarily have to hit them all.

   _____
   _____
   _____
   _____

3. Do the same for a lesson that went very well.

   _____
   _____
   _____
   _____

4. Analyze the difference. What could you add to each lesson to appeal to more types of learners?

   _____
   _____
   _____
   _____

Have *No* Doubts . . . but Be Prepared to Have (Just a Few) Lessons Flop

Imagine you have just signed up for your first-ever whitewater rafting trip. You've never done this before but heard it might be fun. Inside, you are pretty terrified. *What if we hit a rock? What if I fall in? What if I get hurt?* Your mind races into worst-case scenarios. *I mean, people have been hurt before, right? What if I'm one of those people?* You might even start to back out, or at least think of backing out. Then your guide, Tom, shows up. Tom begins to talk about the dangers of rafting. He mentions that he's new at the job but knows how to call for help if needed. He's not kidding. He reads instructions from some note cards he has prepared. You can tell he's a bit unsure of himself, but he tries to assure you with, "Don't worry, we're all in this together." How would you feel in this situation?

This is exactly how students feel when a teacher seems to have doubts that they will succeed in a specific task. Be the experienced whitewater rafting instructor: They smile, they are at ease, and they know the boat will be okay (or at least they say so). They model courage for the team. Carry the belief that your students will succeed even when they do not have this feeling themselves. They are looking for you to do this. Be their whitewater rafting instructor.

The great news is that unlike whitewater rafting, when our lessons flop we aren't risking our lives. And I've learned just as much from flopped lessons as from lessons that went well. Both can be valuable tools for you. The trick is that when a lesson flops, take a breath, get some water, and carve out some time to reflect. You have to take the time to reflect on why it flopped rather than thinking about how unruly the students were that day. Often I found that if a lesson flopped it was because I had forgotten to do a key part of the lesson, such as guided instruction, so the students didn't understand the assignment and behavior issues started to surface. I've flopped lessons, and every teacher you know has flopped lessons. Some just talk about it more than others. Being vulnerable enough to reflect honestly about flopped lessons rather than pointing fingers about student behavior takes a lot of courage and a growth mindset. The best teachers use flopped lessons as a learning tool rather than viewing them as setbacks. If you have a coteacher, it's most powerful if you debrief together. In your reflection or debrief, ask yourself or each other:

- Had you planned well enough? Always start with the lesson plan; don't start with the students. The student behavior is usually a result of the lesson. Was the plan too easy or too hard? Was there not enough talk time, too much teacher talk, or more collaboration needed?
- If the plan was solid, the time was chunked, and the rigor was just right, then what else went wrong?
- How can you use this flopped lesson as a learning tool?

Your Turn

1. Have you ever had a lesson flop? Did you take time to reflect afterward about why it did not go as planned?

   _____
   _____
   _____
   _____

2. What does it tell a class when you come in prepared and confident the day after a lesson flops? What would that indicate about you as a teacher? How would it make them feel?

   _____
   _____
   _____
   _____

3. If a lesson flopped because students didn't understand the concept, what would you do the next day? How could you provide a different way to learn the same concept? (Example: Students could teach each other in small groups with one student "teacher" for every four to six students.)

   _____
   _____
   _____
   _____

Real Conversation With an Eighth-Grade Student

[As I discretely tried to take out my Invisalign while my head was turned to eat some candy.]

Student: Are those your dentures?

Me: No, I'm thirty-four.

Student: So they're not?

PART 4
PARTNERING AND CULTIVATING RELATIONSHIPS WITH STAKEHOLDERS

There Are Better Ways to Have Administration Support You Than This

My ninth-grade French teacher got lost finding the classroom, as it was his first day at the school on the first day of the year. He walked into the room late and asked if this was the ninth-grade French class. I was quite the class clown back then and quickly told him that the room he was looking for was at the complete opposite end of the complex—about ten minutes away. He ran out of the room like he was on fire! About thirty minutes later he came back into the room, led by the principal, whom he had to ask for directions after I directed him toward the gymnasium.

—Stephan, Age 43

Source: iStock.com/Tom Kolodotschko

What do other adults in the school have to do with your classroom management?

Much of your satisfaction with your teaching career will be based on the other adults with whom you work. And the happier you are, the happier your students will be. Most teachers who absolutely love their school do so because they love the colleagues they work with. They've invested time to create respectful and supportive relationships with their coworkers.

I REMEMBER WHEN...

In my second year working Critical Skills, a class of students with moderate to severe disabilities, at the middle school level, a parent came into my classroom and, with little knowledge of my program or my students' skill sets, looked me in the eye and told me that her daughter didn't belong in my class and that she would be giving me a "year." This deeply saddened me because she saw only my students' disabilities and completely disregarded their strengths. With my optimistic outlook, I decided I was going to demonstrate my effectiveness and my students' capabilities, including those of her daughter. In my class we had students whose disabilities ranged from outward ones such as cerebral palsy or Down's syndrome to invisible ones such as intellectual deficiencies. I worked hard with my students to help them meet and exceed their IEP goals. I was determined to do my best to create an honest and welcoming dialogue with this parent.

Hindsight is 20/20. I always invested so much time into my classroom and students that I let the adult relationships suffer. I'll be real with you: This was probably my biggest mistake. I invested a lot of time in my coteaching partnerships, because that was part of my classroom. If I could help you learn from my mistake, I'd advise you to invest time in *all* adult relationships around your school environment.

During my seemingly noble crusade to connect with this parent, I gave her my cell phone number so she knew I was always available to discuss her daughter's progress or troubleshoot ideas. I started receiving angry voicemails and texts from this parent well after 9:00 p.m. She also sent me aggressive e-mails, leading me to feel like I was missing something or doing something wrong.

The family verbally attacked my colleagues and me during meetings. They talked about my other students' physical differences and made assumptions about their capabilities.

These statements were both mean and unfounded. I and many program advocates and specialists saw that their daughter was indeed making progress and working at a level comparable to her peers. I left these meetings feeling depleted and disrespected. Finally, I asked for support from my administrative team and learned how to set clearer boundaries. I now only answer phone calls and respond to e-mails during office hours, for example.

It is my hope that the strategies I learned from this experience can help you when the actions of your own students or their family members make students question their abilities.

Tools to help build positive connections when working with difficult families

- **Set clear boundaries from the beginning.** My second-year experience taught me that if I made myself too available, some parents would overstep obvious boundaries (in this case calling and texting late into the night). I allowed that to intimidate me and felt like I needed to answer right away, which then opened up the dialogue for even more harassment.

    Send out a welcome letter and lay out expectations and boundaries at the beginning of the school year. Some of the guidelines for communication can include what hours you are available by e-mail or phone. This way you can refer to it later if needed, and parents won't feel like you're creating the rule just for them. You have other students who need your attention just as much as the difficult cases, and you do not want to expend all your energy on one family. It is depleting and does not set healthy guidelines for teacher-family interactions.

- **Create open communication.** Make sure that you are transparent with your families and are in communication with them about their child's progress. If families request more detailed accounts of the day or week, create a communication binder. This also provides two-way communication where families can respond and update you on various matters, such as dentist

(Continued)

(Continued)

appointments or that their child didn't get enough sleep the night before. Let parents know from the beginning that they are an essential part of their child's success and thank them for their partnership.

- **Track data and stay organized.** If it isn't recorded, it didn't happen. Keep a running record of student work in a folder along with learning objectives.

  Also keep a communication log of all interactions with difficult caregivers. When I had a parent who was on the border of being abusive toward me through angry e-mails, constant calls, and texts, I started a file that helped me document the timeline of the interactions and helped me feel confident that if it ever went further, I would have evidence to support my experience. It is also important to be prepared to back findings of student progress with student examples and assessments. I have found that color-coded folders make it easy to find what I want to provide to the parent and what I need for my own records. These little organizational techniques help me keep my standing in high-stress meetings.

- **Do not take things personally.** I am the first to admit that this is one of the most challenging things to apply, but it is imperative. Usually when a family is upset, they are worried about their child, especially if they haven't yet accepted their child's abilities or needs. You are merely the person that they see related to their concerns and disappointment, and the easiest person to blame. All too often, they are overwhelmed by the situation, and unfortunately you may get the brunt of their reaction. This does not make you any less of a great teacher! All teachers, no matter how amazing, may end up getting a high-stress parent or advocate at some point in their career. Hopefully, these tools can be your safety net to stay afloat.

- **Listen without interrupting and pause before responding.** Everyone likes to feel heard. It is important to hear your families and validate their concerns even if you do not agree with them. A family's perception is their truth, and it is essential to honor that. Showing empathy and letting the family know you are trying to connect with their words and experience is key. This also helps you not be reactionary and feel like you need to respond right away when asked a question in a high-stress meeting. You can take your time, sit in the silence, and practice key phrases that will be mantras, such as, "You make a good point, let me think about that," or, "I respectfully disagree." No need to overexplain yourself; this can add to the heated interaction. My school psychologist really helped bring this concept home for me when he said to let the parent climb their own mountain of angry. Often they will climb back down on their own, and your listening may help speed this process along.

- **When reporting behaviors, take emotions out of it.** Use and show concrete examples and avoid making statements that could be subjective (e.g., "The student was acting aggressively"). Instead, be specific and only state the observable facts (e.g., "The student pushed another student with his right hand"). When reporting behaviors to a caregiver, try to also point out a positive (e.g., "The student improved their recovery time after a meltdown," or, "The student was able to comply with a direction"). You want the student and family to know that you are on their side while still addressing their behavioral needs.

- **Focus on the positive.** For every challenging family, you have several that support you and realize what a good teacher you are. It can be incredibly challenging, but try to celebrate the good and the fact that there are other families that love and appreciate you. The same year that I had this challenging case, I had another parent rally all my other families to nominate me for the Excellence in Special Education Award. I kept their entries close to my heart to remind me of my effectiveness when times got tough. When handling an upset family, it is easy to get lost in trying to please them and lose all the positives in the process. Keep a positive evidence drawer in your teacher desk filled with student cards and family letters of recognition and pull it out whenever you need a little boost. I know this has been a great asset to me on hard meeting days.

- **Be gentle with yourself; everyone makes mistakes.** There are times that you will drop the ball or make a mistake. It is important

(Continued)

(Continued)

>
> to recognize that as long as you are doing your best and working to do right by your students, that is all you can do. If you are a perfectionist like me, it is hard to not beat yourself up for the one *i* you forgot to dot or *t* you forgot to cross, but I learned that even the best teachers sometimes make missteps. This is how you learn. If you do find that you made an error, it is best to just own up to it, apologize for the oversight, and move forward being your awesome teaching self.
>
> - **Find advocates and support within your teaching community.** Teachers need advocates and support too! Never meet with the parent or advocate alone where you can be cornered or put in an uncomfortable position. Having someone that you trust at the meeting can make you feel empowered and help you from being undermined. I had a case almost go to Due Process—every teacher's biggest fear—and we had a meeting to discuss the facts of the case. I invited my school psychologist because he had a friendly smile and a comforting demeanor, and I would look at him whenever I could feel the heat from the tension of the room. It is important to identify your support system on campus.
>
> Equally helpful is finding guidance and direction in areas that you have yet to experience. As I was facing the unknown, I asked a seasoned colleague who had been through Due Process what to expect. She gave me a rundown of her experience and highly suggested that I had my data organized and easily accessible. This helped me know what to bring with me to the meeting and made me feel more prepared.
>
> - **Practice self-care.** A challenging student, family, or situation can make you feel like you are giving more than you have. You cannot pour from an empty cup; therefore, it is paramount that you take the time you need to recuperate. Do not forget that you are a person with passions outside of teaching, and it is important to nurture that part of yourself as well. Identify your happy place and carve time out of your week to visit it. You need to feel whole in order to be effective in the classroom or when working with a difficult family.

I hope these tips assist you on your path toward being the wonderful teacher you are meant to be! Know there will be days when you feel like an imposter. This is normal; most teachers have these days. The important part is to refer to these strategies and take care of yourself until you feel like the confidence-inspiring educator you truly are.

Jennifer Zimmermaker
9 years' experience
Education Specialist
Mesa Verde Middle School
Poway, California

Work With Parents and Caregivers as Partners

For some of us, the word *parents* has always been that seven-letter *p*-word. As new teachers, we often fear the phrase *student's parents*. Why is this so scary? They are probably older than we are when we first started teaching, and chances are that the only information they know about us is filtered to them through their child's perspective. Just hope that child respects you!

A valuable lesson I learned through years of teaching is that parents and caregivers need to be and can be a valuable resource. When a caregiver respects and admires you, most likely the child will do the same. And, sadly, if a caregiver feels the opposite, more often than not the child will also feel the same. So how do you build partnerships with the adults at home? Remember: Most parents and caregivers act out of love and concern. My mantra when communicating with families is, *They are just doing what they think is best for their child.* If you repeat this mantra you can empathize with where they are coming from.

Tips for Communicating With Parents

- **Fast and frequent communication.** Introduce yourself in the beginning of the year at open house, mail a postcard home, make a phone call, have a parent mixer, etc. The goal is to introduce yourself first, before the parents only hear about you from the student. Chances are you will most likely need the parents' help and support later down the road. The first communication you have with a parent should be an introduction or a quick, positive chat. The first time you speak to or meet the parent should never be a negative phone call, etc.

- **Like their child.** A parent or guardian will never side with you if they feel you do not really care about their child. Most likely, they raised this child. They saw their first steps, heard their first words, taught them how to ride a bike. They love them. You are only seeing a limited view of that child. If caregivers feel like you do not like their child, you will not win. Show concern for every student's situation and progress in your class. Be able to speak of at least two strengths of every child you teach.

- **Be able to defend their child's grade.** Parents and guardians want to understand. If they are upset with a grade, they will ask for documentation. They will most likely not care about the numerous hours you spent on your one hundred other students. Most often, they only care about their child. You should care enough about their child also to have documentation of the child's grading in order, along with work samples. This is your job.

- **Offer support to their child.** Be ready to let the parent know that you are there to help their child succeed. Do you offer tutoring? Podcasts of lessons? Office hours? E-mail support (be sure your district/school allows this)? How are you extending your help to the students?

Staying in Touch With Parents

In any grade level, you want to stay in touch with parents. If you have a positive rapport with parents and a behavior or motivation issue arises with their child, your job will be a lot easier. Ninety-nine percent of parents want to be kept in the loop. If they do not, it's usually because they are used to hearing negative messages from the school and they don't know how to fix this and feel like a failure. Why don't you change that by calling home for something great that their student does? Believe me, that parent will be on your side when you need them in a few weeks. The parent will most likely support you if they like you. If they only hear from you when you have bad news, they will probably not like or support you. Think of a bill collector. You only hear from them when there is bad news. Nobody likes bill collectors. Another reason a caregiver might not show interest in their child's progress could be because the caregiver is working multiple jobs and just doesn't have the time to be very involved.

Here are some creative ways to stay in touch with parents throughout the year. The key is to have high-volume, low-density communication. You want to contact parents often with little bits of information. Then they can never say that the teacher did not make an effort to contact them.

Tips for Creative Ways to Stay in Touch With the Adults at Home

- Send a postcard home during the summer introducing yourself and saying how excited you are to be their child's teacher. Take the first step.

- Make invitations to send home with each student when you have projects to show or presentations. Parents love being audience members.

- Invite caregivers to come for read-alouds. Students can increase their reading level and comprehension by reading to parents too.

- Invite caregivers to come in to help with bulletin boards. Have them write inspirational messages to their child on the board.

- Invite parents to help with fundraisers.

- Depending on the grade level (works well in lower elementary grades), you can invite parents to come eat lunch with their child in the cafeteria.

- Have a parent-only e-mail list that sends out reminders for tests as well as classroom and school events. Then you only have to write one e-mail to communicate with lots of families at once.

- Invite parents to teach a creative concept to the class. For example, a mom who is an art therapist could do some art with the class.

- Get or make a parent signature stamp to put on top of important assignments or tests/quizzes. Add an extra point if the student brings back a parent signature. Parents love to know what assignments their child is completing.

- Have parent guest speakers if their job is interesting or better yet relates to your unit of study.

- Invite caregivers to come in on a peer-editing day. Adults will love to give input to students about their writing.

- Invite parents to chaperone field trips.

- Have a classroom career fair with parents and caregivers of students. Each adult can have a table and talk about what they do.

- Invite a parent to come in to lead a station if you are doing station learning or small group instruction.

- Invite a parent to work with a small group of students. Parents would most likely do well with your students who are higher achieving. You are the one trained on how to work with students performing below grade level.

- Invite a caregiver to read to the class. The students will appreciate the new voice in the room. Give adults the option to bring in a book of their choice.

You can't go wrong. You may want to explain to the class the day before why the parent is coming in so that students behave for their guest. I would say something like this:

Tomorrow, class, I have invited Mrs. Smith, a parent, in to _____. I would not invite a parent to every class, but I trust this class is mature enough to have a guest. It is important that you say good morning to Mrs. Smith and understand that she is dedicating her own free time to help our learning. Make sure you also thank Mrs. Smith for the time she is giving our classroom.

Your Turn

1. What is an event or learning activity you have coming up to which you can invite parents? How can they help the learning in your classroom? Does a parent work somewhere that can donate supplies for a project?

   _____
   _____
   _____
   _____
   _____
   _____

2. Share ideas on low-effort ways you can communicate with parents via apps to keep them in the loop of what is happening in your classroom.

   _____
   _____
   _____
   _____
   _____
   _____

3. Who are your "star" parents who can be an advocate for your classroom? How can they help you with field trips, open house nights, projects, etc.?

   _____
   _____
   _____
   _____
   _____
   _____

Best Practice #38

Make Coteaching Work

....

> This chapter is dedicated to my former mentor, Dr. Orletta Nguyen, who showed me the beauty of coteaching when it works.
>
> —Serena Pariser

You likely will have to work with another adult in your room. This could be a one-on-one aide who is designated to a particular student, or some schools have college students serving as tutors. Or you could have the opportunity to experience the mother of all adult teaching partnerships (drumroll, please): coteaching! This is when one or more credentialed teachers (usually only two) work together to teach a class or multiple classes.

This video shows you what coteaching can look like.

If you have a resource or support specialist in your classroom, as the general education teacher you are the master of content and the other adult is the master of modifications, scaffolds, and interventions. This means that you have the authority to make decisions on content, and they should know best about what each individual student needs. With classroom management, however, ultimately you want to be on the same page with your behavior plan for the classroom so you do not always "outrank" the other adult with decisions and you can truly be equal in this realm.

Many teachers have a difficult time with coteachers at some point in their career; this is natural. Think of your college dorm mate. Unless you were very lucky, you probably have some not-so-delightful stories to tell about that person since you were living so closely with them. It's similar with coteaching. However, not only are you with that person every day, you are also working with them toward a common goal: making sure your students learn to their fullest potential. And teaching can get very personal inside our own classrooms. The key is not so much who your coteacher is (although that is a large part of it—how well you two "gel") but how you learn to interact with one another.

Some teachers in coteaching pairs that I have spoken to thought building a successful relationship was hopeless. They resorted to just ignoring the conflict since it was a work partnership and not a personal one. However, this may be the worst way to handle coteaching. It will make coming to work every day miserable. And it will blow up eventually. The students also notice way more than we think and will sense the tension in the air. Who can learn like that?

On the other hand, successful coteaching partnerships are powerful, delightful, fun, and exhilarating. You get to share the joy of the students every day with someone. There is someone there when Makayla makes that hilarious comment (teaching stories just aren't the same after it happens). There is someone there to bounce ideas off of, plan lessons with, and much more.

Tips for Successful Coteaching

- **Recognize and use your coteacher's strengths.** Every person has different strengths. Does your coteacher have a soothing and engaging reading voice and can differentiate character voices? If so, the two of you could plan for him to read aloud to the students daily. Is your coteacher meticulous, and you're less so? Instead of thinking this trait is annoying, see if he would like to be in charge of a detailed job in the classroom, such as taking roll or grading quizzes. I always found both parties in the room were happiest when they were using their strengths to help the class as a whole. It can also benefit the students if the same teacher does the same part of the lesson each day. It helps that teacher get better and better at that part and offers consistency to the students.

- **Let your coteacher know when she did a great job with something, no matter how small or large.** Everybody wants to be praised. Research shows that employees who are ignored are the most likely to be dissatisfied with their job (even more than employees who are criticized). The most satisfied employees are those who are praised. Let your coteacher know when she did a great job delivering a lesson, dealing with a student, or coming up with an idea. Chances are that she will continue these behaviors and your classroom will be a much more pleasant place.

- **Keep your coteacher in the loop.** You and your coteacher should plan together. Both of you will then be on the same page. I was one of the pioneers of coteaching in my school and advised many coteaching partnerships to help them succeed. When a partnership was not happy, these were the most common complaints:

- She doesn't carry her weight.
- He doesn't tell me what he is doing until the last minute (this makes the other partner feel unvalued, unprepared, and purposeless).
- She cannot control the class, so I have to do everything (most likely this partnership is not using each other's strengths to work together).
- I feel undermined by the other adult in the room.
- He micromanages me.
- She bosses me around.

So many of these issues can be alleviated by planning together and communicating regularly.

- **Recognize that coteaching is a relationship.** My former mentor once gave me some very wise advice: "Serena, you're entering an arranged marriage." The truth is that you have to treat this partnership as carefully as you would a romantic relationship if you want it to be successful. All of the elements of a successful relationship can be applied to a coteaching partnership. Why? Because it is a very close relationship, under constant stress and tension, and the partners are working toward a common goal.

  Think, *What would work in a relationship?* That is probably the answer to what would work in coteaching. For example, if you feel like your coteacher is not carrying her weight, you are probably not communicating your classroom needs (just like personal needs in a relationship). As silly as this analogy may be, it works. Keep this mantra going on in your head: *What would work in a relationship?*

  Realize that you cannot change who your coteacher is, but you can ask him to change specific behaviors that may affect the learning of the class. Everything should be focused on that. Does a behavior of his negatively affect the learning or morale of the classroom? If you feel it does, bring it up respectfully when the two of you are together without students around (never in front of students or during class).

- **Remain united when it comes to student behavior.** When dealing with student behavior—and you will—make sure the teacher who set the consequences is the one to address the behavior and/or speak to the student about the behavior. If one teacher disciplines but another talks to the student about it, it sends mixed messages to the child that one teacher is mean and one is nice. This dichotomy will cause the child to favor one teacher over the

(Continued)

(Continued)

other, or play one off the other one. The teachers will not appear as a united front. For example, if a student acts out and is disciplined by one teacher, the student may seek a more sympathetic ear from the other teacher. In this case, the second teacher should say, "I'm sorry you feel that way. I want to make sure you address these concerns with [name of teacher who disciplined]." Do not engage the student in a conversation, because they need to see the same teacher as both the disciplinarian *and* the understanding teacher. The student needs to see well-rounded teachers who are united.

- **Share paperwork, grading, copies, and phone calls.** Be clear with one another about expectations and divvying up responsibilities. An overworked teacher is an unhappy teacher. Coteachers who split the workload are a solid team. The lead teacher—the adult who holds the teaching credential—should figure out how to split the work. Then it usually works better if the second adult always does the same tasks so there is no confusion. For example, the second adult could always call parents, or could always grade the reading notebooks (just make sure the grading is consistent between classes). Even better, the second adult could always grade a certain period's quizzes or tests and give the teacher a list of grades or enter them manually. This prevents one teacher from feeling like they are always asking the other for things or "nagging them." It also empowers each teacher to know how to do their task well. Figure out what works systematically, then divide and conquer. If you are the coteacher and take initiative and do things consistently without being asked, this can really help the relationship. For example, perhaps you wipe down the desks after class without being asked each day. The video linked to this QR code briefly explains six different ways coteaching can work in a classroom when delivering or supporting a lesson.

Six ways coteaching can look in a lesson to support and challenge learners

Dos of Coteaching:

▶ Make each other a priority.

▶ Listen to each other.

▶ Learn to trust each other.

▶ Plan lessons at least a week in advance (you will most likely have to plan farther ahead when working with someone else).

▶ Use each other's strengths in the classroom.

▶ Be honest and always do what's best for the class.

▶ Put your egos aside in minor conflicts and think, *What's best for the students?*

- Know each other's sensitivity levels.
- Use every adult in the room as a teacher or distributor of knowledge.
- Split the behind-the-scenes class work/preparation and try to each keep the same tasks to maximize efficiency.
- Take initiative and do things without being asked often.
- Settle frustrations behind closed doors as soon as possible with honesty and empathy to be able to move past the issue. Compromise if needed.
- Praise each other for what part of the lesson each did well daily or weekly.
- Thank each other weekly or daily.
- Give each other handwritten thank-you cards every once in a while.
- Be open to learning from one another.
- Let each other flop in front of the class. That's how both will learn.

Don'ts of Coteaching:

- Don't argue or have a disagreement about the lesson out loud in front of the students. Don't debate about what to do or what not to do. Remember that if you're planning together, you should already both be on the same page. Students do not need to see or hear disagreements or lack of planning. There can be times when you flow fabulously together or your class has the same basic structure. It's like you do the same dance. However, it's more fun for the students and more beneficial to the learning if you switch it up once in a while and change teaching roles in the classroom.
- Don't try to wing it. On top of just being bad teaching, it will be a train wreck with more than one person in the room.
- Don't use one of the adults as the disciplinarian and the other as the teacher.
- Don't vent to another in your workplace about how frustrated you are with the other adult.
- Don't hold in your frustrations and refuse to address them. They *will* come out eventually, one way or another.
- Don't talk over each other in the lesson. Know your parts.

▶ Don't correct each other in front of the class. If correction is needed, pass a note or whisper into an ear. All teachers make mistakes. Correcting another teacher in front of the class can be the single most undermining act to do to them, not to mention very embarrassing.

You'll find with one person one way works, but with another a different way may work better. Do what works for both of you, make sure you are both heard and respected in the classroom, and make sure having two bodies in the classroom accelerates the learning.

Your Turn

1. It is almost guaranteed that you will work with another adult in the room at some point in your teaching life, if it hasn't already happened. Think back to a time when you did not see eye to eye with another adult in the room. How did you handle the situation?

   _____
   _____
   _____
   _____
   _____
   _____
   _____
   _____
   _____

2. If you could have a redo, is there a way you could have improved that specific situation?

   _____
   _____
   _____
   _____
   _____
   _____
   _____
   _____
   _____

Lean on Social Workers and School Counselors

All of our students deserve to feel safe, valued, and loved inside the walls of our schools. But many teachers who are just beginning their careers haven't received training in recognizing and developing social-emotional skills in kids. During my first two or three years of teaching, I didn't use the valuable resource of social workers and school counselors. I was too shy and embarrassed to ask for their help because I thought that meant I wasn't a competent teacher. In fact, the opposite is true.

Social workers and school counselors are placed in schools to not only support students but to partner with teachers in supporting the whole child. Sometimes as teachers we have a hero complex and take on a lot of issues concerning students' personal lives, traumas that may have occurred, or feelings of sadness and anxiety students may feel. Thirty-seven percent of adolescents reported clinically high levels of anxiety and depression in 2021, and one in five reported they'd seriously considered suicide (Edutopia, 2022). What does this mean for K–12 teachers? It means trauma is happening as our students are sitting at the desks in our classrooms. It could be happening at home; it could have happened over the past summer; it could be happening at school right now. That's more than we signed up for or are professionally trained to handle. A good teacher is different than a good therapist.

Although schools have always had school counselors, in the past few years social workers have been hired in many schools as well, and some schools may be lucky enough to have more than one. Students today are being exposed to things inside and outside of school that require more school-based mental health services. Here are just a few worrying issues:

- Social media bullying
- School shooter drills (and active shooter events) in grades as low as kindergarten
- School violence
- Higher rates of student anxiety
- Code yellow and red drills in grades as low as kindergarten
- YouTube videos with explicit content
- Loss of family members due to gang violence or health issues, particularly post-COVID
- Political tension
- The constant news cycle amplifying problems in communities and across the globe
- Parent or caregiver stress, overwhelm, or anxiety absorbed by the child

Yes, teachers want to save the world. That's just the type of personality many of us have. But it's not our responsibility to take all of this on. It's important that we lean on the expertise of social workers and school counselors when needed, for a couple of reasons:

- School counselors and social workers not only have professional training in mental health counseling but have many connections to outside resources that the student or family may need. It's actually a disservice to our students not to use them for support when appropriate.
- It is our job as teachers to give students the most appropriate social and mental support. If a student talks to you about something that is a more serious issue, you can simply say, "Do you mind if I talk to somebody about this issue that can help you a little more?" This way you won't lose trust with the student that confided in you and you can get them more support.

You can only handle so much mentally and emotionally. (See Best Practice #55 for information on secondary trauma and compassion fatigue.) There is a lot required of you every day, and the teacher burnout rate is growing. We need to empower teachers to advocate for the support they need to serve all students. So when is it appropriate to ask a social worker or school counselor to help support a student?

- A student confides in you about a social media or in-person bullying issue.

- You have a feeling the student isn't getting proper nutrition or basic resources in their house.

- You find out about any sort of abuse or suspect abuse. For example, if the student regularly comes to school with bruises.

- A student is crying in your class and doesn't want to talk about it. You might just quickly call or check in with the counselor.

- You note an extreme change in behavior from a student that lasts more than a few days. This could indicate something serious is happening in their family or personal life.

- A student is constantly and consistently late or chronically absent, and your phone calls home aren't making a difference. This is especially important in elementary and middle school where caretakers and parents are usually responsible for getting students to school on time. There might be a bigger issue there.

- A student has a close family member or friend get sick or die. You will want to let the school counselor know that this has happened. This is a big one.

Your Turn

1. Have you ever asked a school counselor or social worker for support? If you have, did you do so because you felt they could help the student with more resources than you had access to as a teacher?

   _____
   _____
   _____
   _____
   _____
   _____
   _____
   _____
   _____
   _____

2. Have you ever taken on too much or suffered from a hero complex? (I have.) Why did you do this, and how did it affect your teaching?

   _____
   _____
   _____
   _____
   _____
   _____
   _____
   _____
   _____
   _____

Find a Mentor

Luckily, I never had to find a mentor because my mentor found me. In my third year of teaching, our school psychologist was looking for a classroom to coteach in to gather research for her dissertation. I was approached with the idea and was immediately self-conscious about someone else being in my classroom. I first wondered why I was chosen (Did I need the help? Was there something wrong with the way I was teaching?). Then I became territorial because of all of the hard work I had already dedicated to my class. I had a rhythm that I did not want to break.

To say our first meeting was a train wreck would be an understatement. I was my stubborn self, not wanting any help I didn't ask for, and our school psychologist was frustrated. Little did I know that the woman who I thought was trying to barge into my classroom would be my mentor for many years after. The engagement and smiles she brought to the class were a sight to be seen. The secret to choosing the most beneficial mentor is that they have to be better than you at teaching. I learned I needed her in my life to become a better teacher.

As teachers, we can acknowledge that the most powerful learning for students is one-on-one instruction. This works the same for teacher education. If you want to learn fast, I suggest you find your teaching "guru." Whom you choose as your guru is a very personal decision. The issue is that many teachers don't have the time to sit down and teach another person.

Here's what you can do: Find the teachers that you want to be like one day—shoot for the stars. If you could be the teacher of your dreams, who would you emulate? Now watch them. Visit their classroom and take notes. Listen to how they speak with students. Be vulnerable enough to ask for their advice when needed. Ask if you may have a copy of their lesson plan to try out with your students. Learn how they think.

Depending on how willing they are to help you on your teacher journey, they might sit down with you and go over your plans each week. Make the time to learn from them. Although I had one significant mentor in my life who guided me in my first few years of teaching, each year I choose a different person to learn from. Whom I choose depends on where I am in my career.

I remember one day watching my mentor teach a group of eighth graders. She gathered all of the students to take notes and introduced a concept as they were sitting in a close circle around her. She had their full attention. But instead of standing, she sat at their level in a chair or sometimes even on the floor. This had an amazing effect on the students. They were calm and focused. They didn't feel threatened or talked down to. They were learning with the teacher. I used this strategy with my classes. With a few classes, I even had the students sitting on chairs while I sat cross-legged on the floor while teaching. This method seemed to calm my students while also empowering them. This also gives the teacher the chance to relate to students on their level. I've observed identical results with every group of students I've taught in that manner.

Imitating a few key tactics from your mentor will draw you out of your comfort zone or give you new ideas and stretch you to become the teacher you want to be. Eventually you will incorporate these techniques in future lessons without their help, but in the meantime learning directly from someone else will push you to where you need to be.

I learned from my guru for three entire years before I felt I could work on my own at the level I wanted to teach. Although I did not need her as much anymore, I still e-mailed her from time to time with a question or two. The secret was that I never called her "my mentor." That's a lot of pressure for somebody. I'm sure she knew that she was filling that role, but because I never called her a mentor, we formed a friendship out of choice rather than obligation. I've been told that the word *mentor* scares people because it suggests that they will have to put a lot of obligatory time and energy into you.

Good luck finding the teacher of your dreams and emulating them! You'll find you will not need them one day and will blossom into your fullest self as a teacher, but you will appreciate and grow from their help in the beginning. And one day *you* will become somebody's mentor.

Your Turn

1. Think of a teacher in your life whom you admire. What is it about their teaching that appeals to you? Do you see these qualities in yourself?

   _____
   _____
   _____
   _____
   _____
   _____
   _____
   _____
   _____

2. How can you learn from them without taking up large amounts of your or their precious time?

   _____
   _____
   _____
   _____
   _____
   _____
   _____
   _____
   _____

Watch and Learn

I have always been a visual learner. I learn most effectively by seeing something done rather than having it explained to me or reading about it. To improve as a teacher, I had to *see* better teaching. During my second year of teaching, our school did not have an observation program. This didn't stop me. I would walk up and down the hallways and basically spy on other classes. I wanted to see which teachers I could learn from.

When I found a style I liked, or an appealing way a teacher spoke, or a teacher with a grace about them, or, most importantly, a classroom full of engaged students, I would ask that teacher if I could come and observe them work. I said I wanted to learn from them because I really admired their teaching style and noticed their students were engaged. This empowered the other teacher; everybody enjoys a compliment.

Always ask for permission first; very few teachers will say no, and quite honestly, you probably do not want to learn from that person if they do. Let the teacher know you've heard great things about their teaching and that you would like to come by one period to observe. This will give you an immediate positive rapport with another adult and should give you an open door into that classroom. Sit in on a class or two, take notes, and try the same moves in your classroom.

It's especially powerful to watch a class that the teacher has trouble with as well as one they brag about. This will give you a well-rounded idea of the teacher as a whole and give you ideas on how to improve your classroom engagement and instruction style if needed.

Your Turn

1. How often have you taken the time to watch another teacher you admire in the past few months? If you have not done this, when is a specific time you could watch another teacher? How will you make this happen?

   _____
   _____
   _____
   _____
   _____
   _____
   _____
   _____
   _____
   _____

2. What did you learn from watching that teacher? Can you name one or two specifics that you can use to improve your teaching?

   _____
   _____
   _____
   _____
   _____
   _____
   _____
   _____

Listen With Your Mind

> We have two ears and one mouth so that we can listen twice as much as we speak
>
> —Epictetus

Teachers are notorious for being the worst audience. We just are. We are avid learners, but we do a lot of talking about what we already do in the classroom. I'm guilty. Hey, it's not our fault; we are used to having a captive audience every day. We love to talk, tell stories, and feed others with our knowledge. It is the reason many entered this noble profession. However, when it comes to becoming a better instructor, you need to hold back and listen when conversing with other teachers.

Nine times out of ten, if you're sitting at a table of educators, I can tell you what is going on. Let's see. Each teacher tells a story about a student, a lesson, what went well, what was humorous, and what completely flopped. Listen to what they did well and what worked. Sitting with a group of teachers reminds me sometimes of sitting with my ninety-three-year-old grandfather and his friends telling war stories or stories of their grandchildren. Oh, how their faces light up as they talk about themselves, similar to how a teacher's face lights up as they talk about their class.

Work to listen to these stories of students, tactics, and tricks. Listen during lunch, before and after meetings, and during hallway conversation. Take mental notes. Listen with your mind. We have to remember to think, *How can I use what I am hearing, or how should I not use what I am hearing?* I'm not saying to whip out a notepad and take notes during casual conversation, although that would be humorous. What could you use from these stories in your own classroom? What do you never want to do? Is a teacher talking about something the students loved? Try it. Ask questions and get more specifics. This is free, fast, and real knowledge being given to you. Take it and use it.

Your Turn

1. Think of the last time you had a conversation with another teacher about their classroom. Jot down what the conversation was about.

   _____
   _____
   _____
   _____
   _____
   _____

2. Did you use that conversation to listen with your mind? What could you have done differently to turn the conversation into a learning experience for you?

   _____
   _____
   _____
   _____
   _____
   _____

3. When was the last time you learned something valuable and transferable to your classroom from talking to another teacher? What did you learn?

   _____
   _____
   _____
   _____
   _____
   _____

Earn the Respect of Administrators

This section is one of the longest in the book because it's one of the most important. You have the power to make your administration or school leadership team your best friends or your worst enemies. They can be your biggest help or your biggest obstacle. Your relationship with your administration will directly affect your job satisfaction.

The happiest teachers usually have a great relationship with their administration and feel supported. Honestly, I've been on both sides. I'll say my teaching life was one hundred times more pleasant and easier when my school leadership was on my side. When I worked in charter schools, I had to stay friendly with administration to succeed (and I was lucky to have supportive administration, so this was natural). I did not have a union and actually preferred it that way. When I worked for public schools, I still found that administration wanted to be invited into the classroom, even though your job in public school is not based on merit-based hiring/firing. It's powerful for the kids to have administration supporting what they are doing and learning.

> ### Tips for Earning the Respect of the Administration
>
> - Invite administrators to student presentations; let them see your students at their best.
> - Stay on a positive note with students as well as their parents.
>
> *(Continued)*

(Continued)

- Lead an extracurricular group or club.
- Coach a sports team.
- Invite administration to your room to participate in an engaging learning activity (more details below).
- Give thank-you cards to administration at the end of every school year.
- Show up to work consistently and on time. Respect the work year calendar.
- Host parent nights and other events that include caregivers in your classroom.
- Speak about your students respectfully (administration will hear your tone).

When we teach, we're a part of the web of communication that makes up a school. Often, due to lack of time, our interactions with our administrators are a quick "Hey, how are you?" "Great, thanks" in passing on the way to the restroom or to the office to check our mailbox. Often administrators want to know about the great things going on in our classroom, but we just never get the time or opportunity to tell them. We have to remember that administrators know more about us than we think they do. They hear students talk about us, they overhear teacher conversations, and they have conversations with parents and caregivers. And you'd be surprised how much an administrator can learn about a teacher just by walking past their room a few times a day.

There are times during the year that we may need some support, and, frankly, even some "favors" from administration. I remember a time when I needed a form signed faster than the system would allow. A few of my colleagues and I were doing a ninth-grade, problem-based, interdisciplinary unit around endangered species. This unit was spectacular. Students chose an endangered species in their science class, developed and researched questions in their English class, and researched what the world was currently doing to try to stop that species from going extinct and explained why these efforts might not be working. The students then composed a presentation and proposed a novel solution to save the species. They actually built a geometric biome in their geometry class. Our physical education teachers also got on board and did team-building games around the different species. The students then presented as an entire ninth-grade team in the auditorium to each other. We even had two students who were talented dancers kick off the presentation with an expressive dance with powerful music and a slideshow playing.

During one of our planning sessions, one of our teachers mentioned they'd heard that the local zoo had free tickets for students on field trips.

This was perfect! The problem was that we needed to arrange transportation, and fast. Taking an entire grade level on a field trip takes a lot of work and time, and we only had about a day to make it happen. Getting bus transportation required many forms, signatures, and e-mails, each of which could take a day or two to get. We were stuck in "the system."

It may feel that administrators sit in the office all day making phone calls, taking extended lunches, and joking with their colleagues while sipping espressos. Although a part of me does think they do that just once in a while, many times they are actually dealing with scheduling, policies, and regulations that affect the school at large, as well as financial issues, very angry parents, extreme discipline issues, and budget constraints (just to name a few). The truth is that they *do* care, but they're a little removed from the everyday successes that we are fortunate enough to see as teachers. In all honesty, they miss it a little. Remember, most administrators started out as teachers.

So, here's my point. To navigate your way around the system and "cash in" your favor points when seeking to get around systematic roadblocks, you have to start building a positive relationship with administrators early. I had a lot of points in my bag I had been saving up for years. You will too. Here is my best advice to earn those points:

- **Your students speak louder than you do.** Let's say your students do a really impressive project or problem-based learning unit. This usually happens around the middle to the end of the year. Usually at the end of a project there is a day when the students show off what they have done. Perhaps it's a gallery walk, or a group presentation, or a demonstration. On the day you have your presentations and students show off their work, do you ever invite administration in?

    When I do this, I usually have the class vote to see if they want visitors. (They'll always say yes if they're proud of their work.) You may need to talk the class into this with your best "salesperson" skills, but once the class votes to have administration invited, they will work twice as hard on their projects. I have someone in the class with really nice handwriting compose the invitations. Next, instead of asking administration yourself, choose two to four students from each class who are outspoken and really proud of their projects to hand-deliver the invitations.

    It's extra helpful if you can include a student who is constantly in trouble as one of the deliverers of the invitation. Remember: Students who often get into trouble for talking at inappropriate times usually have advanced interpersonal and people skills. Use this strength and choose this student to be one of the ones to deliver the invitations. Coach them on what to say and what to do if they see the administrator talking to another teacher. Have them practice with you a few times. This is also teaching social-emotional skills they can use in life. There are a couple of reasons it's good to do this:

- Selecting this student as one of the class representatives to deliver the invitations will help build self-esteem and a positive self-image for this student. This could lead to stronger self-management and motivation in your class for the rest of the year. Hopefully, this positive self-image will also spread to other parts of their life. When these students know the whole class is waiting for them to get the invitations delivered, they will not goof around. Trust me.
- Administration wants to see these students succeed. You are showing administration that you are reaching the "unreachable" students in your classroom. In turn, you are indirectly advocating for yourself in a very loud way without having to say a word.

I usually also send an e-mail to administration explaining what they will be seeing, how it is linked to the standards, what we did to lead up to the learning, what the unit was about, etc. In other words, I send them the "adult talk." Having administration show up and be impressed with your students is really powerful for the students.

▶ **Student-led displays of learning at the end of a project.** It's especially powerful if you can have administration see a student-led display of learning. This shows you can empower students. This includes but is not limited to the following:

- Student greeters at the door (especially if parents are also coming). Teach them how to stand, what to say, how to smile, etc.
- Student seaters (if visitors are to sit).
- Students opening words/closing words (if it is a performance).
- Student translators (if many of the parents speak a language other than English) in opening and closing. Have the student translators practice the translation before the day of or consider having two students translate together.
- If you have an ASL program at your school, consider also having a student sign the opening and closing.

Around my fifth year of teaching, I managed to have displays of learning where I could sit back and just watch. I purposely sat a row or two behind the students so they could feel that I trusted them and they were independent. The students did everything. If you can work up to this in your first few years of teaching, administration will notice, and, most importantly, your students will see how much you believe in them to let them lead.

They will notice the smiles and feel like their work was worth watching. Usually, after administration comes, students like to share out with each other the reactions of each administrator. "Did you see how Dr. Gary was smiling ear to ear!? He even said to me . . ." They'll have stories like this.

Administrators often have last-minute meetings and obligations, so it's always a gamble whether or not they can make it. Let your students know this. However, even if administrators can't attend the presentation, in their minds you are already the teacher who inspired that student who constantly gets into trouble. Also, they are able to gauge the level of excitement in the students' voices during the brief interaction with the invitation delivery. Last, you taught students how to code switch and formally interact with adults, which is an important life skill. Administration will start to notice you and might just remember how excited your students were for their project when you find yourself stuck in the system and need a form signed fast. Students can advocate for our classroom much better than we can.

- **Thank-you cards.** You always want to stay on good terms with people who hold the system in place. Give your administrators, department head, administrative assistants, school nurse, and custodians a handwritten thank-you letter around holiday time or at the end of every school year. These are people who help make your classroom happen. A thank-you card is a simple and quick way to acknowledge this. You could also write an e-mail, but a thank-you note is timeless and appreciated.

- **Be proactive.** My mentor once told me that having a supportive administration is almost if not more important than the type of students you have at a school. Some of the lowest-performing schools have some of the happiest teachers due to administrative support. Being proactive is the most effective way to find a supportive administration. With social media today it's all too easy to find someone who knows someone who works at a district or school you are interested in. Try your hardest to get a chance to chat with them on the phone. Ask about administrative support specifically. If you can find two people who work for a particular district or school, even better. See if their answers are consistent. LinkedIn is a great way to find a connection in a school district. You can also use Facebook or other social media tools to ask.

The fact is, in my experience, if people know what you're doing in the classroom, and like what you're doing in the classroom, and see that you're making an effort, the system is easier to work within. People may do things for you faster—if even just a bit faster.

I'm not saying that having a bank of points was the only reason I was able to get the field trip documents signed by all of the required parties in just a fraction of the time it should have taken, but I think it helped. Administration knew if I was asking for something, it would benefit the kids greatly because they had seen my work in the classroom and trusted my intentions. Save up your points; you'll need them one day.

Your Turn

1. How does your administration support you?

   _____
   _____
   _____
   _____
   _____
   _____

2. How could you use the support of your administration to benefit the learning in your classroom?

   _____
   _____
   _____
   _____
   _____
   _____

3. Think of your next class project. Could you invite any of your administration to participate in the presentations? How could this benefit the students?

   _____
   _____
   _____
   _____
   _____
   _____

Real Conversation With Eighth-Grade Students

I only had a few minutes to do grades for the week, and I was desperately trying to save some time. I called all the students up to my desk who had earned an A that week. All ten stellar students gathered around with their eyes wide and ears perked. I wanted to whisper so the others didn't hear and get jealous. I lowered my head and a sly grin spread across my face.

Me: You *all* have *As*. [I smile.]

Student standing closest to me: What? We all have AIDS?!

[All other students look up; confusion and some panic starts.]

Me: No, I said *As, As*!

PART 5

SPINS THAT WILL WOW YOUR STUDENTS

We Don't All Have to Be Magicians

I remember way back in my sophomore year of high school I had a really great substitute teacher, Mr. Lombard. He liked to open the class with magic tricks before Spanish class. There was one trick where he had a ghost made of tissue paper and he made it disappear into a cloud of smoke. My Spanish teacher was out on maternity leave pretty early for the first half of the school year, so we had him for a couple of weeks. It was awesome!

—Derik, Age 34

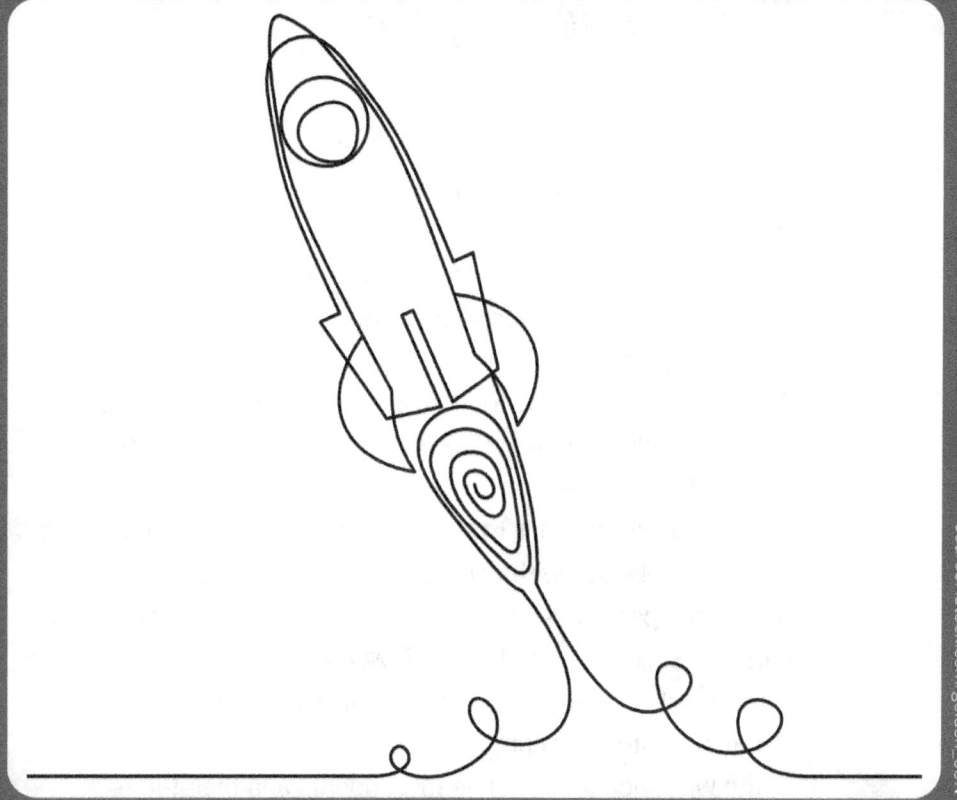

What do spins that set you apart have to do with classroom management?

How do you want your students to remember you? Depending on what grade you teach, by the time the students have you as a teacher, they may have seen it all. They've had strict teachers, they've had fun teachers, they've had boring teachers, and they've had passionate teachers. But they haven't had one type of teacher just yet: you.

We certainly do not need to do magic tricks before every class to make an impression, but if we're moonlighting magicians, we should bring that into the classroom to set us apart. Part 5 contains a few ideas you can use to stand out. These are types of ways to stand out that kids recognize and appreciate, which can mean students enjoy their time in your classroom more and remain engaged and active learners. This can also mean classroom management becomes a bit smoother.

I REMEMBER WHEN...

I remember when I came across a "Dear Abby" column where a reader told the story of running into an honor student working in a grocery store over the summer. Attempting to ring up gravy packages on sale four for a dollar, the student proceeded to charge each packet at forty-four cents, commenting, "That's four for a dollar, right?"

As an educator in my tenth year of teaching, the need for practical application resonated with me. Too often, my students could solve a problem on a worksheet or in a classroom setting but not transfer the skill to real-world application. This need was even more obvious with my group of third to fifth graders in a self-contained special education class in rural Lumber Bridge, North Carolina. Society seems to have lowered expectations for students with disabilities who are also economically disadvantaged, even if out of sympathy and compassion.

But why should this define my students and their future? I frequently submit grant requests for field trips or guest speakers to allow us to maximize opportunities to transfer skills. In 2014 we obtained a class pet from Pets in the Classroom. Striving to maximize this learning opportunity, I e-mailed a local vet who came to answer questions and discuss proper handling of and care for our hamster. We also reached out to a college, hoping that a vet-tech student could come speak to the class. They responded, noting that they could send a "VP of Academic Affairs in the Department of Animal Science." As I shared the e-mail aloud and explained that a VP is a vice president, a student's eyes grew wide and his hand shot into the air. He asked, "Ms. Kellermann, did you just say the *president* is coming?" His peer quickly followed with, "Oh, I know him, that's Barak Obama." Who knew that a tiny hamster could inspire dialogue beyond pet care!? This pint-sized pet led us to a wealth of questions and thinking.

Years later, while completing a short-term Distinguished Awards in Teaching Fulbright fellowship in Botswana, Africa, during the summer of 2017, I was reminded yet again of how integral it is for students to see and apply lessons beyond the four walls of the classroom. My students, a group of young adults between the ages of eighteen and twenty-four, could count *thebe* and *pula* (Botswana currency), yet their understanding was fully realized only once we incorporated these lessons into a training program where they sold oranges from a roadside stand. Now, money had meaning attached to it—a purpose, an exchange of goods, and a renewed motivation.

A phenomenal teacher can devise a new idea to implement, but sometimes having a different voice deliver it brings novelty to the situation. Make an effort to extend learning beyond the classroom by inviting in guest speakers. They can be found anywhere—from professionals at local churches to business owners of local establishments. Let them speak to successes and failures. Let them share the challenges to be overcome and the rewards that come from success or failure. Let students see the inner workings that turn childhood passions into employment realities. People love what they do and are willing to share it to inspire others if we step outside our normal routines and *wow* our students.

Jessica Kellermann
11 years' experience
Fulbright Scholar
Special Education Teacher
Raeford, North Carolina

Host Guest Speakers

To a beginning teacher, having a guest speaker in the classroom may seem like a nightmare waiting to happen. *What if the kids aren't good? What if they say something embarrassing? What if Johnny is having a bad day again?* I completely get it. My second year teaching, my neighboring math teacher invited a guest speaker into his classroom. We had the same group of students. When he told me he was bringing in a guest speaker to talk about a career path they could take, I admired his courage. Our class was, to put it politely, challenging. He seemed excited and beamed as he was telling me about the speaker. After the event, he came to me furious at the students. He told me they had been unengaged and rude, and one student had even thrown a paper ball across the room. That scared me away from guest speakers for a while, until I figured out how to do it.

To be honest, I was lucky to get some help in the beginning from another teacher. She taught me that having a guest speaker can be one of the most powerful learning experiences if you carefully plan, know how to engage the students, and stimulate interaction between the students and the speaker. She showed me that if you choose guest speakers who can add to what your students are currently learning or provide a different perspective, and if you can get the students excited about the guest, it makes all the difference. She gave me the courage to try one, which soon turned into many. The results were amazing and I've been hooked ever since. I can give you a few pointers, but each guest speaker brings a different experience.

I'm going to share my guest speaker success stories. I've never had an unpleasant experience, and all have exceeded my expectations. Here are some guests we've had in the classroom over the years who helped bring our units to life:

- civil rights panel
- career interview panel
- retired judge
- Holocaust Auschwitz survivor (via Skype)
- potential astronaut
- musical therapist
- art therapist
- family doctor

We also invited a unique guest speaker to physically come in during a unit when we were reading *Night* by Elie Wiesel. She was the wife of a deceased German soldier. At first, my class was very against me inviting her. A few of the students booed after I explained who she was. I spoke (not lectured) about what she might be feeling and how she had been a little timid to tell me her background. (There's contextualized social-emotional learning here where empathy is quickly taught and practiced.) We discussed our different opinions about whether her story was worth hearing. I asked them, in a calm voice, to put themselves in her shoes. They listened.

Our guest speaker was elderly and frightened. Her daughter wrote me an e-mail and told me her mother was having second thoughts about coming in. Her story was so personal to her, and she was scared about the reaction of the class, considering the book they were reading. She was afraid nobody would want to hear her story or understand it—or worse, that the students would have an adverse reaction. I could feel her about to back out. I shared this with my classroom. We had a class discussion about what to do. A student suggested we reach out to her. We decided to send her a huge poster sign detailing how excited we were to meet her and have her come in and speak. The students wrote her quick letters about how much they wanted to hear what she had to say.

This was a game-changer. After she got the poster and letters, her daughter e-mailed me and said that the letters were now hanging above her ninety-year-old mother's bed. According to the daughter, her mother said she now felt like somebody wanted to hear her story. I read the response to my class and printed out the e-mail and hung it on the wall. The students got more and more excited as the day of our guest speaker approached.

In a room filled with 125 inner-city eighth graders, you could have heard a pin drop as this woman in a wheelchair told her story. She spoke about the love she had for her father and what she remembered from her youth. I had my students write their questions first on a sticky note and hand it to me. I wouldn't normally do this, but because of the fragility of the speaker and the emotional vulnerability of her topic, I wanted to look at the questions first. Otherwise, I urge you to let your students ask their own questions. The main purpose of this guest speaker was to show the students that in the world there will be conflicts where people on both sides of an issue think they are doing the right thing. It's important to listen to what people have to say, because everybody has a story worth hearing.

Tips for Hosting Guest Speakers

- **Prepare the students to welcome the guest speaker.** For the lady above, I did some background work with my class, and we constructed a graphic organizer relevant to this guest speaker. I also talked a bit about empathy and how the guest speaker must be feeling coming in after our class had just read a book about the Holocaust and knew she had been married to a German soldier.

  If available, we read articles on the people coming in (students had to annotate the articles). The students knew exactly who the speakers were. We also hung pictures of them up in class so the students could put a face with a name and feel empowered when the guests arrived.

- **Share the story.** Be completely honest with your classroom about the conversation you had with person about coming in. Let them know how it happened. I show the actual e-mails on my document camera, describe the conversations, and play the voicemails. The students love hearing that people want to come in and speak to them. This also lets them know that you are talking about them to people in your life. If there is an e-mail chain going back and forth, I show the whole chain. We talk about how the person must be feeling about coming in, and how we should prepare. This teaches emotional intelligence to our students. It's real. We have a great time looking at the correspondence, and they can see the process used to get someone to come in.

- **Be just a little more excited than your students.** They may not get it at first, but they will. If they're not excited, they most likely just don't understand the full picture. Explain it to them. When we first started to write thank-you letters to speakers who had come in, the reaction I got was, "They'll probably just throw them away."

  "They won't," I replied. "I think they'll at least hang them on the bulletin board in their snack room. Adults love that stuff."

  "Yeah, that'd be cool," the kids replied. And they kept writing. I was just a little more excited than they were.

- **Send a letter or card to the guest speaker telling them how excited the students are to meet them.** This will help the speaker if they are anxious and will help them understand where the students are coming from. Teenagers can be scary to speakers! The speaker will come in feeling more warm toward the students.

- **Prepare your students mentally and behaviorally.** I will not discipline my students in front of a guest speaker. I let them know verbally that I will not discipline them and that I trust they'll present themselves respectfully. I want to empower them so they have as much interaction as possible with the guest speaker. I prepare them for how to greet the speaker, how formal to be, how to address them, and how to ask a question. I also advise on how body language can send different signals, what they can ask, what they probably should not ask, and what to do if the speaker gets too nervous. We have a conversation beforehand where students ask me what they really want to know, and I talk to them about how those questions may make the speaker feel. Usually I let them go for it if the questions are worded tastefully (I usually have to change the wording) and do not make the guest feel uncomfortable. These are powerful moments.

- **Trust your students to take ownership.** The students see me taking myself out of the equation and they understand that I trust them. We prepare about two weeks in advance. If you set expectations, do not threaten, and do a great job letting the students know why the speaker wants to come in, the kids will rise to the occasion. Every speaker I've had in my classroom has had a powerful experience. And what's more, the students took ownership. I never have my students come in and just take notes. They can do that with a video. If there's a live person in the room, it's essential to teach them how to interact with that person and how to ask the right questions. That is when the learning happens.

Your Turn

1. How can you prepare your students for guest speakers in the classroom?

2. What message does inviting guest speakers into the classroom send to your students?

3. What is the importance of having guest speakers in your classroom?

Know That Students Are Ready to Have Power and Voice

> In this class we share our thoughts, comments, opinions because we *all* have something important to say.
>
> —Sara, Grade 8

One of the most difficult skills for teachers to master is how to give students power and still maintain control of the classroom. Giving students power goes against our natural instinct as a teacher, but it is rich in benefits. This is especially important today, when we see young adults stepping up in activist roles, becoming voting members of society, and working to fix the problems that they have inherited. Creating active and involved students and giving them power and a voice can start in our classrooms.

This video shows how to give students power and a voice throughout a lesson.

Tips for Giving Students Power (and Still Keeping Control)

- **Give students a structured forum to converse with one another and be a strong facilitator.**

(Continued)

(Continued)

> **Example:** Post around the room sentence starters for discourse (to agree or respectfully disagree) visible at all times for students to use in class or group academic conversations. Examples of sentence starters could be, "I hear what you are saying, but I respectfully disagree because. . . ." or, "I like what you said about . . . , but have you considered . . . ?"
>
> **Nonexample:** Scold students for disagreeing heatedly in academic discourse without offering redirection.
>
> - **Allow students to vote on decisions that do not impede learning.** Keep in mind that sometimes you *do* know best.
>
> **Example:** A vote on whether you have a class lead librarian or everyone helps manage the class library.
>
> **Nonexample:** A vote on whether or not students can walk out of the classroom at their own leisure. (This is probably a safety issue, so you need to make the decision on this one.)
>
> - **Incorporate student choice into your lessons.**
>
> **Example:** Students get to choose their own group leaders within their groups, or students get to choose which short story they want to write an essay about from a choice of four stories.
>
> **Nonexample:** Students choose which students work in the group to finish a task and which do not.
>
> - **Have student leaders in activities.**
>
> **Example:** Have a student keep score during a class activity.
>
> **Nonexample:** Let one student boss around an entire group.
>
> - **Use students as teachers in small groups.**
>
> **Example:** Use the student who scored highest on a test to reteach a concept to a small group of students who did not do well on the same test.
>
> **Nonexample**: Use the loudest student, who may or may not fully understand the concept, as the group leader only because other students listen to them.
>
> - **Let students voice their opinion.** Make sure the squeaky wheels don't have the loudest voice. Let them know there is a time and a place for opinions to be expressed.
>
> **Example:** Allow a student to ask you to slow down if you are teaching too fast for them to learn. Thank them for expressing their learning needs.
>
> **Nonexample:** Allow a class venting session where students all complain about why they shouldn't have to learn a concept. Beware of

classroom mob mentality. If this happens, tell them you are sorry they are unhappy but they need to understand this concept.

- **Do projects where students can set their own pacing.** Check in often and make sure to help the struggling students so they feel successful as well.

    Example: Assign a project where the students create a timeline of when they will have each part of the project completed.

    Nonexample: Allow students to not do work for one week and rush to finish the project at the last minute. This does not teach time management.

Your Turn

1. Discuss a time when either you or a teacher you observed incorporated student choice into a lesson. What did this look like, and how did it affect student engagement?

   _____
   _____
   _____
   _____
   _____
   _____

2. How and when can you give students opportunities to set and monitor their own pacing with a larger assignment or project? How do you monitor students who fall behind or work too quickly? What life skill does this teach students?

   _____
   _____
   _____
   _____
   _____
   _____

3. What are your thoughts on class votes? How would this look in a class? Share an example of when a class vote could be helpful. What message does allowing class votes send to the students?

   _____
   _____
   _____
   _____
   _____
   _____

Show Your Students You Care

> You have been the most caring teacher that I have ever had. I have learned a lot in your class, not just about English but about people.
>
> —Luis, Grade 9

One of the most common complaints students have about a teacher is "My teacher doesn't like me." Sounds childish, right? Guess what? Most students are still children. I hear this complaint from middle school students and high school students just as often as from those in lower grades. Think about it. We adults do this too. Think back to your favorite teacher. I am sure you had a strong sense that they enjoyed your company as a human being. Think back to your least favorite teacher. I'm sure you felt disrespected, ignored, or just not liked. My mentor once told me, "Students remember how they felt in your class, not so much what you did."

How do your students feel in your class? Happy? Loved? Scared to mess up? Talked down to? Silenced? Heard? Constantly yelled at? Like a disappointment? Like the smartest students in the world? Don't just tell them you care; *show* them.

Tips for Showing Your Students That You Care About Them

- **Prepare materials for success.** Have tissues and supplies ready to set them up for success. Show them that you are doing

(Continued)

(Continued)

everything on your end to help them, and you also care if their nose runs.

- **Talk to students.** New teachers almost always talk *at* the class. Experienced teachers talk *to* the students. Listen to the difference.

- **Be firm and caring.** These two characteristics cannot be mutually exclusive. One does not work without the other. If you are too firm, it may seem that you want them to fail. If you are too lenient, they may feel you do not care enough to push them.

  I recommend you make exceptions for some students, privately. Tell them you are making the exception for them specifically. Think of the police officer that pulls you over when you were obviously speeding. You plead your case, and he listens and makes an exception. Would you run and tell the DMV how nice the police officer was? Probably not, but you would like that officer. You would see him as empathetic and having a heart. He most likely told you he was going to "let you go with a warning this time." Do the same with a few of your students *once in a while, and privately.* Give secret extensions. Give a student in need a notebook if he loses his. If you do this, that student will love you! Make sure you use this tool very sparingly. Tell the student that you are making an exception because you want to see him succeed, and do not let the other students see or you will have a battle on your hands. Care enough to do what the child needs.

- **Give returning students a few minutes.** When the students come back from a break or long weekend, give them a few minutes to catch up with their friends. They are going to do it regardless, so why not structure it? I usually set a timer for four minutes and thirty-five seconds or some odd number like that (just to let them know I am controlling the structure), and I tell them to ask each other how they spent their holiday break. Sometimes they roll their eyes and say, "Wow, thanks." I then admit that it's not a lot of time and jokingly add on another second. That usually gets a laugh. Most times I'll set it up like this:

  Teacher: I think I'd like to give you five minutes to talk to your tables about your break. Do you think you'll be able to refocus on the learning today if I give you that time?

  Class will always say yes.

  Teacher: Let's do this. Tell me right now. If you think you're going to have trouble refocusing after I give you five minutes, could you raise your hand? You're not in trouble, I just need to know who may need a little extra help. [said with a smile]

  Almost always, a student or two will raise their hands. Basically, they don't want to let the class down so they're revealing themselves.

Teacher: Okay, great. I will be sure to help you out a bit. Thanks for letting me know. Okay, here we go!

Start the timer, project it, and let the kids talk about their break and catch up without a prompt. Just give them time to get it out, share, and connect. More often than not, students won't start talking right away, and some might go on their cell phones instead. You can simply say (with a smile on your face), "Oh no! I don't hear enough talking. I guess you don't need this time?" Kids will almost always start talking immediately, some even dramatically loud because they appreciate the humor in how you said that. Giving them an opportunity to talk to each other also creates a community of friends, which leads to a community of learners. How often do students get to talk and create friendships during class?

You can talk to them, too, if you like, at their desks. Look out for students sitting alone and not talking to anybody. When you see this, discreetly ask a kind student in the class to go over and ask them about their break. This is a great opportunity to help students feel like they belong.

It's a good idea to project the time on the document camera so students can see how much time they have to talk, and also in case a supervisor walks in and wonders what is going on. Since you are structuring the talk time, you can get right back into learning after the five minutes. And letting the kids socialize will earn you lots of respect. When you stop the timer, the students should be back in their seats and extra ready for you since you did them a favor.

When you let kids catch up, you're building a healthy community where students are getting to know one another in an unstructured setting and "unclogging" anything they just have to get out of their brains so they can fit learning in. Also, they will most likely laugh a bit, so they will be lowering their affective filters before they learn. It will benefit their learning in many ways. Now you can enjoy your Day 1 of more focused learning after a break. It works. It will seem like you have given them a gift, and your lesson will be much easier.

- **Let students know when they do a good job.** It's that simple. Chances are, unless they have spectacular parents, they already hear all about how they need to do better, be more like their more responsible sibling, or study harder. Compliment them when they do a good job, act in a pleasant way, do well on a test, are kind to a classmate, or answer a question using critical thinking. Students will perform more for you when you recognize their strengths. Start small if you have to. Even if you simply compliment somebody's handwriting, you'll be surprised what effect that can have.

Remember: If you are waiting for students to fail, they will fail. If you are recognizing their strengths, you are helping them succeed. Point out what students do right, not just what they do wrong. They already get enough criticism.

It's easy to show you care when the student is likeable. However, what do you do with those students who just get under your skin and push your buttons? You have to see their *strengths*. Breathe, and think about the students' strengths. This is your job. Learn to respect every student.

Your Turn

1. How do you *show* your students that you care?

   _____
   _____
   _____
   _____
   _____
   _____
   _____
   _____

2. Do your words and your actions match?

   _____
   _____
   _____
   _____
   _____
   _____
   _____
   _____

3. Is there a student in your classroom that may feel like you don't like them as a person? How can you change this in an authentic way?

   _____
   _____
   _____
   _____
   _____
   _____
   _____
   _____

Laugh Together, Learn Together

....

This is the funniest class I've ever been in.

—Jayden, Grade 8

Laughter can be effectively used in a classroom to increase learning as well as build relationships.

I remember one particular time during my second year of teaching when the entire class laughed. I was disciplining the class, big surprise, and suddenly the whole class burst out in laughter. There were all looking right at me. I turned red and asked why they were laughing, and then I tried to get them to stop. This moment may be a teacher's biggest nightmare.

One empathetic student pulled a hand mirror out of her backpack and let me see what was causing the hysterics. I had somehow rubbed blue marker from my hand onto my nose. Rudolph the Blue-Nosed Reindeer was trying to scold them! Most eventually stopped laughing because they felt so bad for me, but some still kept giggling. I can only imagine how silly I looked with my stern face, disciplining the rowdy class with a bright blue nose. This is the only laughter I remember hearing in my classroom that year.

Now I laugh with my classes on a daily basis. My students say my laugh sounds like a dolphin. It actually does.

Do your students know what your laugh sounds like?

Usually, it's at the beginning of class (for about two minutes) when I let students share any good news or interesting stories, such as Black Friday shopping stories, crazy things their younger brothers and sisters did that weekend, or just funny things they've noticed around school. One time when I asked the class about their weekend, an eighth-grade student shared that her uncle had hired a clown to come scare her mom as a practical joke. The clown came prancing into her house, and her mom apparently got so scared she literally passed out. I asked immediately if the mother was okay (she was). Needless to say, that story left me with a million questions and gave the students and myself a good laugh.

Laughter breaks down barriers, brings people together, and relieves anxiety and stress. Laughing makes students feel safe and helps shy students lose their fear. People don't laugh when they're stressed or anxious. I know if we're laughing, we're relaxed and ready to learn. We laugh now as a class for a specific purpose. Students are not afraid to laugh in my class, but they know never to laugh directly at someone. They see me laugh all of the time. We laugh together and we learn together.

Companies are starting to realize this. There is a push in the corporate sector, especially among managers and leaders, to utilize laughter to strengthen relationships with coworkers to maximize productivity. Shawn Achor, Harvard teacher and leading happiness expert, recently published *The Happiness Advantage* (2010), a book exploring how happiness is one of the leading factors of performance. He teaches a happiness course to companies worldwide showing corporate leaders how happy workers significantly increase the performance of a company.

Teachers can use this valuable insight as well. A teacher who can get students to laugh can get students to open up and learn. Below are some "funny" tips to help you.

> A teacher who can get students to laugh can get students to open up and learn.

Tips for Infusing Productive Laughter

- **Have a stuffed class pet.** When I taught middle school, I had a different stuffed animal every year as our class pet. I put it in the front of the class and dressed it up some days. I had our class rat (we named him Ratatouille) in a Halloween costume when fall arrived, a Santa hat when December approached, and swim gear when it got hot. It always made students chuckle when they came in. The students will notice it immediately, and it will be a great conversation starter. Even better if the costume can relate to what you are learning. Even my high schoolers loved our Mr. Giggles (a stuffed lion). They stopped by my classroom year after year to ask what he was up to.

- **Humorous surprise prizes.** Why not make some of your classroom prizes or incentives humorous? Add some funny prizes. Only have a few of these, though, or the class won't trust your prizes. A girl in my class once won a tiny packet of soy sauce and her face lit up. The whole class was thrilled, and we all had a good laugh together. Make sure the student who wins the prize shows the class so you

(Continued)

(Continued)

can laugh together. You can give them a real prize after if you wish. You could have a big box with an opening for the student to reach in and pull out a prize. Or, think more creatively and have a fishing rod and a shower curtain on the ground representing a lake. Students "fish" for a prize (you clip something to their rod). The point is that the sky is the limit.

- **Tell funny stories.** Occasionally tell a funny story about something that has happened to you. Make sure it's a learning experience so the students understand why you are telling them about it and know that you're not just a boundary-free, too-much-information teacher. Sharing with students makes you more human. Even better if you can weave a relevant story into a lesson. Be careful that your story is appropriate for students. And please, no sob stories. The students don't need to know *all* your business.

Your Turn

1. Do you agree that laughter can increase learning and productivity in a classroom? Why or why not?

   _____
   _____
   _____
   _____
   _____
   _____
   _____
   _____
   _____
   _____

2. How do your students have fun in class while they are learning? Brainstorm three new ideas!

   _____
   _____
   _____
   _____
   _____
   _____
   _____
   _____
   _____

Give Gifts Without Strings Attached

Whether you like it or not, you will probably spend more time with the students in your class than even your closest friends during the school year. A wise teacher takes advantage of this opportunity to make the student-teacher relationship healthy and positive for both parties. I always think of my students as part of my extended family, in a sense. You will spend birthdays and other holidays with the students in your classroom. Show them you care on these holidays, and there's nothing wrong with giving them a little gift every once in a while. For example, on Valentine's Day, I gave each student a wooden pencil with hearts and "Happy Valentine's Day" written on it.

Gifting is also a great way to remind students to say thank you when receiving a gift. If a student did not thank me when I handed them the pencil, instead of scolding them I gave them the benefit of the doubt. I would say overly loudly to the next student, "You're welcome!" and usually the students who forgot would bashfully say, "Oh, sorry, thank you, Ms. Pariser!" In return, many students started giving me candy or other small gifts to show that they cared as well. You're then indirectly teaching gratitude and giving just for the sake of giving. Around the winter holidays, I might hand out one Hershey's kiss to each student and say "Happy Holidays."

Don't break the bank, but a tiny gift goes a long way—yes, even for high school students. It shows them you care, you are human, and you wish them well. If the gift is small, I usually joke about how I spent all the money in my bank account and bought all I could afford on my teacher's salary. They appreciate the chuckle and graciously take the piece of candy with a smile. It's a win-win situation. The secret is do not spend so much that you make the students feel guilty or like they owe you something. After all, you may be spending your hard-earned money on supplies. Spend the amount of time and money you like (I usually spend five to ten dollars per holiday, tops, for all the students). A bag of pencils or pens, or a little something sweet goes a long way. As with all gifts, it's the thought that counts. Students do not expect gifts from teachers at school, so you'll look like a hero and show you care.

Your Turn

1. Teachers may have varying opinions on gifting. What is your stance?

   _____
   _____
   _____
   _____

2. What does gifting tell your students?

   _____
   _____
   _____
   _____

3. How could gifting maximize learning in your class?

   _____
   _____
   _____
   _____

4. How do you feel when you give someone a gift "just because"?

   _____
   _____
   _____
   _____

5. How do you feel when you receive a gift "just because"?

   _____
   _____
   _____
   _____

Empower Students With Student-Led Conferences

> We all have a voice in this classroom.
>
> —Maddie, Grade 8

Student-led conferences are becoming commonplace all over the country. Many classrooms and schools have had great success with changing their traditional parent-teacher conferences into parent-teacher-student conferences led by students. In these cases, the student not only is at the conference but actually leads it. This is a dramatic shift for all parties from traditional teacher-led conferences, which most students fear and do not even attend, to a format that gives agency to students.

Are you ready for student-led conferences? Only you know the answer to that, but here are some tips to help if you are.

What are the essential parts of a student-led conference?

> These videos show what a student-led conference can look like at different developmental levels:
>
> Kindergarten: https://vimeo.com/49170218
>
> Middle school: https://vimeo.com/45140230
>
> High school: https://vimeo.com/43992567

- The student and their parent(s) or caregiver(s) are both in attendance at the conference.

- The student does most of the talking and can even lead the conference. Teach them how to greet their parents and introduce you to their parents. You can see an example of this in the middle school video in the sidebar.

- Display a sample of work the student has mastered as well as a sample of what they are focused on learning currently or will be learning in the near future. Students select these samples.
- Students set one or two goals for themselves and express them at the end of the conference. Goals are then shared with the grade-level team so all adults can help students meet the goals. This can be easily shared through a Google Doc and not an in-person meeting.
- Students could write a letter to their parent or caregiver thanking them for coming to the student-led conference.

Benefits of student-led conferences include the following:

- Builds confidence in students at school and at home
- Gives students an opportunity to take pride in their success
- Gives students an opportunity to advocate for their learning
- Increases student agency
- Greatly increases student participation
- Allows students to share what they have learned
- Increases student engagement in class because they have vocalized and analyzed their learning goals and have a rationale for them
- Fosters a stronger relationship between parent and student
- Promotes self-awareness (a skill that will benefit students in job settings and relationships with other people throughout their life)
- Increases parental involvement in school (parents more likely to attend if they know the student will be leading the conference)

FAQs about student-led conferences:

Q: What about students who have parents and caregivers who cannot attend a conference?

A: The student would lead a conference with the teacher. Or a conference can be recorded for the caregiver to watch later.

Q: What if there are behavior, motivation, defiance, or work completion issues that need to be addressed during the conference?

A: The high school video in the sidebar shows a great example of how to handle this while still empowering the child. This can be seen at the 2:10 point in the video. It's a gentle dance that involves giving the student an opportunity to accept responsibility, become accountable, and find solutions without humility or shame. The student should be talking the most during this part as well, but they may need some prompting, questioning, guidance, and help with finding solutions. You do not want the child to shut down in any way during this part.

Your Turn

1. Have you ever held or observed a student-led conference? If yes, what were your initial thoughts and/or how did it turn out?

   _____
   _____
   _____
   _____
   _____

2. How would you feel as a parent if you were invited to a student-led conference?

   _____
   _____
   _____
   _____
   _____

3. How would you feel as a student if you had to prepare and lead a student-led conference?

   _____
   _____
   _____
   _____
   _____

4. How would student-led conferences affect the behavior and engagement in your classroom?

   _____
   _____
   _____
   _____
   _____

Use Peer Mediation to Teach Conflict Resolution Skills, Foster More Positive Classrooms, and Make Your Life Easier

> Peer mediation offers a chance for students to work with other students to help them resolve problems, arguments, disagreements without having to get the teacher or the administration involved.
>
> —Janet Reno, former U.S. attorney general

In a society of cancel culture, it's essential that we teach students how to resolve conflict and communicate effectively. Peer mediation is like training wheels to be able to solve conflicts independently, calmly, and empathetically. It prevents us from having to solve minor issues and teaches students how to find solutions and compromise with each other *without* your help. Teaching your class how to peer mediate creates more student agency and independency, and it leads to a stronger community of learners. Peer mediation is a skill that students will carry throughout their lives to help them have healthier relationships with friends and family.

Here's an example of what peer mediation could look like in an elementary school.

Here's an example of what peer mediation could look like in an upper middle or high school.

I'll admit, teaching peer mediation does takes more time up front, but it will pay dividends in the long run for both you and your students. It will reduce the amount of time you spend intervening in minor conflicts, especially as the year goes on and students get more skilled at mediating their own issues. Also, kids today need to have conflict resolution skills to be successful at work and in life.

Peer mediation will dramatically help with classroom management because you will no longer have to waste time and energy asking Consuelo to give Aria her pencil back, or telling Jake to apologize to Sydney for accidentally bumping her chair. The most fundamental benefits of peer mediation include the following:

- Effectively resolves student conflicts
- Enables students to develop lifelong conflict resolution skills
- Encourages students to accept responsibility for their actions
- Empowers students
- Increases self-esteem
- Prevents escalated tension
- Helps students develop their moral framework during the years they attend school
- Builds empathy
- Teaches students to listen without interruption
- Gives students a voice
- Provides a sense of safety
- Shows your students that you trust them
- Improves your classroom climate
- Saves you time and energy

Peer mediation is relatively new and can be carried out in a variety of different ways. Most schools that use peer mediators train a group of responsible students to help other students resolve their issues. But what if we shifted our thinking and trained *all* of them? Training all of your students provides them with essential skills and saves you the time of having to wait for a designated peer mediator to show up in your classroom. Either way, you can start small and build as you start to see successes and feel comfortable. If you are a middle or high school teacher, you could even just start with training a few students in just one class and build from there. Elementary school teachers, you could first train a few responsible students in your class and build from there. It's really up to you.

Tamra Nast, a former elementary school teacher, shares how she used peer mediation in her fifth-grade classroom:

Based upon research on conflict resolution and peer mediation skills and programs, I created the "Solve-It-Spot." Our school made the decision to train all students in conflict resolution skills and then have students each choose their personal peer mediator as situations occurred.

We asked them to choose someone of good character who would be honest so the situation could get resolved, not necessarily the student's best friend. The students lived up to our expectations and were very thoughtful in choosing the person who would be able to help them in each situation. Interestingly, it was not always the same person.

We trained all students during the first month of each school year. We designed our peer mediation program to align with our social, emotional, and character development standards. When we first began, teachers were skeptical about spending time out of their teaching day to do this training. However, we discovered that teachers were able to save time in the long run. The smaller conflicts were resolved through students going to the "Solve-It-Spot" in the classroom or on the playground, and the teachers only needed to step in for serious situations. Because of its success, the "Solve-It-Spot" moved to other elementary schools within the district.

> Although there are a few different ways to do peer mediation, a general rule of thumb is that if the conflict happens during class time, the mediation should be done *outside* of class time. A cooling-off period often helps, especially since the students know the issue will be addressed soon. If the conflict happens during recess, the mediation can be done immediately.

Here are the guidelines Tamra and her students used:

Step 1: Look at the other person. (Eye contact and active listening; standing or sitting in the spot)

Step 2: Tell them calmly what happened and how you feel about it. (Using just facts and "I" statements)

Step 3: Tell what you did to keep the problem going.

Step 4: State what you will do so this doesn't happen again.

Step 5: Each person involved completes a reflection sheet and submits it so that the teacher has a record of the solution reached by the students.

Tamra's class used laminated spots or hula hoops so the students could stand or sit in them to calm down. They had spots painted on the playground for conflicts that happened during recess. Students could choose a peer mediator to join them if they needed a third person to mediate.

The program helped by offering students constructive choices for resolving their conflicts. Peer mediation offers students real tools that they will use throughout their lives to be successful in interpersonal interactions. According to Tamra, "High school students who have been trained have shared with me that they use these skills all of the time, in some way, when conflicts arise with their family and friends. Peer mediation should be used to address minor peer-to-peer issues to prevent tensions escalating into larger issues."

Coaching students through peer mediation will help your classroom management in general because not only will your students start to rely on each other for minor issues, you will have more energy.

Your Turn

1. How could training your students in peer mediation positively affect your classroom climate?

   _____
   _____
   _____
   _____

2. Does peer mediation seem like something your students would be interested in learning?

   _____
   _____
   _____
   _____

3. What would peer mediation look like logistically for you? Would you have an area inside or outside of your room set aside? Would you create a space for mediation on the playground?

   _____
   _____
   _____
   _____

4. How could peer mediation not only empower your students but save you time and energy?

   _____
   _____
   _____
   _____

Get Students to Behave When You're Covering a Colleague's Class

....

I like your point thing-a-mijigy.

—Sarah, Grade 5
(after I covered her class one day)

I have never been opposed to substitute teaching and don't find the classroom management the hardest part of the job. Barely any paperwork is involved, the lesson is done for you, if you can't connect with a student you are only there for one or two days, and you can work when you want. Finding the restroom in each different school was the most frustrating part of substitute teaching for me, not the classroom management. I credit much of my ease with substitute teaching to the subbing classroom management system I developed and used when I had to cover a colleague's class during my prep. I used it in every classroom, every subject, every grade. It usually works. Most schools are working on ways to not take away teacher prep time, pay teachers a bit extra when they have to cover, or even have the principal or vice principal step in and cover for the day (this is a beautiful thing to see). But the reality is that we might have to cover a colleague's class of students we don't know. The good news is that there is a way to get students to respect you and complete the assigned work when you are covering.

#51. Get Students to Behave When You're Covering a Colleague's Class

Here's a trick I use that works 95 percent of the time to make your life much simpler when you are covering a class: Enter the class smiling. Students don't see happiness as weakness; in fact, they take it as strength. Your smile will shock them because they are used to guest teachers coming in with a different affect. If you can go in early, talk to the first student who arrives (believe me, it won't be the naughty ones that show up first) about anything you're unsure of. They'll answer all questions for you. Do this quietly so you don't get one hundred different answers from other students trying to help. Then, as they come in, get them seated. Say to the class, "Good morning! My name is Ms./Mr. _____." (Have it written on the board always.) Point to your name. Students will have more respect for you if they know your name. It also shows you have your act together if you have it written down already.

Continue with, "Now, I cover classes a little differently. You know your teacher better than I do. Think of me as a messenger. I report back one score to your teacher. The score is a whole class score out of 10. Ten is the best. Your current score will always be on the board." Then write a large 10 on the board and draw a box around it.

Now say, "You are now at a 10 as a class. If you stay like this, I will report to your teacher that you were a 10-out-of-10 class. However, let's say someone is talking at an inappropriate time or not doing their work. Then it would fall to a 9." Draw a line through the 10 and make it a 9. The class may groan.

"The great thing about this is that you can go back up! Once you are on task again, you go right back up to a 10!"

The lowest score I've ever reported was a 6, and I've even had classes at 11. The students will always ask how a class earned an 11. I reply, "Well, they were so polite to both me and each other." Believe me, you will have students so polite the entire time. Sometimes even jokingly polite, and that's okay.

You can also give them a list of three criteria they will be graded on. Usually I write this on the side:

You are scored on:

1. Following instructions

2. Respecting your classmates and the adults in the room with your words and actions

3. Noise level at appropriate volume

That's it. Write a 10, knock it to a 9, 8, 7 (only one number decrease or increase at a time). And tell them when the number is going up or down. Simple. You should end with a number between 7 and 10 every time. Let the students know you want them to end on a 10. Be rooting for them rather than using the system to exert control over them.

Why does this work?

- Students have a chance to redeem themselves if they mess up.

- It's not personal. You are not disciplining them individually. Personal disciplining probably won't work with subbing since you most likely do not have a connection with the students.

- It uses positive peer pressure. I guarantee you will hear "Juan! Shhh! Quiet! We want our score to go up!"

I've used this for classes from third grade to eleventh grade. By using this method, you're empowering the students. They are taking control of their behavior (they should always be able to see the score) instead of you writing down names of who is naughty or nice. It works if they believe that you want them to do well. Try it and see. It's simple and will lessen your stress when covering classes.

Make sure you report the class number to the teacher over e-mail or leave a note at the end of the period or the day. Sometimes classes will compete against each other to see who can get the highest score.

Your Turn

1. What are your thoughts on this system? Why do you think it works?

   _____
   _____
   _____
   _____
   _____
   _____
   _____

2. Does this system empower students or take away their power?

   _____
   _____
   _____
   _____
   _____
   _____
   _____

3. What valuable lessons can the students learn using this system?

   _____
   _____
   _____
   _____
   _____
   _____
   _____

Best Practice #52

Surprise!

In her article "Why Humans Need Surprise," Suttie (2015) points out that surprises increase the amount of dopamine released in our brains, leading to more vitality in our lives. In turn, surprises lead to more vitality in your classroom engagement. We wrap gifts to hide what is inside, and we still have surprise parties. We love getting taken on surprise outings or, for the lucky few, surprise dates. Some of us watch mysteries; others read mystery novels. When life gets too predictable, we get bored. Although structure and consistency are very powerful and work, great teachers know how to intertwine a bit of surprise to keep the spice alive. As a teacher, I use the element of surprise often. It worked when we were kids; it works when we are adults. Most importantly, it works with students. It's fun!

Remember: You were hired to create fun, engaging, and rigorous lessons that you deliver to the class. Creating lessons with an element of surprise will make your job a bit easier and be more fun for you! When I say *surprise*, I do not mean balloons have to fall from your ceiling (although, how fun if you could make that happen!). There are many surprises you could employ.

A video showing how surprises can increase engagement and wonder in students

Tips for Adding an Element of the Unexpected Into Your Lessons

- **Mystery prize.** If there is a prize for a learning game or activity you have planned, have it out somewhere where the students can see it, but covered. Put a sheet over it and place a sign on it that says "Mystery Prize" or "What could this be?" Another idea would be to buy one of those fancy covers restaurants put over plates to keep dishes warm. You could buy one on Amazon or find one in a thrift store and yell "Voila!" as you reveal the prize. The point is, make the students wonder. Even if the prize is just a candy bar or bookmark, the excitement itself makes it a bit more fun for both you and the students. Just make sure the prize is not located in a spot where an impulsive student could prematurely rip off the sheet and wreck your surprise.

- **Let them guess.** Give the students two minutes to predict what is under the tray or sheet. You'll be surprised how invigorating these two minutes can be. Be prepared for some really outrageous answers that make you and the class laugh. Laughter brings a classroom together.

- **Create a trail of hints.** Before you read a class novel or start a new unit, make the students wonder what the book will be, or what the lesson will cover. Give them little clues each day. Do an activity that hints at what is to come. You'll find students will start coming up to you in the hallway trying to guess what the book or unit is. Remember the *Of Mice and Men* example I shared in Best Practice #18? This is one solid way to incorporate surprise in your lessons.

- **Pique interest with a prop.** If you plan to use a piece of realia in your lesson, have it out and exposed so the class wonders what you are doing that day. Realia are props that help the learning. Any artifact can be realia. For example, if you are doing a lesson that entails showing the class a project that was completed last year, have that project on display. This will be a focal piece as students walk in the door. Or, if you are using a live turtle in your lesson that day, have the turtle in front with a sign that says, "I wonder how this turtle will be part of our learning today." The students will wonder, be entertained, and be surprised.

- **Stay one step ahead of the class.** One of the first times I wanted to read a novel with a class, I used the element of surprise. I had an underlying fear that some students would groan or roll their eyes when I announced the book title, not because it was an uninteresting book, but because with thirty-two students in the classrooms, the odds were this was likely to happen with at least two students. I decided to add surprise to make everyone, I sure hoped, excited.

(Continued)

(Continued)

I piled all of the class novels on the carpeted floor in front of the board and placed a shiny silver cloth over them. I taped a piece of bright construction paper on top of the cloth and drew a huge question mark on it. The only way I can describe what happened when my eighth-grade students came into the room is to tell you to imagine a room full of flies and a big bowl of honey. They came in and circled around the shiny lump. I had to remind them many times not to touch it. This drove them crazy. A few put their head to the carpet and tried to peek underneath the sheet; others tried to poke at it with a pencil (thus obeying the no-touch rule). "I think I know what it is, guys!" a student shrieked. I wanted them to sweat a bit; you could feel the excitement in the room. When I whipped off the shiny cloth ten minutes into the lesson, they screamed, cheered, and could not wait to get their hands on the books. Would I have had that same initial engagement by just passing the books out? Of course not.

The secret to being able to add the element of surprise is being one step ahead of the class. You have to know the next unit that you are going to teach, or know how you will determine the winner in a class competition, or be certain what novel you will read next. To sum up, the element of surprise not only adds fun and excitement to the classroom, it also shows the class that you are prepared and in charge—a win-win situation.

Your Turn

1. Think back to the last time somebody surprised you with something great. How did you feel building up to the surprise? How can the element of surprise increase engagement in the classroom?

   _____
   _____
   _____
   _____
   _____
   _____

2. Do you personally believe that the element of surprise can increase engagement? Why or why not?

   _____
   _____
   _____
   _____
   _____
   _____

3. Think back to a specific past lesson. How could you have incorporated a surprise to increase engagement or add excitement into the class?

   _____
   _____
   _____
   _____
   _____
   _____

Real Conversation With a Fifth-Grade Student

Teacher: Okay, yesterday the girls lined up first, so today the boys line up first.

Female Student: But they already get higher pay than we do!

PART 6
STAYING AFLOAT

Remembering a Teacher Who Hit Her Breaking Point

My first-grade teacher tied one of our classmates to his chair because he would keep getting up and running around while she was teaching. The boy would run around and hit people when we were quiet and listening to what she was teaching. She honestly just wanted him to sit in his chair so she could get through the lesson. Everybody in the class was pretty happy she did that. This was in the 1980s before anybody got in trouble for anything. She was a good teacher, too.

    She used something lying around. It wasn't like it was premeditated or anything. I think she was at her breaking point with him.

—Jenna, Age 38

How does staying afloat relate to classroom management?

We never want to reach our breaking point. Staying afloat is all about controlling the amount of stress we let into our lives during the school year. We don't want to have the urge to tie our students to their chairs. But even the best teachers can hit their breaking point if they don't take care of themselves throughout the school year, both mentally and physically. In Part 6 I'll explain some key ways to keep yourself healthy so you can give your best self to your students. When you take shortcuts with yourself, it is reflected in your teaching. You won't have as much patience, energy, and enthusiasm for your students.

I REMEMBER WHEN...

Watch Rebekah Madren give a few suggestions for staying afloat.

It was the fall of 2005, and I was expecting my quiet commute to my school in the Paris suburbs, but the trains were stopped and the train stop was chaotic. Some commuter trains had been vandalized in protest of a deadly incident that had led to a state of emergency and violent rioting in France. Two immigrant teenagers had been unjustly electrocuted while running from local police, and the immigrant community was angry over years of ongoing issues surrounding immigration.

I had come to the City of Light to learn about second language education as a Fulbright exchange teacher. After three years of teaching middle and high school French in the U.S., I wanted to see how languages were taught in Europe, and drink coffee in cute cafes on the side. I was assigned to a middle school in the Parisian suburbs. But, voila! I found myself teaching in the heart of a national issue.

The next few weeks were difficult and beautiful as I navigated this unforeseen situation. Ten years later, as a teacher, I see where I failed and succeeded in trying to keep the learning going in my classroom during this national crisis.

My first mistake was that I had expectations. I was a skilled, hard-working teacher and assumed I would have another smooth year. Never did I imagine circumstances powerful enough that I could not fight through them. Let go of expectations of what type of school year you will have.

Secondly, I blamed myself for what happened in my classroom after the rioting began rather than taking a look at the bigger picture. What I know now is that we can't always be perfect. Sometimes a misbehaved class is a result of something larger going on. My school was comparable to an inner-city school in the U.S. Add a national crisis, and some days I could not teach a single lesson to my chaotic classes. I felt guilty and unqualified as my students' learning halted.

I should have allowed myself room to fail forward during this time. Even the seasoned French teachers struggled to manage their classrooms.

The one thing I'm proud of during this time was the fact that I reached out for help. As teachers, sometimes we can't do it completely alone. I talked to my local American friends about my anxiety, and they fed me dinners as they took time to deepen my understanding of the history of immigrant issues. I kept in touch with my teaching mentor in the U.S. to get moral support. I also swallowed my pride and asked my French colleagues for help with classroom management. Teachers are caregivers, and we need to support each other.

On my days off from school, I did what only Paris could offer. I played duets with a violinist friend and frequented French movies, small concerts, and museums. I ate as well as I could with my anxious nerves and walked all over exploring the city for exercise. We teach from the overflow of a full life, and I did the things I love to do.

To do this job, we need to preserve the peace inside of ourselves. My biggest success was that upon my return to my school in the U.S., I saw the incredible value in my teaching role amidst my simple, peaceful community. A teacher plays an irreplaceable part in maintaining a stable community. We teach, we nurture, and we inspire to preserve peace and prosperity. It might sound cliché, but we need to keep our cups full to pour into students, for the future is formed in our classrooms.

Rebekah Madren
20 years teaching experience
Fulbright Scholar
Patuxent River, Maryland

Balance Your Life

> You can't pour from an empty cup.
>
> —Anonymous

Watch this video with tips for keeping a work-life balance during the school year.

Read about the realities of teacher self-care with Angela Watson.

It took me four years to fully understand this quotation. In my first year teaching, my principal found me one Friday evening around 8:30 p.m. in my classroom working. When he entered, I was secretly excited that he could see how dedicated I was. He stuck in only his head and said two words: "Go home." This habit of staying late in my classroom lasted my first few years. In addition to the many hours I put in at school, I exercised rarely, often worked late into the night at home, ate poorly, and just did not take care of myself. What happened? I snapped at my class when they misbehaved, did not have the energy they needed, and became more and more worn down.

The bottom line is the title of this best practice: Balance your life. In order for you to take care of your classroom, you have to take care of yourself. Eat right, exercise, and get enough sleep. That's easier said than done, however, especially because many of us have families, responsibilities, and full lives outside of school. Yet there has to be a body-mind-spirit balance. I did not have that balance during my first few years. After I made a conscious effort to balance my life, I noticed that my teaching improved dramatically. I was the best teacher I could be once I regained balance.

Students deserve a teacher who is healthy and rested. I was still working hard, but I also got into an exercise routine, started going to bed at a reasonable hour, and paid closer attention to what food was going into my body. Face it—you have to be in tip-top mental shape to win this race. So how do you do it? Do you just not finish your work? There's a quote from Anne Lamott that sums up the concept of work-life balance beautifully: "Almost everything else will work again if you unplug it for a few minutes, including you."

Tips for Keeping Your Balance

- **Exercise.** Schedule exercise into your calendar. There will always be something that comes up, but exercise! Whether it is walking, running, yoga, Pilates, or your home treadmill, do it at least twice a week. It will come in handy when Alex flips his water bottle on the desk one too many times. Instead of losing your cool, you will notice that you actually have patience.

- **Keep one "get out of jail free" card.** Shhhh . . . this one is a secret and only to be used once in a while when you're really in a bind. Is there something that has been sitting on your desk waiting to be graded for more than three weeks? Chances are the students do not remember. Realize that you will never be able to grade everything. Focus on the present assignments that specifically assess essential skills. Is there a pile of papers that don't necessarily link to a standard, or have you done another assignment that assesses the same skill? Skip grading this pile and move forward. This will free your mind for more relevant assignments. Skipping a hurdle or two can help you win the overall race. It's okay, really.

- **Prioritize and prep.** Use your prep to actually prep! I make a list of what I have to do in my prep; otherwise, I can get involved with one task for too long. Prioritize what you have to do that will get you ahead. Make a list and stick to it.

- **Respond to correspondence immediately whenever possible.** Respond to e-mails, papers, and phone calls as soon as possible. Once these start to build up, it's like credit card interest and it will snowball. I used to get my mail and fill out the forms right in the mailroom to avoid a stack forming on my desk and becoming a visual stressor. Respond immediately if you can. This will also make you a more efficient and valuable employee.

- **Ask for student assistance sparingly.** If you start to feel unbalanced or are particularly tired or ill, it's okay to tell the students that you need their assistance to work with you. This will actually help you appear human in their eyes. Use this sparingly to avoid losing credibility, though.

- **Separate your work life from your personal life.** In a 2016 study, Google attempted to address the work-life balance debate to conclude who was healthier, people who separate work and life—known as *segmentors*—or people who integrate work and

(Continued)

(Continued)

life—known as *integrators* (Boch, 2014). The results of the study were based on measuring life satisfaction. The study concluded that those who segmented were twice as happy as those who integrated. This means people should develop interests outside of work. Turn off your work e-mails when you are enjoying your own time. Schedule specific office hours on set days after school for your students to be able to contact you. Make time for you so you can develop higher life satisfaction and thus be a better teacher for your students.

- **Focus on what matters most to you.** The bottom line is that we could all spend five or more straight years in our classrooms and find things that need to be done, such as reorganizing cabinets, cleaning, etc. What matters the most to you? For me, it was the lessons. I would perfect the plans. This helped keep engagement high and behavior issues low. Know that there are many distractions in the classroom, and you have to know what you *need* to get done and how to do this while still managing to take care of yourself.

The demands of teaching every day can and will eat you alive if you do not take care of your emotional health, your physical health, and your overall well-being. You cannot use lack of time as an excuse. Make time. You can and you will be much happier and a better teacher for your students. They *will* notice a difference. Figure 53.1 presents a self-care inventory you can use from my book *Real Talk About Time Management: 35 Best Practices for Educators* (2018).

Figure 53.1 Self-Care Inventory

1. How often do you skip daily exercise?

   _____ Very often _____ Sometimes _____ Almost never

2. Are you getting enough sleep?

   _____ Most of the time _____ Could use more

3. Do you drink enough water each day?

   _____ I try to _____ I need to do better

4. How often do you find yourself relying on caffeine to get through the day?

   _____ Very often _____ On occasion _____ Not often

5. How often do you skip breakfast and/or lunch and rely on junk food?

   _____ Very often _____ Sometimes _____ Almost never

6. Do you schedule or partake in downtime activities each week? Yes No

   If yes, list your three favorite downtime activities.

   a) _____ b) _____ c) _____

7. How would you rate your ability to delegate tasks to students in your classroom?

   _____ Could be better _____ Really good

8. How would you rate your skill at saying "no" to doing things that you don't care about or that will take time away from your primary teacher's tasks?

   _____ I'm good at it _____ I need to learn how to do it better

9. How well do you handle emotions like fear, sadness, or worry?

   _____ I think I handle them well _____ I need to work on doing better

10. Are you a person who is curious about things and enjoys exploring new ideas, skills, and people?

    _____ Yes, that's me! _____ It depends on a variety of factors _____ Not for me

11. How would you rate your skills in speaking up about events and issues that bother you at school?

    _____ Not good at this _____ Need help to do this _____ I seldom hesitate to express my opinions

12. How would you rate your sense of humor?

    _____ Poor _____ Good _____ Excellent

13. How would you rate the quality of the social interactions and relationships you have at school, outside of school, and in life in general?

    School: _____ Excellent _____ Good _____ Fair _____ Not good at all

    Outside: _____ Excellent _____ Good _____ Fair _____ Not good at all

    Life: _____ Excellent _____ Good _____ Fair _____ Not good at all

Your Turn

1. Do you think it's possible to have a balanced work and personal life?

   _____
   _____
   _____
   _____

2. How balanced is your work and personal life right now?

   _____
   _____
   _____
   _____

3. Brainstorm and discuss specific changes that you want and need to make.

   _____
   _____
   _____
   _____

4. Pull out your schedule and schedule in activities that will preserve and balance your body, spirit, and mind and enable you to become a better teacher. Schedule them in just as you would a staff meeting. Make these activities a priority.

   _____
   _____
   _____
   _____

How to Turn Around a Potentially Difficult Parent or Caregiver Meeting

We teachers all have hard meetings and difficult parents and caregivers. We get questioned and feel put on the defensive sometimes, and chances are we will have to defend ourselves. We may have to rectify a situation. Difficult meetings with parents are where our true strength comes out. They are where our words can be daggers or saviors, where we will experience tears and laughter. We all mess up in meetings sometimes, but through practice teachers can get better at handling difficult ones.

I remember my first angry parent meeting. It was the last week of school. A girl in my class was upset because she felt that she deserved a higher grade. I was conducting the three-ringed circus I called my classroom. Grades had already been submitted, the students were finished with their work, and I was struggling to just keep them in their seats until the end of the school year. Two strangers' faces appeared in the door. Not only did they look like I had just killed their dog, they were very powerful-looking women who could have crushed me with their bare hands if they really wanted to. I could see their resemblance to the angry student. Was it her mother and aunt? Her mother and her cousin? From the furious looks on these women's faces, it didn't matter. I was about to be told

A deeper look at addressing difficult parent meetings with empathy

off and humiliated in front of my own ninth-grade class. What could I do? Call the office for help? Run? I considered how far I could get. I knew I could probably at least run faster than they could.

In my attempt to remain professional and not hide under my desk like I wanted to, I asked them if we could step outside. I moved away from the door so the students could not see their demeanor as they (I'm not sure how else to put it) told me off. Boy, did they let me have it. They angrily lectured me for what seemed like an eternity. Luckily, an administrator was walking by and entered the conversation to support me. I'm not sure what my class was doing besides listening as well as they could to their teacher being told off. After this meeting, I knew I had to make some changes. This could never be repeated. My biggest mistake was not informing the parents of the student's grade when it had started to slip. I was just too busy. I know now that it's essential to inform a parent when a student's grade is slipping quickly. Let's fast-forward to a meeting later in my teaching career.

A student in my class was frustrated with the grade she had earned. I knew her low grade was because she was talking too much in class and not doing her work to the best of her ability, but she felt she had been wronged. She vented to her parents, and her parents asked for a meeting with me.

The number one rule is to not become defensive, and the number two rule is do not become arrogant. Body language is important; make eye contact and nod your head when a parent makes a point. Do not cross your arms. Empathize with the parent or caregiver. Be on *their* side. They love their child and will fight for what they think is right. It is not you they are angry with, it is the grade.

If a student says their parent would like a meeting with you, say to the student, "Your parents would like a meeting with me? I think that's a good idea so we can see how to help you succeed."

Call the parent or caregiver. Say to them,

> Mr/Mrs. [parent's name]? This is Ms./Mr. [your name], the teacher of [student name], and I'm wondering if you have a moment? [Student name] mentioned to me that you would like a conference? I'm so glad she did because I was just about to call you. I'm glad we can work together to figure out the best way to help [student's name]. We both want her to succeed. When is a good time for you to come in?

Be sure to ask if they have a moment as it's important to show respect for their time.

After you schedule the time, try to refrain from discussing any more on the phone; this can be handled during the conference. It is up to you, but I always preferred to have the student in the conference as well. They feel like they are part of the solution when they are given a chance to be heard as well. After all, it is the student you are teaching every day, not the parent. I found these were the meetings that worked best. Have documentation ready and prepare for the meeting, otherwise you will just be talking in circles. Have samples ready of student work and documentation of assignments not turned in, etc.

Okay, now at the meeting be prepared and know that the parent may come in angry and ready to fight. The goal of the meeting is to listen, listen, listen. Empathize and diffuse. Do not go to a meeting ready to "win a fight." You'll have an angrier parent on your hands and administration will likely become involved, which is not what you want. Let's jump to the actual conference now.

Parent and student walk in. They both seem angry, ready to argue. You have bottled water ready for both, which surprises them. If it's chilled, brownie points! You have the student's grade already printed out (but flipped over so it doesn't upset her right away) and samples of her below-quality work. Show them that you are leading the meeting, but make sure they are heard. Here's how it could go:

> Shake hands with both parent and student before you sit. Say, "Mr. Xiong, thank you so much for coming in today. I understand you are both concerned for Sarah's low grade. I am just as concerned. Sarah, could you tell us what is going on?"

> Empower the student and let them talk. Do not interrupt; just listen. If the student says something that is accusatory or just not accurate, respond with, "I'm sorry you feel that way."

> Then, start your part by sharing a student strength. You might say, "Sarah, I really value having you in class because you always raise your hand even when the others may not participate as much. It's nice to have a student as brave as you are in class every day." Think of at least one student strength before a meeting.

> You continue: "However, sometimes you use that strength at inappropriate times. There have been times where we had to complete assignments and you were talking with a friend. This has caused a lower grade. Would you agree with that statement?" Most students would agree here. "So I would like to help you raise your grade. What can I do to help you talk less?"

> The student will probably either shrug her shoulders or ask you to change her seat at this point. Most likely, the parent will probably jump in now and ask that you contact them if this happens again.

Bingo! You have just gotten what you need.

First of all, you empowered the parent. Now when you call home, the parent will most likely be on your side. Remember that the parent asked you to call home. Secondly, the student knows that you and the parent are working together to help her. You just empowered both the student and the parent when they were originally coming in ready to fight. The student will most likely do better in class now without you ever having to call, or maybe you will just need to make an occasional call.

> ## Tips for Successful Parent and Caregiver Meetings
>
> - **Listen, listen, listen.** Show parents that you are listening by nodding your head yes. Put yourself in their shoes and understand their side. A parent wants to be heard and understood.
>
> - **Be prepared with grades, work samples, and other documentation.** Use this as support, not as a weapon.
>
> - **Work *with* them.** Take the position that you are working *with* parents. You want the best for their child.
>
> - **Come to an agreement.** Let the parent know you respect their child and come to an agreement where you and the parent are working together for the student.
>
> - **Schedule sooner than later.** It's much easier to be the first to bring attention to a situation in a meeting rather than having to respond to an angry parent phone call. They'll end up thanking you instead of wondering why you've waited so long to call them. Remember that they love their child.
>
> These tips could have saved me from wanting to hide under my desk.

Your Turn

1. In your opinion, what is the biggest obstacle when it comes to working with parents or caregivers? How can you overcome this obstacle?

   _____
   _____
   _____
   _____
   _____

2. Think back to a parent or caregiver interaction you have had that didn't go as well as planned. With the knowledge you now have, is there anything you could have done differently to improve that interaction?

   _____
   _____
   _____
   _____
   _____

3. Now think back to a parent or caregiver interaction that went exceptionally well. How did you contribute to this happening?

   _____
   _____
   _____
   _____
   _____

Be Aware of Secondary Trauma and Compassion Fatigue

S. E. Hinton, a famous author, once said, "Nothing can wear you out like caring about people." In our profession this is so very true. We may come home not only physically exhausted but mentally and even emotionally drained. Teaching is a beautiful but simultaneously taxing profession.

In my book *Real Talk About Time Management: 35 Best Practices for Educators* (2018), I discuss both secondary trauma and compassion fatigue because they relate so closely to one another. I've recapped some of those thoughts here.

Secondary Trauma

When I taught eighth grade, I had a student we'll call Mark. I had a soft spot for Mark. He was smaller than the other boys and always seemed to be having a giggle about something. He loved to skate but didn't seem to have any other hobbies. He had the street smarts of a twenty-year-old, easy. He didn't particularly love academics and held a steady *F* in my class most of the year. At one point, he and I worked together to guide him up to a *C-*. He beamed and bragged that this was a highlight in his academic career. Mark would joke with me often, and we had a strong connection and a mutual respect for each other. This is the foundation for connecting with any student academically.

Although Mark was excited about earning a *C-* in my English class that one semester, I knew the work wasn't done. I had bigger plans for Mark academically. Mark had very high emotional intelligence. He knew exactly how to get under any teacher's skin. I was thankful he hadn't chosen me as a victim. I'm not sure exactly what he did in his mathematics and science classes, but I found him constantly in the dean's office during those periods. He would give me a peace sign, raise his eyebrows, and flash a big smile as I walked by on my way to prep.

I had Mark in my first period, so I was lucky to be able to connect with him first thing in the morning, before everything seemed to spiral downward for him. One day Mark did not show up to class. I asked his girlfriend where he was, as she seemed to keep better tabs on him than his parents. She looked down and didn't respond at first. My stomach dropped. Then she said she hadn't heard from him, either.

A few days later Mark's girlfriend came up to my desk. She said Mark had made some very poor decisions and was at the wrong place at the wrong time. He had been involved with an attempted car theft. He was in juvenile detention and would be there for a while.

The day went by, and on my drive home I started crying. The tears poured down my face. I started sobbing so hard I could barely drive. I imagined little Mark surrounded by teenagers much larger than he was. He wouldn't get by with his jokes there. Deep down, I knew that he probably wasn't going to make it. I feared he would end up in jail, and I couldn't save him. I never saw Mark again. To this day, I do not know where Mark is and have not heard anything further about him.

That evening, after I wiped away the tears, I felt heavy. I lay down in my bed and slept. Sleeping is all I had the energy to do because of the weight of the heavy emotions I was experiencing. It was only 5:00 p.m.

At the time of this incident, I didn't know what was happening. I thought it was a normal part of teaching and I was just upset about a student. Now I know that what I was experiencing is commonly referred to as *secondary trauma*. According to the National Child Traumatic Stress Network (n.d.), "Secondary trauma is defined as the emotional duress that results when an individual hears about the firsthand trauma experiences of another."

Sixty-seven percent of our students have experienced trauma. If you work with high-needs students, the percentage is probably greater. There's a pretty good chance some of these students are going to tell us about their trauma, or we are going to be their teacher when it happens. As much as we love our students—our Marks—we need to take care of ourselves. The rest of the class still needs us to be centered, focused, caring, and compassionate teachers. If we aren't aware of secondary trauma before we step into the classroom, it's more than likely we will silently suffer from it without knowing what is happening. If we are experiencing secondary trauma, we aren't performing at our optimal level.

You care about your students and you want to be the best teacher you can be for them. When I suggest ways to prevent secondary trauma from wearing you down, I am helping you stay strong because you still have the rest of the class to teach and your family to take care of at home. It's okay to feel good and still care about your other students.

Prevention

We can strengthen our minds and bodies *before* we hear about traumatic events. Methods for this can include but are not limited to the following:

- Meditation—it will strengthen your ability to regulate your emotions and actually "pad" your brain to be able to better process. Let's get more meditation rooms in schools! Teachers need it.
- Exercise and healthy nutrition—a strong body has a better ability to regulate emotions.
- Professional learning—school counselors can help train staff to increase awareness and offer wellness strategies.
- School community—school leaders can be trained on secondary trauma and cultivate a school environment in which teachers have support.

Intervention

Being around, experiencing, or hearing about trauma affects your body as well. There's a saying that "issues stay in our tissues." It's true. So it's important to get the emotions of secondary trauma out of your own body. Keep in mind that it can be difficult to tell if something is secondary trauma or if we are just tired from the day. Here are some ways to get secondary trauma out of your body:

- Practice yoga.
- Use employee assistance programs (EAPs) for counseling services.
- Enlist a self-care partner to help monitor your progress.
- Get out into nature.
- Go exercise (a.k.a. gym therapy).
- Journal it out.
- Talk to your school counselor about strategies.
- Talk it out. (Be careful with this one—a counselor or therapist is best for talking it out so we don't spread the secondary trauma to others.)
- Use a roller to move your tissues in your body.

- Literally just shake your shoulders and whole body to reset your nervous system.
- Do some stretching exercises.
- Talk into a voice recorder on your phone; delete the recording when you are finished.
- Dance it out. Just moving your body to music helps release trauma and boost serotonin.

The point is whether you dance, talk to a friend, journal it out, or do some sort of exercise, don't just fall asleep or forget about it. You need to get the trauma out.

> Counselors and therapists are trained in processing secondary trauma. Unfortunately, most of the time teachers are not.

While doing research for this book, I found people in all professions who shared their stories of secondary trauma. I heard from people who work with seriously ill children, veterans of war, caretakers who work with trauma every day, and medical professionals who deal with families suffering from grief and loss.

Treating secondary trauma appropriately is especially important for teachers because, as mentioned earlier, 67 percent of the students we work with have been exposed to some sort of trauma. The chances of us experiencing secondary trauma are high. And we work with children—*children*! Let's give them what they deserve.

Compassion Fatigue

Compassion fatigue relates directly to secondary trauma, but it's slightly different. Compassion fatigue, in a nutshell, happens when our bodies and minds just can't take it anymore and we lose empathy and compassion. It can look like when a teacher often snaps at a class for minor infractions or rolls their eyes when they hear of trouble a student is going through. This is not a place we want to be as a teacher, but it can happen. Unlike secondary trauma where we hurt because we've heard about someone else's pain, with compassion fatigue we *stop caring* as a defense mechanism for survival. While secondary trauma can set in directly after we hear about a traumatic event, compassion fatigue usually takes years to surface.

As teachers we need to take measures to prevent and overcome compassion fatigue because our students need us to be the compassionate, caring advocates we started out as. Their minds are young, malleable, sensitive, and impressionable. They need our positivity and love daily to grow up to be mentally healthy adults. Some of our students spend more time with us during the school year than with their parents or close friends. We can't adequately teach the next generation if we aren't taking care of our bodies and minds. One doctor of pulmonary and critical care medicine I spoke to described compassion fatigue by saying, "Compassion fatigue is not just numbness. It becomes irritation and exasperation with people who are suffering" (Pariser & Deroche, 2020, p. 181).

The difference between the advice for dealing with compassion fatigue versus secondary trauma is that you are not "getting it out" when dealing with compassion fatigue. When you experience compassion fatigue, you'll need to manage your health over the long run for prevention of future occurrences. Some suggestions for preventing and managing compassion fatigue include the following:

- Exercise and eat properly.
- Get enough sleep.
- Take a personal day when needed—seriously, take one.
- Spend time with family or close friends.
- Take a break from grading for a weekend.
- Develop interests outside of work.
- Seek counseling from a trained professional to help you work through the buildup of emotions.

Mother Teresa understood compassion fatigue. The American Institute of Stress (2018) reported that "[Mother Teresa] wrote in her plan to her superiors that it was *mandatory* for her nuns to take an entire year off from their duties every 4-5 years to allow them to heal from the effects of their care-giving work."

Your Turn

1. Have you experienced secondary trauma or compassion fatigue? What did it feel like in your body?

   _____
   _____
   _____
   _____
   _____
   _____

2. What preventative strategies can you adopt to strengthen your mind and body to help prevent secondary trauma and/or compassion fatigue?

   _____
   _____
   _____
   _____
   _____
   _____

3. How are the remedies for secondary trauma and compassion fatigue similar and different from one another?

   _____
   _____
   _____
   _____
   _____
   _____

Cultivate Healthy Relationships With Colleagues

Believe it or not, getting along with your coworkers is extremely important to your success inside the classroom and for keeping yourself sane. The longer we teach, the more we realize that we absolutely do need our coworkers for support. Colleagues can cover a class, lend an extra ream of paper, co-chaperone a field trip, help deal with a student, provide an experienced view on a difficult situation, spell you for a few minutes when you have to use the restroom during class, or just provide emotional support for those challenging days. Burning bridges with a coworker can jeopardize your success as a teacher. Imagine if you were in a disagreement with another teacher one year, and then the next year you were placed beside her classroom, or even assigned to be her coteacher. Being on good terms with all of the employees at your school will help your personal career.

The Golden Rules for Healthy Relationships With Colleagues

- Don't gossip.
- Use a respectful tone when speaking to other adults.
- If you mess up, apologize as soon as possible.

- Resolve issues through conversation before they escalate.
- Watch what you e-mail, text, or post to social media. Consider it saved forever and forwarded.
- Do not try to solve disagreements with a coworker over e-mail or text. Face-to-face conversation is a priceless tool and can clear up many misunderstandings quickly.
- Use the chain of command. Always go to the coworker first, and then to the supervisor only if needed. Supervisors should be used if the conflict cannot be resolved or if there is a legal issue involving a student or adult.

Your Turn

1. Have you ever had a coworker gossip to you about another coworker? If yes, how did that make you feel? How did it make you feel about the gossiping coworker?

   _____
   _____
   _____
   _____
   _____
   _____

2. As technology becomes the more acceptable means of communication, why is it important to remember that miscommunications and disagreements should always be handled in face-to-face conversation, especially in the workplace?

   _____
   _____
   _____
   _____
   _____
   _____

3. Have you ever had a disagreement with a colleague that escalated because text or e-mail was used instead of face-to-face conversation?

   _____
   _____
   _____
   _____
   _____
   _____

How to Navigate Colleague Conflict

In *Answers to Your Biggest Questions About Creating a Dynamic Classroom* (2022), my co-author Victoria Lentfer and I discuss colleague conflict, because unless you are the luckiest teacher alive, you will most likely experience a disagreement with a colleague at some point during the school year.

Here's how we explain it: Schools are organizations that are filled with people all working toward a common goal. However, you will most likely have a conflict, perhaps only a minor conflict, with another colleague at some point in your career. One of the most important things to remember is that people who work in a school are generally compassionate people. That is one of the factors that sets the profession apart from others. Teachers are not usually in it for the money or the personal gain. They are in it for the kids. However, as the school year goes on, it can get stressful at times, teachers can get tired, and frankly sometimes teachers do not see eye to eye with a colleague. This is where the work has to come in.

Most importantly, handling conflict in a healthy way requires empathy. Try to see where the other person is coming from. Put yourself in their shoes for a few moments. Is there a perspective that you might not be considering?

Now, consider the stakes. If the outcome of the conflict will affect how you do your job or how your students learn, it's worth working toward a resolution right away. If it's more about your ego or a need to be "right," consider talking it through once both parties have cooled down.

Finally, when you engage in conversation with a colleague with whom you disagree, try to use as many "I" statements as possible instead of "you" statements. For example: "I feel like we should take the students

Teachers discuss keeping positive colleague relationships

> Usually a conflict with a colleague should be solved with an honest, face-to-face conversation, not a text or an e-mail. Texts and e-mails can be forwarded, misinterpreted in tone, or misunderstood. They can also feel like an attack.

to the zoo because it would bring the learning to life for our biology unit. I understand this would mean they would miss soccer practice on Tuesday, but is there another way the students could gain the skills they need to play in the game?" Compare this to a "you" statement, such as, "You always put soccer first. Why can't you see that this field trip is more important than a soccer practice?"

Tips for Handling Colleague Conflict

- Focus on the problem at hand and finding a solution.
- Be willing to compromise if is a colleague you work closely with.
- Listen to what they are saying and how they are feeling before you respond.
- Use your compassionate voice to take control of the situation. Try to listen with an empathetic ear.
- Have this conversation away from students and away from other colleagues, if possible.
- Do not personally insult the other colleague during the conversation. Focus on the specific issue at hand, not on them personally. This will only escalate the issue.
- Be sure to not point fingers; again, focus on finding a solution.
- For major conflicts, you might consider asking somebody you trust from administration to be a mediator during the conversation, although you shouldn't ask them to solve the issue for you. Use this tactic sparingly.
- If you are having a conflict, think, *What's best for the students*? if that applies.
- Consider if the colleague is perhaps just tired, stressed, or a bit on edge from being stretched too thin.
- If the conflict is purely about saving your ego, consider letting it go.

Your Turn

1. Have you ever had a conflict with a colleague? Was it resolved? If so, how?

2. Have you ever wished you had handled a colleague conflict differently?

3. Have you ever let a conflict go that wasn't worth addressing?

Real Conversation With an Elementary School Student

Me [introducing myself to a very young student I didn't know]: Hello. My name is Ms. Pariser. If you can't remember that, you are welcome to call me Ms. P for today. *P* like *potato*. Can you repeat my name back to me?

Student: Your name is Potato.

Handy To-Go List of Fifty-Seven Teaching Dos and Don'ts

DO...	DON'T...
1. Build mutually respectful relationships from Day 1.	1. Try to demand respect on Day 1.
2. Teach students not to shame, laugh, or ridicule each other from Day 1.	2. Let the ridiculing happen because it "wasn't that serious" and hope it goes away.
3. Learn student names as soon as possible.	3. Have students realize that you do not know their names as the school year progresses.
4. Set routines and structures early, even before they are needed.	4. Wait until structures and routines are needed before creating them.
5. Use "I" statements. (Examples: "I need you to . . ." or "Do me a favor and . . .")	5. Use "you" statements. (Example: "You need to . . .")
6. Use student data to create a purposeful seating chart early in the year.	6. Make a seating chart without using student data.
7. Have student pictures up somewhere in the room.	7. Fail to have any class or student photos visible anywhere in the room.
8. Praise the positive often.	8. Focus on the negative behaviors in a classroom.
9. Redirect encouragingly when students make mistakes.	9. Shame students for making mistakes.
10. Include DCD students in every single activity your classroom does to create a sense of community.	10. Exclude DCD students from participating in some activities with the rest of your classroom.
11. Find out what a challenging student is interested in or thrives on outside of school by asking questions.	11. Not seek to find anything out about a challenging student.
12. Know that if a student is not doing work in class, it's mostly either a skills/knowledge, resources, or motivation barrier and you can intervene accordingly.	12. Take it personally when a student does not do work in class.

DO . . .	DON'T . . .
13. Praise behaviors you would like to see continued.	13. Focus on the negative with your words to the class.
14. Know that some students are connection kids and you need to connect with them nonacademically first before they will learn from you.	14. Ignore taking time or effort to build a relationship with connection kids and expect them to learn from you.
15. Reward students.	15. Tell a class of students that they do not deserve a reward.
16. Provide authentic audiences for projects.	16. Have students complete a project and just turn it in to the teacher for a grade.
17. Use a behavior contract (pitched carefully) for students who are consistently not following class expectations and disrupting learning for the rest of the students.	17. Continue with the same consequences for your most challenging students.
18. Connect curriculum to the real world.	18. Fail to connect your curriculum to the real world.
19. Use trusted sources to keep learning and growing to improve your practice.	19. Stay stuck in the same pattern, routines, and thinking year after year.
20. Keep the pace up: Use chunks of ten to twenty minutes in your lesson plans for elementary and middle school, and chunks of thirty to forty minutes for high school.	20. Teach too slowly.
21. Use arm's length voice with students.	21. Speak so every student in the classroom can hear you when you are working with students in small groups or one-on-one.
22. Incorporate ample opportunities for students to stop and collaborate with each other on what they are doing or creating when they are using technology.	22. Fail to add an aspect of student collaboration when using technology.
23. Stay one or two steps ahead of the class.	23. Always be playing catch-up in your classroom and scrambling to get a lesson prepared the morning of.
24. Do project-based units that last two to eight weeks throughout the year	24. Spend most of the year not tying the curriculum to the bigger picture.
25. Do problem-based units that last two to eight weeks throughout the year to tap into students' curiosity about the world around them.	25. Avoid doing units that ask students to think about problems in the world around them.
26. Use quick formative assessments to take a snapshot of what students have retained to drive instruction.	26. Teach an entire lesson without any type of formative assessment.

(Continued)

(Continued)

DO...	DON'T...
27. Be a warm demander teacher.	27. Fail to be a warm demander teacher.
28. Teach in ways other than direct instruction often.	28. Do direct instruction for most or all of the class period.
29. Take risks in your lessons.	29. Always keep students in their comfort zone.
30. Empower your students to succeed when you will not be there.	30. Miss many days of work.
31. Use creative discipline once in a while.	31. Keep your creative or fun side from showing in your class.
32. Use nonverbal cues to keep students quiet during a test or silent reading.	32. Raise your voice or talk in a classroom that is supposed to be silent.
33. Prepare students for groupwork by giving them a clear written description of the task and giving each one an individual role (if needed).	33. Fail to communicate clear tasks for groupwork.
34. Have creative and well-planned lessons.	34. Have dry and unprepared lessons often.
35. Include at least three types of engagement styles in each lesson.	35. Have only one engagement style in your lesson.
36. Use a lesson that has flopped as a learning tool by spending time reflecting on what could have been done differently.	36. Fail to take the time to reflect if a lesson flops.
37. Have fast and frequent communication with parents.	37. Only communicate with parents when a student is not doing what is expected.
38. Take time to plan with your coteacher.	38. Hope coteaching will just work out without planning or communication.
39. Lean on the expertise and resources of social workers and school counselors when needed for students.	39. Try to help and "save" all of your students without the expertise or resources social workers and school counselors can provide.
40. Find a mentor who is better than you at teaching.	40. Fail to have a mentor.
41. Ask other teachers if you may observe their class, if only for a few minutes.	41. Fail to take the time to observe other teachers.
42. Take mental notes about what you can try in your own classes when talking to a group of teachers.	42. Only tell stories of your own classroom with other teachers.
43. Invite administrators to student presentations, but keep in mind they might be busy and not able to come.	43. Teach behind proverbial closed doors so administration is not aware of the great things your students are doing.

DO...	DON'T...
44. Invite relevant guest speakers into your classroom to bring the learning to life, and prep your students for what type of questions to ask the speaker beforehand.	44. Fail to invite guest speakers into your classroom because you don't trust that your students will behave.
45. Allow students to vote on class decisions that do not impede learning.	45. Always make the decisions for the class.
46. Show students you care in your actions, not only in your words.	46. Only tell students you care with your words.
47. Laugh with your class.	47. Keep your class serious all of the time and not allow laughter in the classroom.
48. Give gifts.	48. Tell your students they don't deserve anything.
49. Empower students with student-led conferences.	49. Always lead the conferences.
50. Use peer mediation to foster more positive classrooms and teach students skills that will help them succeed in life.	50. Try to solve all student conflicts.
51. Be prepared for success when covering a colleague's classroom.	51. Expect that students will misbehave when covering a class.
52. Sometimes add the element of surprise to your lessons to increase engagement and vitality in your classroom.	52. Fail to include surprises in your lessons.
53. Schedule exercise into your calendar, especially during the busiest parts of the school year.	53. Fail to take care of yourself because you do not have the time.
54. Be prepared for difficult parent meetings.	54. Show up at a potentially difficult parent meeting unprepared.
55. Be aware of the signs of compassion fatigue and secondary trauma and how to prevent them and intervene if needed.	55. Fail to be aware of the signs of compassion fatigue and secondary trauma.
56. Resolve issues with other adults through quick empathetic conversation, not text or e-mail.	56. Attempt to try to resolve an issue through text or e-mail to avoid face-to-face conflict.
57. Focus on finding a solution to the issue when resolving a conflict with a colleague.	57. Blame each other for what happened without being focused on finding a solution when experiencing colleague conflict.

The End . . . of the Beginning

The end of the beginning is a great place to be. When you do not have to spend countless hours picking up paper balls after class, or calling parents to alert them about negative behavior, you can actually start getting creative without fear. It's a beautiful thing to spend your precious time writing lesson plans knowing the class is on your side rather than being your enemy. I sometimes have posttraumatic first-year flashbacks where I remember the boy rocking side to side, or how the class seemed more threatening than any adversary in any war fought over the past hundred years.

A talented ninth-grade teacher, now a middle school principal, once told me something that stuck. She said the goal of a teacher is to "teach themselves out of a job" by the end of the year. This means you've created a real community of learners who depend on each other for help—not on you. This means they can resolve small conflicts, stay motivated without constant redirection, collaborate, share confidently within their groups, and demonstrate higher-order thinking skills.

I can always gauge a successful school year if the kids don't notice when I walk out of the room because they are too engaged in learning with each other in academic collaboration. They are usually in project- or problem-based learning units and, as my mentor used to say, "on autopilot." Sometimes, in the last month of school, I'll test this and walk a few feet away from the class and wait. Usually they don't notice I've walked away because they are too engaged in their final projects. They also don't need me to resolve minor conflicts because they have learned these skills. They also don't depend on me for constant praise because they have developed their own sense of self-esteem. Those moments are when I get shivers and my eyes may even tear up a bit. I feel like this because I know they have a much better chance of being fine out there in the real world if they don't need me anymore. It's a bittersweet feeling that we'll all experience. Most years I've gotten this result, but not every year. If we don't get this result at the end of a school year, it's okay. Teaching is one of the few professions that gives us a chance to start fresh each year, recreate ourselves, change what didn't work, and keep doing what did work. We get a clean slate and a new chance at the beginning of every school year to try to be the teacher we want to be. Few other professions can say that.

I am a teacher through and through, and the students and I are traveling side by side on this learning journey. There are many things I still have to learn, and I work on them daily. How do I use technology in the classroom to maximize learning and increase engagement? How do I challenge the most gifted child without separating him or her from the class? How do I work with adults as successfully as I do with children? These questions are what push me every day to become better at my chosen profession. I use my own experience to listen, to keep learning, and to find mentors. One of the most beautiful aspects of teaching is that we are always learning. We are always growing as teachers, and our students are always growing. Good luck in your journey, and perhaps we will meet someday, somewhere along our paths. Here's to you and your dreams! I hope sharing my real experiences helped you reach a little higher.

—Serena

Real Advice: Teacher to Teacher

Every day's a new day. Always give your students the opportunity to make good choices. Be flexible; things happen, and go with the flow. Smile and show students that you care; you may be the only person who does. Also, be calm and patient.

Ms. Saft, 6 years' experience, Early Childhood Education Specialist, Kimbrough Elementary School, California

In many cases, teaching can be and often is stressful. There are days when you will be angry, frustrated, anxious, and emotional. Do something about it. Take a break, write about your feelings in a journal, go to the movies, the theater, et cetera. Most important, do something physical; try yoga, take a long walk, jog, or work in your yard.

Dr. DeRoche, 30 years' experience, Former Middle School Teacher and Principal, University of San Diego, California

As teachers, we cannot fully understand our students until we put ourselves in their shoes.

Ms. Hambira, 15 years' experience, High School Teacher, Kgari Sechele Senior Secondary School, Botswana

I think one of the most powerful behavior management techniques is for the students to like you and want to be in your class. I always work on that first, making the class a fun and loving place to be. If students like you and respect you, then they care what you think and want to please you. If you teach through intimidation and fear, you may get temporary results, but at what price?

Mrs. Perez, 21 years' experience, Kindergarten Teacher, Jefferson Elementary School, California

Project-based learning allows students to become aware of the benefits of working together in this world, allowing for peace not only to be possible, but inevitable.

Mr. Kemp, 10 years' experience, High School Teacher, Vista High School, California

Take time to get to know each student personally—greet each one by name every day while smiling and looking them in the eyes; talk to each student when you have a chance and listen to them without judging. Be your authentic self, and don't be afraid to share a little of who you are with your students. Then you will have real relationships with your students, you will be happier in the classroom, and you will find you have fewer disciplinary issues.

Mrs. Swan-Gerstein, 11 years' experience, Former Elementary Vice Principal, Integral Elementary School, California

Be yourself. Don't be afraid to laugh at yourself in front of the students. Admit when you are wrong, but always be firm, consistent, and fair, and love them.

Mrs. Mello, 11 years' experience, Middle and Elementary School Teacher, Golden Hill Elementary School, California

Don't judge someone on who they are when they are thirteen. We never know what path each kid will eventually take, and we have to try our best to be a nice stop on the path. It's taken me a long time to figure that out. Also, start fresh every day. Don't hold grudges. Pacing helps classroom management, too. I try to change activities every ten to fifteen minutes to keep minds active and engaged.

Mrs. Register, 10 years' experience, Middle and High School Teacher, Cajon Park School, California

It's important to cultivate an atmosphere in which mutual respect is practiced. You listen to and respect the students' voices, and they show each other and you respect. They don't have to like everyone or you, but they need to practice respect. The working world needs people who will work with others to get the job finished. Prepare your lessons well. The best prevention is a well-prepared lesson.

Mrs. Pariser, 34 years' experience, Retired High School Alternative Education Teacher, Hampdon Academy, Maine

One thing that helped me a lot is being prepared: lesson plans, planning, resources. Remember you are there to teach and not to gain popularity or friendship. Popularity comes from having your learners intrigued, which comes from being prepared and going the extra mile, especially as a new teacher.

Mr. Sawyers, 5 years' experience, Middle and High School Teacher, Windhoek High School, Namibia

The result of imposed authority by teachers is reflected in student behavior when you ask them to teach junior [younger] students. Senior [older] students are found to be more focused on maintaining discipline by using elevated voice pitch than on attaining the learning outcomes of the assigned task. Some of our seniors [eighth-grade students] were assigned a task to teach juniors [third-grade students]. They were as rude or as kind as their teachers. It was like "monkey do what monkey sees."

Mr. Sijapati, 9 years' experience, Elementary and Middle School Administrator and Teacher, Creative Academy, Nepal

---

It can be overwhelming with trivial details when organizing your classroom at the beginning of the school year. Make it your own! Do what works for you. For example, if having space on the floor for students to work on their bellies using clipboards is important to you, then be sure to have an area for floor work.

Ms. Vaites, 21 years' experience, Elementary School Teacher, Greenfield Middle School, Massachusetts

---

The first year teaching first grade was a real challenge, as I hadn't yet figured out the key to proper classroom management skills. But, as with all things, I tested out many different methods until I found what really worked. Using reward systems, like Class Dojo, has made a world of difference in my classrooms, and the children really feel more self-accomplished and responsible, and they develop an understanding of their ability to achieve and succeed.

Ms. Reinblatt, 7 years' experience, Early Elementary School ESL Teacher, Uskudar SEV American School, Turkey

---

What's worked for me, with connecting with students, is understanding they are already very accomplished people. I don't tell them what to do and what not to do. I share my stories and listen to their goals and dreams. While listening to them, I don't judge. Listening helps me to deeply connect.

Ms. Rai, 5 years' experience, Inspirational Youth Speaker, India

Do everything you can in the beginning of the year to create a sense of community within your classroom. This takes time at first but goes a long way when your students feel ownership of the room and group!

Mrs. Pariser, 8 years' experience, Elementary School Teacher/Counselor, Akiba Schechter Day School, Illinois

Identify a student in the classroom who's a leader, even if the student leads in a negative way. Get to know that student and become friends—get the student on your side. Then the other kids will follow!

Jackie Hicks, 10 years' experience, Middle and High School Teacher, Cortez Hill Academy, California

In my second year of teaching, I decided to take a different approach to that of the traditional authoritative teacher; I was enthusiastic, kind, and positive. I resolved not to raise my voice. As a result, I found that my students became more kind, positive, and enthusiastic as well.

Mrs. Beck, 7 years' experience, Middle and High School Teacher, Gompers Preparatory Academy, California

Make sure to practice self care and nurture your needs as a person. It's important to identify passions outside of teaching and continue to pursue those as well. I now get monthly massages and pedicures; I practice meditation and being present in the moment; and I do things I love that make me feel most alive, such as writing poetry and going to the beach, concerts, and farmers' markets. When you honor your own needs, it allows you to feel more whole, therefore making you a better teacher for your students.

Mrs. Zimmermaker, 9 years' experience, Education Specialist, Mesa Verde Middle School, California

References

Achor, S. (2010). *The happiness advantage.* Random House Inc.

Adams, S. (2014). The 10 skills employers most want in 2015 graduates. *Forbes.* https://www.forbes.com/sites/susanadams/2014/11/12/the-10-skills-employers-most-want-in-2015-graduates/?sh=384078592511

American Institute of Stress. (2018). *Definitions: Compassion fatigue.* https://www.stress.org/military/for-practitionersleaders/compassion-fatigue

Anderson, A. R. (2015). A little appreciation goes a long way: Why gratitude is the gift that keeps on giving. *Forbes.* https://www.forbes.com/sites/amyanderson/2015/11/03/a-little-appreciation-goes-a-long-way-why-gratitude-is-the-gift-that-keeps-on-giving/?sh=7230168d7aaf

Boch, L. (2014). Google's scientific approach to work-life balance (and much more). *Harvard Business Review.* https://hbr.org/2014/03/googles-scientific-approach-to-work-life-balance-and-much-more

Carnegie, D. (1981). *How to win friends and influence people.* Pocket Books.

Child Trends Inc. (2015). *5 soft skills that help youth succeed at work.* https://www.childtrends.org/publications/5-soft-skills-that-help-youth-succeed-at-work

Delpit, L. (2013). *Multiplication is for white people.* New Press.

DeRoche, E. (2013). *The skills game.* http://sites.sandiego.edu/character/blog/2013/11/12/skills-game/

Education Week. (2021). *Top U.S. companies: These are the skills students need in a post pandemic world.* https://www.edweek.org/technology/top-u-s-companies-these-are-the-skills-students-need-in-a-post-pandemic-world/2021/03

Edutopia. (2016). *Multiple intelligences: What does the research say?* https://www.edutopia.org/multiple-intelligences-research

Edutopia. (2022). *What's the role of teachers in supporting mental health?* https://www.edutopia.org/article/the-doctor-is-in-your-classroom/

Intervention Central. (n.d.). *Response to intervention—RTI resources.* https://www.interventioncentral.org/

Karpinski, E. (2021). *Put happiness to work.* McGraw Hill.

Kelley, W. M. (2003). *Rookie teaching for dummies.* Wiley Publishing, Inc.

Mager, R., & Pipe, P. (1997). *Analyzing performance problems.* CEP Press.

Marzano, R. J., Marzano, J. S., & Pickering, D. J. (2003). *Classroom management that works.* ASCD.

National Child Traumatic Stress Network. (n.d.). *Secondary traumatic stress.* https://www.nctsn.org/trauma-informed-care/secondary-traumatic-stress#:~:text=Secondary%20traumatic%20stress%20is%20the,disasters%2C%20and%20other%20adverse%20events.

Pariser, S. (2018). *Real talk about time management: 35 Best Practices for Educators.* Corwin.

Pariser, S., & DeRoche, E. (2020), *Real talk about time management.* Corwin.

Pariser, S., & Lentfer, V. (2022). *Five to thrive: Answers to your biggest questions about creating a dynamic classroom.* Corwin.

Suttie, J. (2015). Why humans need surprise: A new book argues that surprise, whether good or bad, is critical for bringing vitality to our lives. *Great Good Magazine.* from https://greatergood.berkeley.edu/article/item/why_humans_need_surprise

Teaching & Learning Transformation Center. (n.d.). *Creating effective group work: Tips, tricks and resources.* University of Maryland. https://www.umdsmartgrowth.org/wp-content/uploads/2018/07/group_work_handout.pdf

Thiagarajan, S. (2006). *Thiagi's 100 favorite games.* Pheiffer.

Urban, H. (2004). *Positive words, powerful results.* Simon & Shuster.

Index

Achor, Shawn, 241
Advocates, for teachers, 190–91
Angry students, 35, 37
Aristotle, 104
Advancement via individual determination (AVID) students, 33, 37

Behavior modification systems, 72, 84, 98
Best Practice: Bringing Standards to Life in America's Classrooms (Zemelman), 110
Bodily-kinesthetic learners, 173
Boundaries, establishing classroom, 13

Chain of command, coworker conflict and, 287
Child Trends, Inc., 4
Chunking, 110, 113, 114
Classroom structures, setting, 23–25, 63
Contextualizing learning, 128
Coworkers, 185, 241, 286–88
    conflict with, 287

Data, 33, 39, 41, 137, 148, 143, 168, 190
    tracking student, 188
Defiance, 28, 90, 91, 155, 248
    discipline for, 156
Delpit, Lisa, 139
Differentiating Instruction in the Regular Classroom (Heacox), 109
Discipline, 63
    books on how to, 109
    in coteaching, 200
    creative, 155–59
    using sparingly, 13
"Do Schools Kill Creativity?" (Robinson), 169
Due Process, 190

Engagement styles, 173
English language learners, 34, 39
    where to seat, 40
Extrinsic
    motivation, 69–70, 87, 97
    prizes, 84–85

Families, 16, 17, 192–94, 251, 254, 270, 282, 284
    of challenging children, 80
    classrooms as, 17, 74, 149, 153, 244
    communicating with, 88, 187, 192, 194
    suffering grief and loss, 205, 206, 283
    working with difficult, 186–91, 279
The First Years Matter (Radford), 109

Gardner, Howard, 173
GATE (gifted and talented) students, 36, 37, 39
    where to seat, 33–34
Google
    searches, 123, 133, 177
    tools, 118–20, 133, 248
    work environment at, 51, 271
Grumpy students, 52
    where to seat, 34, 35, 37, 53

The Happiness Advantage (Achor), 241
Happy students,
    where to seat, 35–36, 52
Heacox, Diane, 109

Icebreaker activities, 21, 123
Interpersonal learners, 175, 177–78
Intervention Central, 90
Intrapersonal learners, 176
Intrinsic motivation, 68–70, 84, 86, 87, 97, 104
"I" statements, 28–31, 75, 253, 289

Kellermann, Jessica, 224–25
Kirschbaum, Jeff, 104
Kozol, Jonathan, 109

Learning
    engagement styles, 172–79
    problem-based, 127
    project-based, 126–27
The Learning Challenge (Nottingham), 110
Lessons
    adding element of unexpected in, 260–62
    chunking in, 114
    flops, 180
    infusing creativity into, 169–71

pacing, 113–15
preparing, 12, 122–25
risk-taking in, 148–49
sample plan with different engagement styles, 177
Letters to a Young Teacher (Kozol), 109
Linguistic learners, 175, 178
Logical-mathematical learners, 174

Madren, Rebekah, 269
Mentoring in Action (Radford), 109
Metaphysics (Aristotle), 104
Motivation
    extrinsic, 97
    intrinsic, 68–69, 97
    performance barriers and, 68
Multiple intelligence
    theory, 173
    quiz, 177
Musical learners, 174
Mysteries, 158, 260, 261

Names, learning students,' 19–21, 37
Naturalistic learners, 175
Nelson, Jane, 110
Nguyen, Orletta, 92
Noise levels in classroom, 160–63
Nottingham, James, 110

Of Mice and Men (Steinbeck), 105

Parents, 192–94. *See also* Families
    communication with, 187
    involvement in discipline, 155
    winning over, 196
    working with difficult, 186–279
Perez, Erika, 48
Performance barriers/problems, 69, 71–72
Pets, 224, 241
Pictures, learning student names using, 20
Planned absences, 152
Point system, daily, 166
Positive, focusing on the, 51, 60, 74, 189
Positive Discipline in the Classroom (Nelson), 110
Preparation
    lesson, 12, 122–25
    mental, 122–25
    of students for guest speakers, 228–29

Prizes
    behavior contract rewards, 92
    extrinsic, 84–85
    mystery, 260
    surprise, 241
Problem-based learning, 127
Project-based learning, 127
Project planning, 126

Radford, Carol, 109
Recognition, for students, 51.
    See also Rewards
Respect
    of administration, 215
    treating students with, 63–64
Rewards
    behavior contract, 92, 96
    extrinsic prizes, 84
    mystery prizes, 261
    surprise prizes, 241
Risk-taking
    in lessons, 148–49
Robinson, Ken, 169

Seating charts
    creating, 20–21, 32–41
    flexible seating, 39–40
    learning names and, 20
    sample, 35
    tips for making, 37
Skills
    performance barriers and, 68
    social, 244
    transfer to real-world applications, 224
Steinbeck, John, 105
Substitute teaching, 256
Surprises, 85, 106, 107, 128, 241, 260–63

Team-building activities, 21. *See also* Icebreaker activities

Unplanned absences, 152

Visual-spatial learners, 174
Vocal students, 36
Voice
    arm's length, 116–17
    giving students, 231

Helping educators make the greatest impact

CORWIN HAS ONE MISSION: to enhance education through intentional professional learning.

We build long-term relationships with our authors, educators, clients, and associations who partner with us to develop and continuously improve the best evidence-based practices that establish and support lifelong learning.

Confident Teachers, Inspired Learners

JONATHAN ECKERT

Focus on feedback, engagement, and well-being to support comprehensive growth while elevating the essential work of educators.

JOE SCHMIDT, NICHELLE PINKNEY

Facilitate contentious conversations by approaching civil discourse through the lenses of courage, understanding, belonging, and empathy.

CHASE NORDENGREN

Find actionable solutions to classroom management and culture, engaging lesson design, and effective communication.

JOHN HATTIE, DOUGLAS FISHER, NANCY FREY, SHIRLEY CLARKE

Discover how working with other people can be a powerful accelerator of student learning and a precursor to future success.

To order your copies, visit **corwin.com/teachingessentials**

No matter where you are in your professional journey, Corwin books provide accessible strategies that benefit ALL learners—and ease the many demands teachers face.

CAROL PELLETIER RADFORD

Equip teachers with the tools they need to take care of themselves so they can serve their students, step into leadership, and contribute to the education profession.

AMANDA BRUEGGEMAN

Develop student-centered approaches, promote collective efficacy, engage in coaching conversations, and prevent burnout while promoting student learning.

SERENA PARISER, VICTORIA LENTFER

Find actionable solutions to classroom management and culture, engaging lesson design, and effective communication.

STEPHANIE SMITH BUDHAI, KRISTINE S. LEWIS GRANT

Help teachers pivot instruction to ensure equitable, inclusive learning experiences in online and in-person settings.

CORWIN